# Community-Based Conditional Cash Transfers in Tanzania

A WORLD BANK STUDY

# Community-Based Conditional Cash Transfers in Tanzania

## Results from a Randomized Trial

David K. Evans, Stephanie Hausladen, Katrina Kosec, and Natasha Reese

**THE WORLD BANK**
Washington, D.C.

ISBN (paper): 978-1-4648-0141-9
ISBN (electronic): 978-1-4648-0142-6
DOI: 10.1596/978-1-4648-0141-9

*Cover photo:* Katrina Kosec. Used with permission from Katrina Kosec; further permission required for reuse.
*Cover design:* Debra Naylor, Naylor Design, Inc.

### Library of Congress Cataloging-in-Publication Data

Evans, David K., 1975-
    Community-based conditional cash transfers in Tanzania : results from a randomized trial / David K. Evans, Stephanie Hausladen, Katrina Kosec, and Natasha Reese.
        pages cm. — (World bank studies)
    Includes bibliographical references and index.
    ISBN 978-1-4648-0141-9 (pbk. : alk. paper) — ISBN 978-1-4648-0142-6 (ebook)
    1. Tanzania—Social policy. 2. Tanzania—Economic policy. 3. Transfer payments—Tanzania. I. Title.
    HN797.A8E935 2014
    303.309678—dc23                                                                      2013045167

# Contents

## Figures

**Tables**

# Acknowledgments

This project is the result of great effort on the part of a large number of parties. Although the authors of the report are David Evans (World Bank), Stephanie Hausladen (Harvard University), Katrina Kosec (International Food Policy Research Institute, or IFPRI), and Natasha Reese (University of Virginia), this impact evaluation benefitted at various stages from experts at the World Bank, IFPRI, Tanzania Social Action Fund (TASAF), and elsewhere.

At TASAF, the evaluation has been supported by the Executive Director Ladislaus Mwamanga, as well as the former Executive Director Servacius Likwelile. Amadeus Kamagenge has led TASAF input to the evaluation, and his entire team has contributed with substantive and logistical support to the evaluation.

From the World Bank, the program and evaluation have benefitted from several World Bank task team leaders, particularly Samantha de Silva, Anush Bezhanyan, and Ida Manjolo, as well as other key staff, including Myrtle Diachok and Manuel Salazar. Berk Ozler designed and shared the survey for the TASAF II vulnerable groups evaluation, on which the household survey for this evaluation was based. Janmejay Singh consulted on the community score cards supplementary intervention, and Julie Van Domelen consulted on the focus group questionnaires and other elements of the qualitative evaluation. Margaret Grosh and Dena Ringold provided extensive and helpful comments as peer reviewers. Michele Valsecchi also provided valuable comments. Brian Holtemeyer at IFPRI and Anna Popova provided excellent research assistance. Arianna Legovini, who leads the World Bank's Development Impact Evaluation Unit, provided helpful guidance.

This project is being implemented by TASAF. The project and evaluation were supported by the Japan Social Development Fund (JSDF). The impact evaluation also received support through the Trust Fund for Environmentally and Socially Sustainable Development (TFESSD), the Spanish Impact Evaluation Fund (SIEF), the International Initiative for Impact Evaluation (3ie), and the Consultative Group on International Agricultural Research (CGIAR) Research Program on Policies, Institutions and Markets (PIM).

This project has benefitted from the careful analysis of the Public Affairs Foundation, led by Dr. Sita Sekhar. The Public Affairs Foundation carried out a community score card (CSC) analysis of the community-based conditional cash transfer program. Our section on community score cards is adapted directly from their report.

The authors accept full responsibilities for errors in the report.

# Abbreviations

| | |
|---|---|
| 3ie | International Initiative for Impact Evaluation |
| AIDS | acquired immune deficiency syndrome |
| CB-CCT | community-based conditional cash transfer |
| CCD | community-driven development |
| CCT | conditional cash transfer |
| CMC | community management committee |
| CSC | community score cards |
| ETT | effect of treatment on the treated |
| FBO | faith-based organization |
| HIV | human immunodeficiency virus |
| IFPRI | International Food Policy Research Institute |
| ITT | intention to treat |
| JSDF | Japan Social Development Fund |
| LGA | local government authority |
| LGDCG | Local Government Development Capital Grant |
| MIS | Management Information System |
| MUAC | middle-upper-arm circumference |
| NGO | nongovernmental organization |
| SIEF | Spanish Impact Evaluation Fund |
| TASAF | Tanzania Social Action Fund |
| TFESSD | Trust Fund for Environmentally and Socially Sustainable Development |
| TSH | Tanzanian shilling |
| VA | Village Assembly |
| VC | village council |
| VEO | village executive officer |
| WHO | World Health Organization |

# Executive Summary

Given the success of conditional cash transfer (CCT) programs elsewhere in the world, in 2010 the Government of Tanzania—via the Tanzania Social Action Fund (TASAF)—rolled out a CCT program in three districts. Its aim was to see if, using a model that relied heavily on communities to target beneficiaries and deliver payments, the program could improve outcomes for the poor the way centrally run CCT programs have in other contexts. What follows is a summary of the pilot program, the methodology used to evaluate it, and its major impacts.

1. The program was piloted in three poor districts (Bagamoyo, Chamwino, and Kibaha), selected in part for their poverty relative to other parts of Tanzania (see figure ES.1).

**Figure ES.1 How Do the Study Population and the Rest of the Country Compare?**

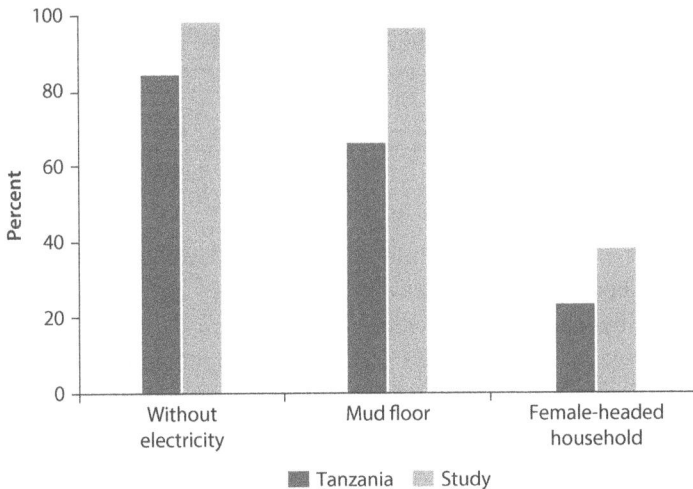

*Source:* World Bank data.

2. The program provided benefits for these poor households based on the number of vulnerable children (age 0–15) and elderly (age 60+) therein. Payments were made every other month, or six times each year (see figure ES.2).

**Figure ES.2  How Large Were the Bimonthly Payments to the Families?**

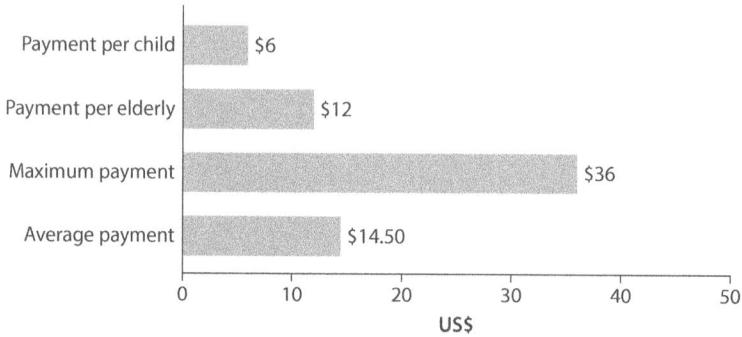

*Source:* World Bank data.

3. To receive payments, households had to comply with certain conditions. Locally elected community management committees monitored compliance with these conditions and penalized participating households that did not comply (see table ES.1).

**Table ES.1  What Were the Conditions that Households Needed to Meet?**

|  | Education | Health |
|---|---|---|
| Children (age 0–5 years) |  | Visit clinic 6 times per year |
| Children (age 7–15 years) | Be enrolled with 80% attendance |  |
| Elderly |  | Visit clinic 1 time per year |

*Source:* World Bank data.

4. Given scarce resources, TASAF randomly selected 40 villages out of 80 eligible villages in the three study districts to be treated under the pilot program. Communities selected the most vulnerable households to participate before learning which villages were randomly selected to participate in the program. This provided a group of comparison households in the 40 untreated villages.

   A baseline survey was carried out in early 2009. Transfers began in January 2010. A midline survey was carried out in mid-2011 (18–21 months after transfers began). An endline survey was carried out in late 2012 (31–34 months after transfers began).

   A community score card exercise (in which communities rated themselves), two rounds of focus groups, and a set of in-depth interviews complemented the quantitative evaluation (see figure ES.3).

**Figure ES.3  Impact Evaluation Design**

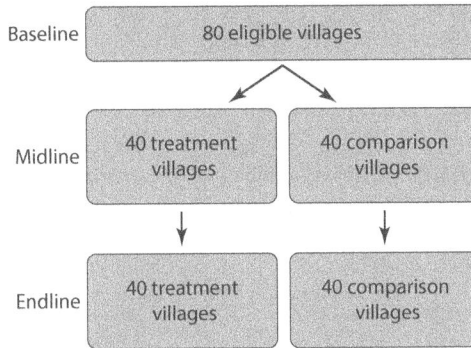

*Source:* World Bank data.

5. Treatment and comparison households were *comparable* at baseline, with few significant differences across a wide range of characteristics. In the final analysis, we compared changes over time in treatment and comparison households (a method called difference-in-differences) to adjust for small baseline differences, like those shown here (see figure ES.4).

**Figure ES.4  How Similar Were the Treatment and Comparison Households before the Program?**

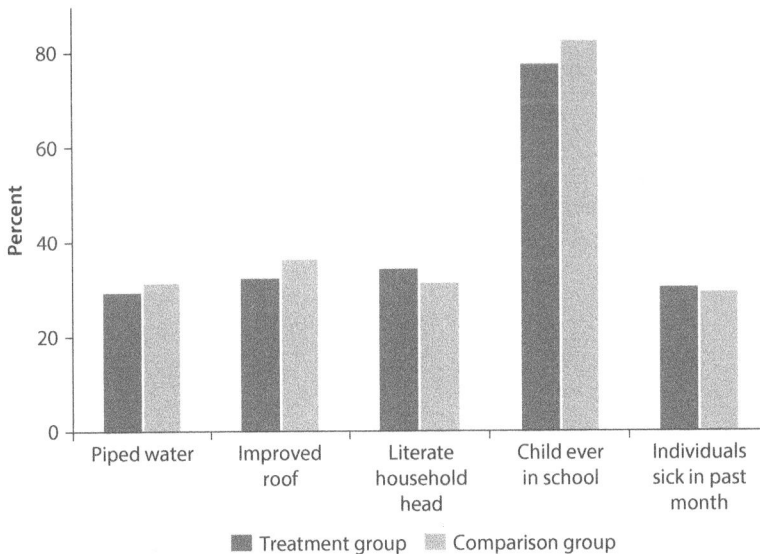

*Source:* World Bank data.
*Note:* All differences are nonsignificant.

6. After an initial surge in clinic visits among treatment households, 31–34 months into the program (at endline), participating households were attending clinics less often but were *healthier*: their members were 5 percentage points less likely to be sick (averaging across all ages), and children age 0–4 were 11 percentage points less likely to be sick (see figure ES.5).

**Figure ES.5  How Much Less Sick Were Members of Treatment Households Relative to Members of Households in the Comparison Group?**

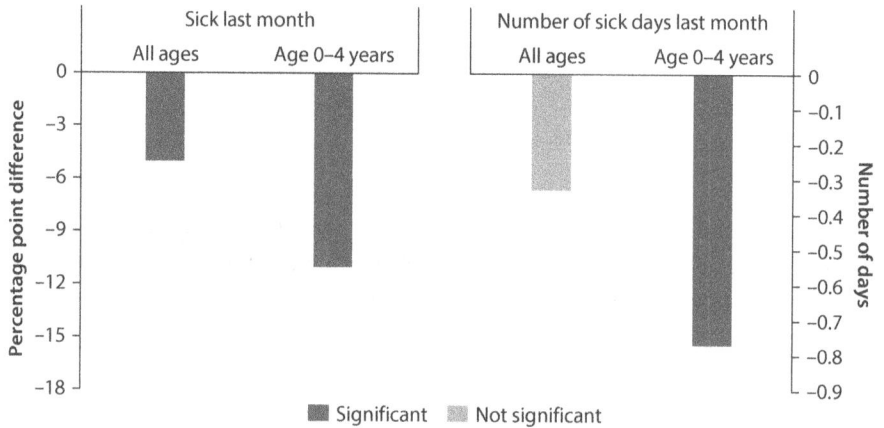

*Source:* World Bank data.

7. *Health* improvements due to the CCT program are even more marked for the poorest half of treatment households: the poorest of the poor. They experienced a half a day per month reduction in sick days (averaging across all ages), and poor children age 0–4 in particular had a full day per month reduction in sick days (see figure ES.6).

**Figure ES.6  How Much Less Sick Were Members of the Poorest Half of Treatment Households Relative to Members of the Poorest Half of Households in the Comparison Group?**

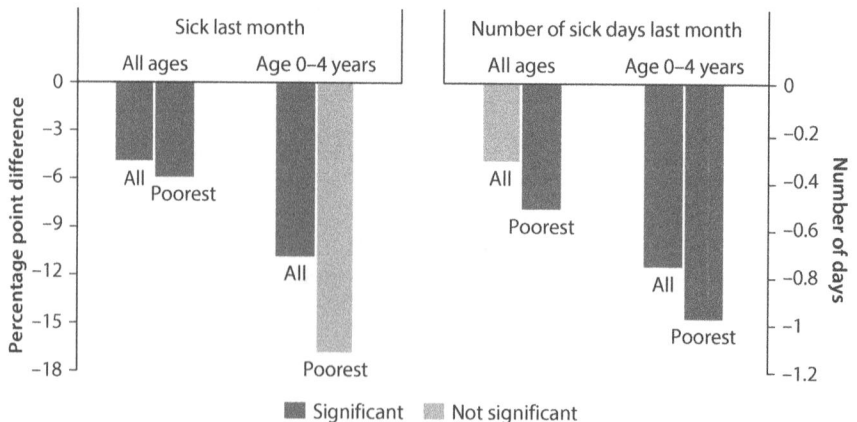

*Source:* World Bank data.

8. In *education*, the program showed clear positive impacts on whether children had ever attended school or if they completed primary school. Through qualitative data collection exercises, communities reported that the program had dramatic, positive impacts on school attendance. While these positive impacts on absenteeism were not observed in the quantitative data, only 12 percent of children were reported to be absent during the previous week at baseline, so student absenteeism may not be a major problem. Furthermore, the program's conditions only required 80 percent attendance at school (see figure ES.7).

**Figure ES.7  How Much Better Did Treatment Group Children (Age 0–18 Years) Do in Literacy, Attendance, and Completion?**

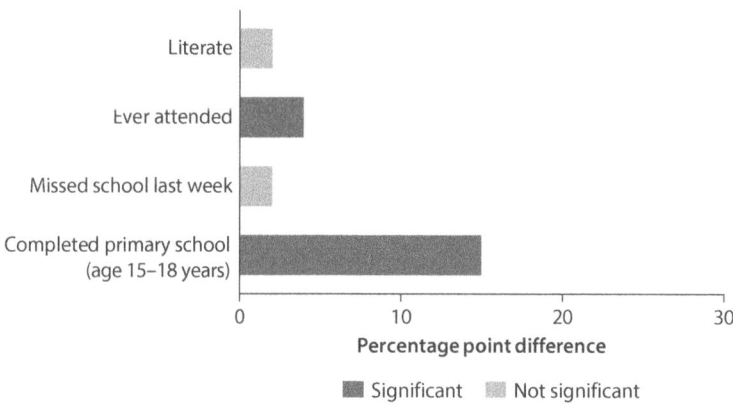

Percentage point difference

■ Significant    ▨ Not significant

*Source:* World Bank data.

9. The primary school completion effect is particularly striking for girls, who were 23 percentage points more likely to complete primary school than were their comparison group counterparts (see figure ES.8).

**Figure ES.8  How Much Better Did Females in Treatment Households Do in Literacy, Attendance, and Completion?**

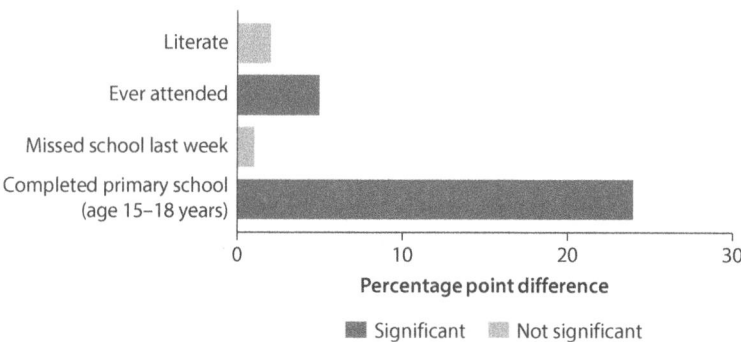

Percentage point difference

■ Significant    ▨ Not significant

*Source:* World Bank data.

10. In addition, *literacy rates* increased significantly for children who were out of school at baseline (see figure ES.9).

**Figure ES.9  How Much Better Did Students Out of School at Baseline in Treatment Households Do in Literacy, Attendance, and Completion?**

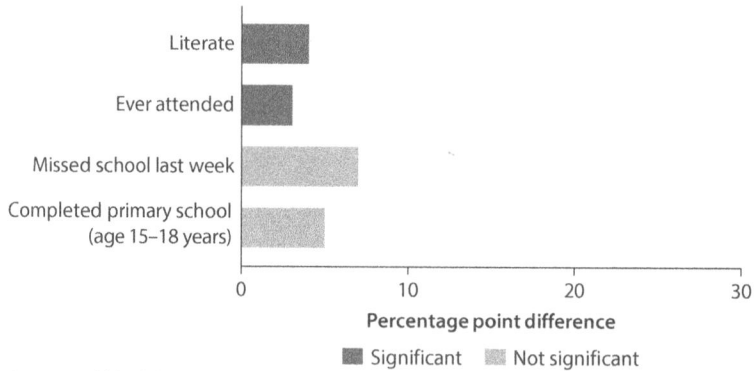

*Source:* World Bank data.

11. Some of the most consistent changes observed have to do with *health insurance*. Treatment households were much more likely to finance medical care with insurance and much more likely to purchase insurance than were their comparison counterparts. This is important because having health insurance can substantially reduce out-of-pocket expenditures for medical care and increase the propensity to seek treatment for health problems (see figure ES.10).

**Figure ES.10  For Someone Sick in the Last Month, Did You Finance Treatment with Health Insurance?**

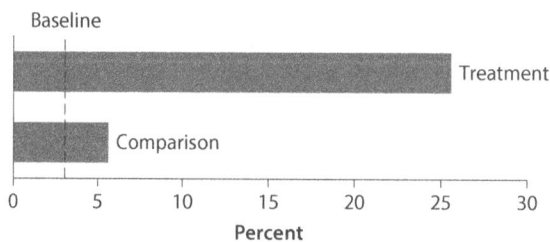

*Source:* World Bank data.
*Note:* Treatment and comparison both achieved significant increases.

12. Increases in expenditures, either on food or non-food household items, were not significantly higher for treatment households, with the exceptions of *insurance* and *children's shoes*. Households, on average, were much more likely to purchase children's shoes. This was especially true for the poorest households (see figure ES.11).

**Figure ES.11  Does the Child Have Shoes?**

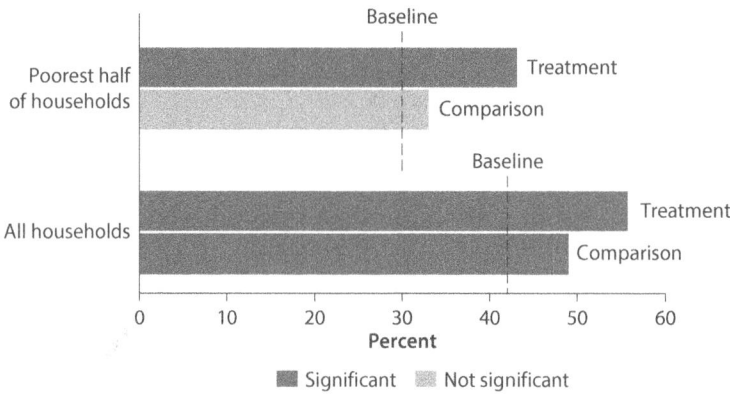

*Source:* World Bank data.

The quality of housing materials improved in treatment villages but more slowly than it did in comparison villages.

13. The program did not significantly affect savings or spending on average, although the poorest half of treated households saw a fivefold, highly significant increase in *nonbank savings* (see figure ES.12).

**Figure ES.12  What Share of Households Have Nonbank Savings?**

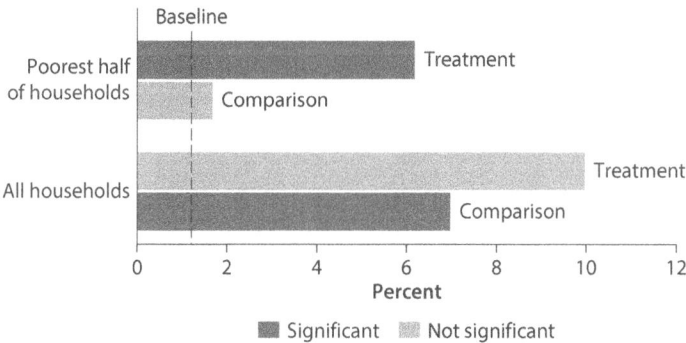

*Source:* World Bank data.

14. Treated households invested in more *livestock* assets. Focus groups revealed that households purchased chickens and other animals and used them to create businesses (for example, selling eggs or chicks) or in order to have easily sellable, productive savings (see figure ES.13).

**Figure ES.13  How Much Did the Program Affect Livestock Asset Ownership?**

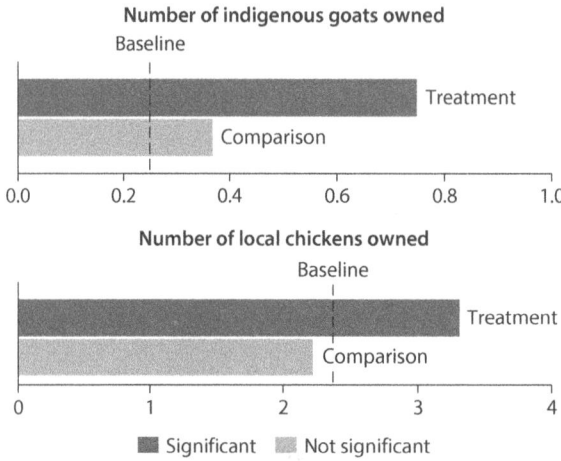

Number of indigenous goats owned

Number of local chickens owned

■ Significant  ▨ Not significant

*Source:* World Bank data.

15. Because this program relies so heavily on communities—to target, to deliver transfers, and to monitor compliance with conditions—there was concern as to its impact on community cohesion. In fact, treatment households were more likely to have attended village council meetings, to have contributed labor to a community development project (for female recipients), and to express trust in a range of community members (see figure ES.14).

**Figure ES.14  How Much More Do Individuals in Treatment Communities Trust These Groups than Do Individuals in Comparison Communities?**

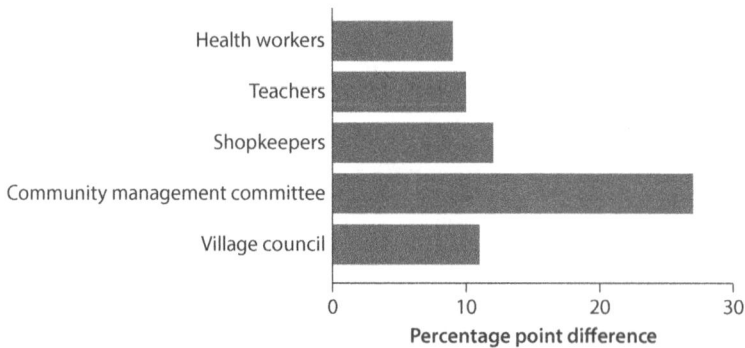

Percentage point difference

*Source:* World Bank data.
*Note:* All categories achieved significant increases.

On the whole, the community-based CCT program led to improved out-comes in both health and education. Households used the resources to invest in livestock, in children's shoes, in insurance, and—for the poorest house-holds—in increased savings. This suggests that the households focused on reducing risk and on improving their livelihoods rather than principally on increasing consumption. There is also evidence that the project had positive effects on community cohesion.

# Background

## Motivation for Project

Conditional cash transfers (CCTs) have proven immensely effective in alleviating extreme poverty and improving health and education outcomes for children around the world (Fiszbein and Schady 2009; Baird et al. 2013). Evidence from across Latin America—and now growing evidence from other parts of the world—has demonstrated that CCTs can be an extremely effective mechanism for improving outcomes for families, children, and entire communities. In Africa, the evidence base remains more limited. For example, conditional cash transfers have improved health and education outcomes for children in Burkina Faso (Akresh, de Walque, and Kazianga 2012, 2013) and for adolescent girls in Malawi (Baird, McIntosh, and Özler 2011).[1]

An increasing number of African countries are interested in implementing CCTs and have vulnerable populations that might benefit immensely from them. However, this raises the important question of what is the best way to operate CCT programs in different institutional contexts—especially those in which the central government would find it difficult to administer all aspects of the program. This project introduced a model of CCTs that relies heavily on local communities to target and to administer the program—more so than most CCT programs in the past. Because initial project funds did not have sufficient resources to benefit all low-income households, the project design included random assignment of which villages would initially receive the cash transfer program, accompanied by a rigorous impact evaluation. In the time since this project was launched, a host of CCT programs have grown up around the African continent. This project seeks to add to the evidence base informing these and future programs.

## Project Description

### Overall Objective

The overall objective of the pilot was to test how a conditional cash transfer (CCT) program could be implemented through a social fund[2] using a community-driven development (CDD) approach, and to learn about what systems may need to be in place to achieve positive results for highly vulnerable populations. This project represents the first time that a social fund agency was used to implement a CCT program in Africa, and the first time that a CCT program was delivered using a CDD approach in Africa. Specific objectives of this pilot project included (a) to develop operational modalities for the community-driven delivery of a CCT program through a social fund operation; and (b) to test the effectiveness of the community-based CCT model and ensure that lessons from the pilot inform government policy on support for vulnerable families.

### CCTs and the CDD Approach

Conditional cash transfer programs provide grants to poor and vulnerable families contingent upon specific family actions, usually investments in human capital such as keeping children in school or taking them to health centers on a regular basis. There is clear evidence that successful CCT programs increase enrollment rates, improve preventive health care, and raise the household consumption of beneficiaries (Fiszbein and Schady 2009). There is also some evidence that CCT programs benefit not only beneficiary families, but also other, nonbeneficiary families living in the same communities (Angelucci and De Giorgi 2009). This means that the benefits of CCT programs for beneficiary families represent only a share of their overall benefits.

The community-driven development approach, which gives control over planning resources and investment decisions to community groups and local governments, has been shown in other contexts to improve the effectiveness and efficiency of service delivery. As such, many social funds rely on and make efforts to build community capacity for delivery of a range of social and economic services at the local level.

In the Tanzanian case, the capacity of many local communities has already been strengthened by the Tanzania Social Action Fund (TASAF). TASAF was established in 2000, as part of the Government of Tanzania's strategy for reducing poverty and improving livelihoods by stimulating economic activity at the community level. TASAF's first phase of work (TASAF I) began in 2000 and oversaw community-run projects (for example, construction and rehabilitation of basic health care facilities, schools and other small-scale infrastructure) which gave local communities experience in managing funds, employing contractors and labor, monitoring, and reporting. TASAF I was completed in 2005, having built a foundation for further community-driven development.

Considerable central government capacity has typically been viewed as a prerequisite for administering a system of CCTs to millions of poor households and ensuring that funds are utilized properly. The CCTs in Latin America and South Asia typically have come about under a strong central administration. Since central capacity is more limited in many low-income countries, new modalities of CCT delivery are needed. The pilot leveraged the management capabilities of TASAF to oversee the program, and leveraged the capacities of community organizations—strengthened during the first phase of TASAF (TASAF I)—to implement it. Again, communities supported under TASAF I had already successfully managed projects, making them relatively good candidates to operate a community-based CCT. Lessons from the pilot will potentially have broad operational implications both for low-capacity countries worldwide that are considering novel social protection plans, and for donor-supported social fund portfolios.

In the community-based CCT pilot, the community organizations handle many of the activities related to implementation and operation of the CCT, including:

- Screening of potential beneficiaries,
- Communicating program conditions to potential beneficiaries,
- Transferring funds to individual beneficiaries, and
- Applying peer pressure for compliance with the program conditions.

### Poverty and Vulnerability Targeting

The CCT pilot was implemented in the districts and communities targeted under TASAF I. TASAF I targeted the poorest and most vulnerable districts of Tanzania using a rigorous selection process. Regions were ranked using several indicators (poverty level, food insecurity, primary school gross enrollment ratio, access to safe water, access to health facilities, acquired immune deficiency syndrome [AIDS] case rates, and road accessibility). Districts were then prioritized within the regions using an index of relative poverty and deprivation constructed using data from Tanzania's 1992 Income and Expenditure Survey.

In addition, participatory assessments were conducted to gain an understanding of the coping strategies used by the poor.

Potential elderly beneficiaries in a control community in Kibaha district, 2012.

Community-Based Conditional Cash Transfers in Tanzania • http://dx.doi.org/10.1596/978-1-4648-0141-9

## Coverage

At the household level, eligibility criteria for beneficiary households were based on household characteristics of the very poor that were defined by communities themselves through focus group discussions. The precise targeting criteria are defined later in this section.

The CCT pilot operated in three districts—Bagamoyo (70 kilometers from Dar es Salaam), Chamwino (500 kilometers from Dar), and Kibaha (35 kilometers from Dar), as shown in map 1.1.

The pilot covered 80 communities (40 treatment and 40 control). At the time of the baseline survey, there were 1,764 households and 6,918 individual beneficiaries. All 80 communities within the three districts had community management committees (CMCs) that received financial training from TASAF during TASAF I, and had successfully managed at least one TASAF-supported project.

**Map 1.1  Map of Project Areas**

*Source:* World Bank data.

The CMCs in the pilot communities comprised of between 6 and 14 members, male and female, who lived in the community. In the midline survey, 58 percent of households reported that a CMC member was a neighbor, and 23 percent reported that a CMC member was a blood relative.

The communities were randomized into treatment and control groups, stratified on community size and district. In other words, among communities of a similar size and in the same district, each community had an equal likelihood of becoming a treatment community (that is, the potential beneficiaries identified would receive cash transfers during the evaluation phase of the project) or becoming a control community (that is, the potential beneficiaries would not receive cash transfers during the evaluation phase of the project). The randomization methodology maximizes the likelihood that treatment and control communities are similar in unobserved characteristics as well as in measured characteristics. Beneficiaries in control communities received benefits after the formal evaluation was concluded.

### Project Cycle and Key Stages of Implementation

Key stages of the CCT process are elaborated below and illustrated by figure 1.1.

1. *Community Sensitization and Supply Capacity Assessment:* Prior to the targeting of beneficiaries, an extensive communications and training program on the CCT program was conducted by TASAF at the regional, district, and community levels.

**Figure 1.1 Project Cycle for Community-Based Conditional Cash Transfer**

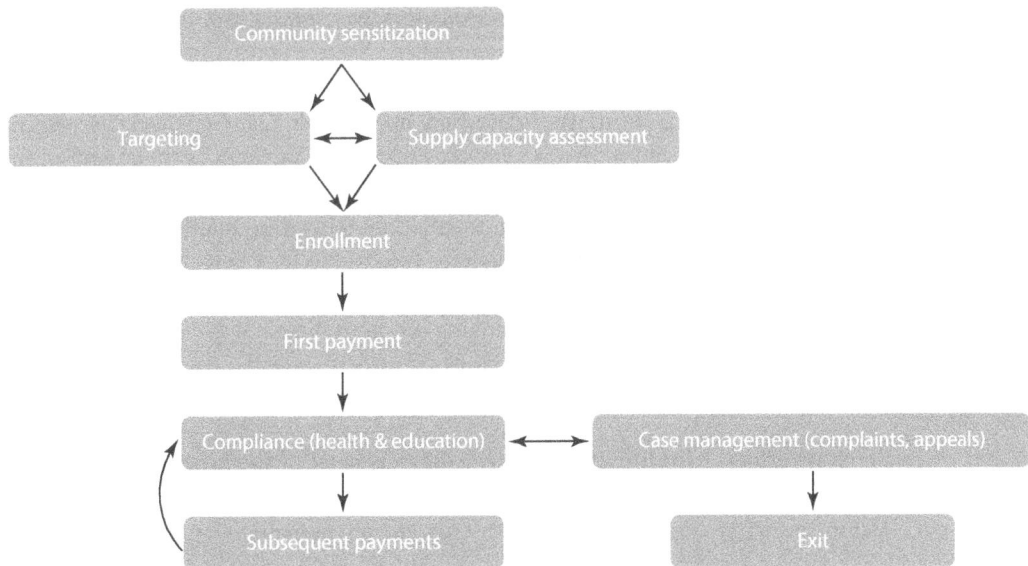

*Source*: World Bank data.

2. *Targeting:* The targeting process aimed at identifying, selecting, and prioritizing the poorest and most vulnerable households. Rather than purely using a centralized system for identifying the most vulnerable on a nation- or district-wide basis, the social fund relied on a system that combined means-testing with reliance on the community's knowledge to target the most vulnerable at the community level.

Targeting was done by community management committees (CMCs) under the oversight of the Village Council (VC), the local governing body, and with the endorsement of the Village Assembly (VA), which consists of all adults who live in the village. The CMC was democratically elected by potential beneficiaries and endorsed by the VA. Targeting was done using screening forms designed to identify vulnerable children and elderly people based on the following criteria, which were defined by the communities themselves.

Vulnerable children were defined as follows:

- One parent or both parents deceased
- Abandoned children
- Having one or two chronically sick parents (for example, human immunodeficiency virus [HIV]/AIDS)
- Chronically sick children, despite having two parents alive.

Vulnerable elderly were defined as follows:

- Elderly with no caregivers
- Poor health
- Very poor.

The CMC used these poverty indicators to identify the poorest (approximately) half of households in the community. Next, the CMC—under the supervision of local government authority (LGA) facilitators and the guidance of the VC—collected data from the identified households using a special screening form for first verification by proxy means test. LGA facilitators then verified the accuracy of collected data. With these data, TASAF performed proxy means testing on a sample basis to ensure that targeted beneficiaries qualified.[3] Households were divided into three groups: eligible, ambiguous, and rejected. Validation of the list of eligible households was done by the Village Assembly, allowing for community validation. Priority ranking of households was conducted in the event that the number of beneficiaries exceeded available resources, along the following criteria:

First priority:        Households with a child as head of the household
Second priority:    Households with an elderly person as head of the household
Third priority:        Households with only elderly persons

The final list of households was then endorsed by the VA. Random selection of the control and treatment communities was done after vulnerable households

Potential beneficiaries in a control community in
Bagamoyo district, 2012.

were identified in all 80 communities, in order to ensure comparability between vulnerable households identified in the treatment and control communities.

3. *Enrollment:* The enrollment of beneficiaries was carried out in each community, with the enrollment process lasting between one and three days, depending on the total number of beneficiary households in the community. The enrollment team identified who would receive payments in each household (usually the mother of the children in the household if present), updated family information, linked children and the elderly with schools and health centers, provided an orientation session about the program, and provided identity cards. Data collected during enrollment was entered into a Management Information System (MIS), which generated the official lists of beneficiary households. Table 1.1 shows the number of households enrolled by district.

**Table 1.1  Interviewed, Eligible, and Invited Households**

| District | Households interviewed | Households eligible | Households invited to enroll |
|----------|------------------------|---------------------|------------------------------|
| Bagamoyo | 13,397 | 6,836 | 1,335 |
| Chamwino | 10,122 | 4,766 | 692 |
| Kibaha | 7,174 | 4,130 | 472 |
| Total | 30,693 | 15,732 | 2,500 |

*Source:* World Bank data.

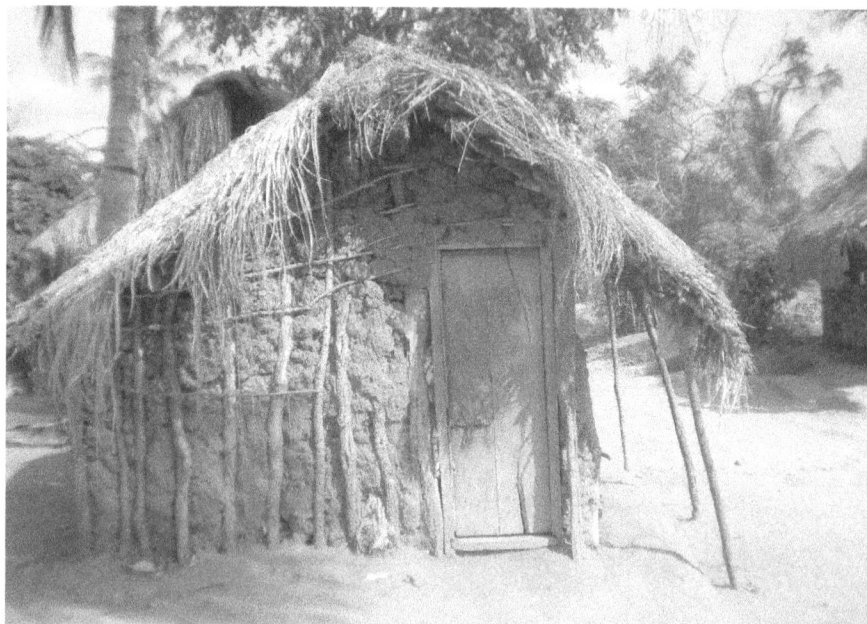

A beneficiary's home, 2013.

4. *Payments and Flow of Funds:* Payments to beneficiary households are made bimonthly (every two months), ranging from a US$12 minimum to a $36 maximum depending on the number of people in the household. Figure 1.2 shows the distribution of transfer amounts, as reported by the households. These figures were based on the food poverty line,[4] and calculated as follows:

- US$ 3 per month for orphans and vulnerable children up to 15 years of age (approximately 50 percent of the food poverty line). Initially this was T Sh 3,600, but later that amount was revised to T Sh 5,100 to account for inflation.
- US$ 6 per month for elderly at least 60 years of age (100 percent of the food poverty line). Initially this was T Sh 7,200 but was later revised to T Sh 10,500.
- No household was to receive less than US$ 6 per month, and no household was to receive more than US$ 18 per month.

The first payments were made in January 2010, and continued every two months since then. Funds are routed to communities through the local government authorities (LGAs). The governance picture in Tanzania varies widely, with some local governments having sophisticated planning and budgeting processes, while others with low capacity have inadequate planning and budgeting capabilities. In districts where the local government was certified compliant via Tanzania's Local Government Development Capital Grant program,[5] payments were disbursed by TASAF to a bank account managed by the LGA, which disbursed the funds directly to the community-managed accounts. If the local government was

**Figure 1.2  Distribution of Household Transfer Size**

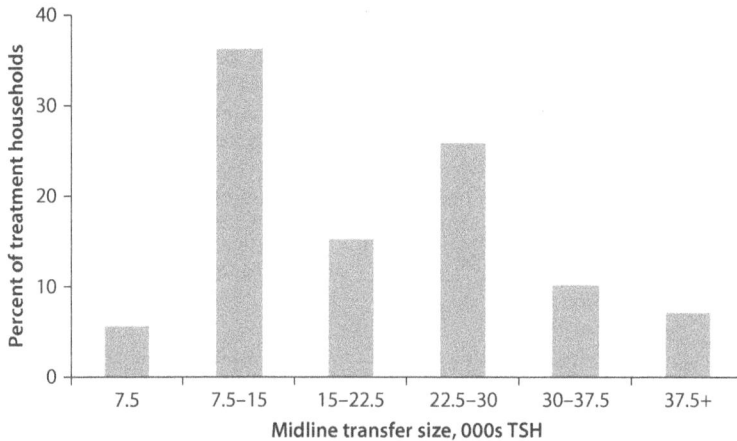

Source: World Bank data.

not qualified to receive capital development grants, TASAF disbursed the funds directly to the community-managed accounts. The community management committees are then responsible for making payments to beneficiary households.

5. *Conditions and Monitoring Requirements:* The role of conditions is to ensure that children go to primary school and that both the elderly and children visit health facilities, fostering long-term improvement in their education and health indicators. The details of the conditions are described in table 1.2 below, followed by a description of monitoring requirements.

Monitoring of conditions began after the first payment was disbursed to beneficiaries in January 2010, and then was done every four months. The monitoring process was conducted by TASAF and the CMCs, with support from schools, health centers, and district staff. Monitoring forms were completed by schools and health centers, collected by the communities, and delivered to TASAF (through the district authorities) where monitoring data were entered into the MIS, and the payment list was generated.

If beneficiaries failed to comply with the conditions, a warning was issued to them by the CMCs. This, however, did not yet affect their payments. If after the next monitoring period (eight months after the first payment), beneficiaries still failed to comply with the conditions, payments were reduced by 25 percent and a second warning was sent. After two warnings were issued, beneficiaries that failed to comply were suspended indefinitely, but allowed to return to the program after review and approval by the communities and TASAF.

The CMCs played a key role in monitoring conditions, as they were responsible for collecting the monitoring forms from schools and health clinics, and conducted awareness sessions for the beneficiaries on a regular basis. They also made regular home visits to stay abreast of developments in beneficiary households in order to update the records as changes occurred in the households, and delivered warnings when conditions were not being met. As of September 2011, over

**Table 1.2  Conditions to Receive Benefits from Conditional Cash Transfer Programs**

| Sector | Beneficiary | Conditionality | Frequency of required compliance | Frequency of compliance monitoring |
|---|---|---|---|---|
| Education | All beneficiary children 7–15 years old | Enrollment in primary school | Once a year | Once a year after the enrollment period ends, by filling out compliance form |
| | All beneficiary children 7–15 years old | Individual attendance | 80% attendance of total school days | Six times a year, by filling out compliance form |
| Health | Children 0–5 years old | Visit to health facility to monitor growth | Six times a year | Six times a year, by filling out compliance form |
| | Children 0–2 years old | Vaccination and growth monitoring | | |
| | Elderly (60+ years old) | Visit to health facility for basic check and orientation | Once a year | At the end of annual visit, by filling out compliance form |

*Source*: World Bank data.

86 percent of beneficiary households reported that a member of the CMC had visited their household at some point since the program began in January 2010. About 93 percent of people claimed to have received their transfers from the community office, while 3.5 percent said that the CMC came to their house to deliver the payment, and the remainder received the payment in some other way.

6. *Case Management:* Case management covers the range of appeals, complaints, and other issues arising during the course of the program. Households that believed they met the beneficiary criteria and were unfairly excluded from the pilot could appeal to the local government authorities or TASAF. Beneficiaries could submit complaints to TASAF and the local government authorities on issues relating to payments, quality of education and health care services, and management of the program by community members, local government or TASAF staff. Other social welfare issues that come to light through the program (for example, violence or abuse in the households) were referred by the community to the relevant government ministry at the district level using existing procedures for dealing with such issues.

7. *Exit Policy for Beneficiaries:* Households were included in the program for the duration of the pilot provided that they complied with the conditions. They could also leave or be asked to leave the program for the following reasons:
- If they chose to opt out, and have informed the community management committee
- If the household no longer had an elderly person or a child under age 15 that was in primary school
- If household members failed to comply with conditions after a warning had been issued three consecutive times for children, and two consecutive times for elderly people

- If they moved permanently to another community where the program was not operating
- If the household representative had presented false information related to eligibility and/or committed fraud against the program.

### Pilot Monitoring and Evaluation

Monitoring activities for this pilot fell into two major categories, which comprised routine monitoring and a community score card exercise.

### Routine Monitoring and Reporting Activities

These were carried out as part of implementation by TASAF and local government authorities, with input from communities, to ensure that activities were being carried out as planned, proper targeting had taken place, and funds were properly disbursed. TASAF submitted quarterly financial management reports, and conducted semi-annual audits of community accounts. TASAF is subject to independent financial audits led by Tanzania's auditor general, and also undertakes systematic process and technical audits (all of which have been highly satisfactory to date). Information provided by the community management committees on monitoring of conditions was randomly cross-checked against submissions from the schools and health facilities.

### Community Score Cards

A module on community score cards (CSCs) was used as part of the intervention itself to enhance the accountability and process monitoring of the CCT roll out. CSCs are simple community monitoring tools that blend different participatory monitoring approaches and social accountability techniques (such as social audits and citizen report card surveys). They have proven to be powerful instruments to exact accountability and promote transparency in rural contexts.[6] The CSC process consists of four elements:

1. Input tracking—in which a mini social audit is undertaken at the community level that attempts to match project/program inputs with actual outputs and disbursement. In the context of the CCT pilot it means tracking disbursements and timing of CCTs to stated beneficiaries and cross-checking targeting efficiency. For the schools and health centers themselves, it tracks key infrastructure and materials that are available (for example, classrooms, medicines, and medical equipment)
2. Community performance scorecard—in which different focus groups (for example, CCT beneficiaries, nonbeneficiaries, youth, elders, men, women) in each community rate the performance of different elements of a program (in this case the CMC management, CCT system, and the participating school and health facilities) on different performance criteria (such as transparency, fairness, timeliness, or adequacy), as well as the services being provided (for example, teachers, health personnel, supplies, and medicines)

3. Self-evaluation score card—the community management committee that is administering the CCT and the schools and health centers participating in the program themselves give a self-assessment of how they see the system performing (these could be similar to the criteria above, but normally one finds that providers rate themselves differently compared to beneficiaries)

4. The interface meeting—providers (CMC, health staff, and school teachers) and the community are brought together to share their results, discuss the findings, and jointly plan how to make the process work better. This action plan can then feed back to TASAF management and ideally would help modify the operation of the pilot in subsequent rounds.

The use of CSCs in the context of the community-based CCT pilot (or CB-CCT) is warranted for several reasons. First, given that the administration of the CCTs is community-based, it is also important to have a monitoring and accountability mechanism at the community level that can help to ensure transparency and oversight of the process. Second, as this pilot tests the CB-CCT model, there is a need for feedback on the process from the grassroots level. Third, the CSCs provide a simple evaluation of the quality of health and school facilities that can supplement the supply side capacity assessment. Finally, the CSCs provide a means for empowering vulnerable households besides the cash transfers.

Implementation of one round of CSCs was managed by the local government authorities in partnership with TASAF and covered a sample of treatment communities.

## Impact Evaluation Description

The primary objective of this evaluation was to test the combined effectiveness of (a) a CCT program in Tanzania and (b) the CDD model of administering a CCT program. If either of these parts failed, then the CCT would be ineffective at improving outcomes for vulnerable households.[7] In other words, the primary objective was to observe whether this community-based model of CCTs could achieve health, education, and consumption gains in the way more centrally administered models have done elsewhere. These research questions are derived from the CCT program's logic model, a schema of which is presented in table 1.3 below. In this model, a set of inputs are translated through program implementation into the delivery of conditional grants to eligible Tanzanian households. These outputs may then affect participants' behavior in terms of health and education investments, consumption, attitudes toward education and health services, and interactions with their community more broadly. If successful, the program would contribute over the longer term toward societal goals like the reduction of vulnerability and a reduction in the intergenerational transmission of poverty, although these longer-term effects are beyond the timeframe of this evaluation.

This impact evaluation focuses on two main areas:

- Household-level outcomes, including program impacts on the health and education of household members and related impacts in the areas of employment and time use, consumption, transfers, savings, and household-level decision making, attitudes, and preferences
- Community dynamics, including program effects on social capital and potential conflicts, traditional solidarity systems, quality and utilization of services and perceptions of service providers, and other communitywide impacts.

### Evaluation Methodologies
#### Quantitative Evaluation

The evaluation uses random assignment of the program at the community level, comparing the changes in outcomes of beneficiary households in 40 randomly selected treatment communities over time to the changes in outcomes of households that *would have been* beneficiaries (had their community been selected) in 40 control communities. The 80 communities were drawn from Bagamoyo, Chamwino, and Kibaha districts. At the time of selection, this was the number of communities in those districts that had managed a TASAF-supported project and therefore had training and experience in financial management, monitoring, and implementation of small-scale infrastructure projects.

In each community, meetings were held to ensure understanding among households and community leaders about the purposes of the impact evaluation (that is, to increase knowledge and inform future planning) and the reasons that treatment could not be universal (a lack of sufficient program resources).

The selection of treatment and control households followed the following process:

*Phase 1: Selection of program communities.* In this phase, the team compiled information for all communities in the three program districts on their population, the existence of the infrastructure necessary to accommodate the increase in demand for community education and health services that a CCT would induce, and the experience and quality of CMCs. This information was necessary to both stratify the sample and ensure that program communities were suited to the requirements of the CCT, including provision of services and enforcement of program conditions.

*Phase 2: Identification of eligible households.* In this phase, the potential beneficiaries in all program communities (not yet divided into control and treatment communities) were identified. CMCs and Village Councils prepared ranked lists of households based on the criteria for vulnerable households that had been previously determined in discussions with TASAF communities. These lists informed the selection of recipient households in treatment communities and of households for data collection in control communities. Expectations of

**Table 1.3  Logic Model for Impacts of CCT Program**

| Resources | Implementation events and action | Direct products of program | Outcomes | Longer-term impacts |
|---|---|---|---|---|
| • TASAF capacity<br>• Health and education service providers<br>• CMC capacity<br>• CCT program financial and technical resources<br>• Social capital in communities<br>• Committed households | TASAF<br>• Determine scope, eligibility criteria, conditions, and so on<br>• Disburse to CMCs<br>• Provide information, education, and community to CMCs<br>• Report to central government and funders<br>• Manage program information via MIS<br><br>CMC<br>• Identify beneficiaries<br>• Communicate conditions<br>• Monitor compliance<br>• Manage cash transfers<br><br>Service Providers<br>• Provide health and education services<br>• Report compliance | • Poor households in selected communities receive transfers<br>• Households more aware of positive health and education practices<br>• CMCs able to effectively carry out program functions | • Improved educational outcomes<br>• Improved health outcomes<br>• Increased consumption<br>• Improved (or at least unharmed) community cohesion<br>• Increased community capacity to address social problems | • Reduced vulnerability<br>• Decreased intergenerational transmission of poverty<br>• Increased income-earning potential of poor households |
| Best measured by process evaluation | | | Best measured by impact evaluation | |

*Source*: World Bank data.
*Note*: CCT = conditional cash transfer; CMC = community management committee; MIS = Management Information System; TASAF = Tanzania Social Action Fund.

residents in all 80 program villages were managed by providing clear communication from the start that not all communities could participate. (Ultimately, additional resources were secured so that transfers could be rolled out to control communities immediately after the endline survey concluded, in November 2012.)

*Phase 3: Selection of the treatment and control communities.* Once eligible households were identified in all 80 program communities, 40 treatment communities were selected at random. Random selection was stratified on known community characteristics (such as subdistrict and community size) to ensure comparability between treatment and comparison communities.

*Phase 4: Selection of the treatment and control households.* The design team used the total share of the eligible population across all selected communities to ensure proper coverage among all treatment communities. CMCs received a cap on how many households in the community could participate in the program based on a combination of community population and poverty map projections.

*Phase 5: Data collection.* There were many more program beneficiaries (in treatment communities) and potential beneficiaries (comparable households in control communities) than could feasibly be interviewed. Once all communities were assigned into the treatment or comparison groups, power calculations identified the need to interview an average of 25 households per community.[8] In cases where participating households (that is, households that *would* receive treatment, whether in a treatment or control community) did not exceed that number, the team interviewed the full sample of target households in that community. In communities with more than 25 participating households, the team collected data on a random sample of 25 households.

Household indicators are supplemented with several modules of community indicators. At midline, information on the education and employment of community leaders was gathered as well as on their effectiveness in mobilizing the community (for example, by measuring the number of community meetings and the number of projects carried out by the community). At endline, surveys of community health facilities (completed by the facility head), community primary schools (completed by the head teacher), and a focus group with community leaders on issues related to governance and institutions were added. These provide important information on how the program affected community leadership and how preexisting community capacity (at baseline) affected program impacts.

### Qualitative Evaluation

This evaluation also incorporated qualitative evaluation methodologies. The qualitative and quantitative approaches are complementary, and their integration is an important characteristic of the evaluation design. Qualitative research offers a number of strengths for evaluating CCTs that quantitative methods do not. Qualitative methods may be especially useful to understand program impacts that are harder to measure through a quantitative survey: for example, changes in social relations and community dynamics, intrahousehold relationships and gender issues, how people view and interact with local program agents, and why and how participants respond to the program design, incentives, training, or other implementation aspects. They also help to build theories about why things happened the way they did (as measured in the quantitative work). Several distinct qualitative methods were employed:

*Phase 1:* Between November of 2010 and February of 2011, a community score card (CSC) exercise was implemented in 20 treatment communities across the three pilot districts. This exercise involved focus groups of varying sizes which rated program performance on criteria such as transparency, fairness, timeliness, and adequacy, and rated the overall quality of services including availability of teachers, health personnel, supplies, and medicines. Following this scoring by community members, CMC members, health facilities staff, and school staff were asked to evaluate themselves. Finally, an "interface meeting" was held, which involved sharing of the findings in a communitywide meeting, followed by the community drawing up an action plan for improving the operation of the pilot in subsequent rounds. Results from the CSC exercise are detailed in chapter 5.

*Phase 2:* Between July and September 2011, a series of focus group interviews were carried out in six of the treatment communities. Focus group interview methods are well suited for understanding how people think or feel about a program, and evaluating how well programs or projects are working and how they might be improved. The focus group communities were selected from the same sample frame as the household survey treatment communities, with purposeful selection of communities by general characteristics (for example, population, ethnic group, geographical location, successful/less successful at program implementation), looking for variety of experience rather than statistical representativeness. Rather than have one communitywide focus group, where power and incentive differences among participants might preclude effectively eliciting in-depth information, there were several separate focus group interviews carried out in each focus group community representing groups of stakeholders: health care providers, Village Councils, CMCs, service providers, beneficiaries, and nonbeneficiaries. The beneficiaries and nonbeneficiaries were divided into male and female groups due to sensitive topics in these focus group discussions. This also allowed for triangulation of viewpoints between the groups. Lessons from these focus groups are detailed in chapter 6.

*Phase 3:* Between July and August 2013 (approximately 1 year after the endline survey), we carried out nine focus group discussions in three communities in Bagamoyo, 20 in-depth interviews in three communities of Kibaha, and 19 in-depth interviews in three communities of Chamwino. We selected communities by employing a *typical* and *deviant* case selection method. We selected one typical treatment community in each district by minimizing the sum of deviations from the mean on 12 dimensions: (a) the baseline values of the following six variables; and (b) the change from baseline to endline on the following six variables:

1. Average food consumption in last week in community
2. Average non-food consumption in last year in community
3. Average literacy rate in community
4. Average attendance rate at school among school-age children in last week in community
5. Average number of health clinic visits per person in community
6. Average share sick in last 4 weeks in community

We then selected a deviant treatment community in each district by maximizing the sum of deviations from the mean on the same six dimensions. Finally, we selected one control community in each district by selecting the control community nearest to either of the two treatment communities selected in the district.

In communities in which we carried out focus group discussions, we carried out three types of discussions:

- Community leaders: VC, CMC members, head teacher, doctor or most responsible health care provider from health clinic, and any other leaders;
- Beneficiaries: a group of 5–7 beneficiaries of the program;
- Nonbeneficiaries: a group of 5–7 nonbeneficiaries.

In communities in which we carried out in-depth interviews, we carried out seven types of interviews:

- Village chairman (VC) or other village committee member
- Village executive officer (VEO)
- Community management committee member
- Head teacher
- Head of health facility (clinic or dispensary)
- Beneficiary (elderly)
- Beneficiary (parent of beneficiary child)

Lessons from these interviews are described throughout chapter 7.

### Household and Individual-level Impacts—Issues and Indicators

In order to measure quantitative changes in treated communities, we used a number of indicators related to education, health, consumption, and transfers. For education, each child's current school enrollment, a measure of frequency of attendance, her current standard (grade level), her standard the previous year (to measure grade progression), and end-of-year test scores were measured. In health, information on clinic visits, recent episodes of disease or illnesses and the steps taken to treat them, and the ability to perform daily activities were gathered. For children, we also gathered information on height and weight to check for malnutrition: short-term malnutrition leads to reduced weight (for a given height), called "wasting," while longer-term malnutrition leads to reduced height (for a given age), called "stunting." Several other questions characterize household perceptions of the quality of local service providers.

For consumption, we measured the number of meals consumed as well as how much and what kinds of foods households consume in a week, to observe whether the transfers affect food consumption. Cash transfers may also affect whatever systems already exist to transfer assistance to the poor. We gathered data on cash and in-kind transfers from individuals, nongovernmental organizations (NGOs), and the government during all survey rounds to examine how the magnitude and nature of those transfers may have shifted in response to this external program. We also ask about vulnerable households' savings to see whether the transfers allow the households to build a buffer against adverse shocks.

Potential beneficiaries in a control community, gathered at a community meeting in Bagamoyo district.

Beneficiaries in a treatment community in Chamwino district, gathered to sing about the census and women's empowerment.

In addition to the quantitative data from the household survey, the qualitative analysis provides complementary information on program impacts at the household level. Issues explored include the following: beneficiary views on program effectiveness and impact, perceptions of timeliness and amount of the transfers, reports of any irregularities, time use trade-offs for children, potential effects on intrahousehold transfers, empowerment effects (for example, confidence, awareness, changes in household decision-making processes), motivational factors (that is, besides cash, what might influence the decision of parents to send children to school, or the elderly to make regular health care visits?), issues around benefits and compliance directed to orphans, the elderly and other potentially vulnerable household members, work incentives, time demands on women, and attitudes toward the education of girls and women.

### Evaluation of Community Dynamics—Issues and Indicators

Impacts at the community level were investigated using both quantitative and qualitative techniques, covering two main areas: (a) general community characteristics and dynamics, and (b) impacts on health and education services. In terms of general community dynamics, the household and community survey modules measured social capital impacts in terms of social cohesion and membership in social and community groups, as well frequency and attendance at meetings, forms of local decision making, perceptions of trust, and number of disputes and crime. The focus group discussions further probed community dynamics in terms of the relationship of the CCT program to traditional solidarity systems and any changes in social relations within the community resulting from the program.

In addition to these general community dynamics, the evaluation explores changes in perception and quality of local education and health services as a result of the program. The household survey asked about service quality and availability. The qualitative methods queried issues involving provider-user interactions, which included involvement of CCT beneficiaries and nonbeneficiaries in decision making regarding school management and health care provision.

### Integration, Synergies, and Phasing
#### Integration of Different Methodologies and Instruments

To achieve maximum effect, the different areas of research focus (household impacts, community dynamics, and program processes) were integrated into the different methodological instruments rather than being treated as separate evaluations. Elements of each area were incorporated into the quantitative household survey as well as the focus groups and the structured interviews, while the community scorecard exercise reveals elements of all three areas. This increases the value added of the mixed-methods approach through triangulation and complementarity. For this reason, in the write-up of final results (in chapter 7), quantitative and qualitative findings are merged to provide a more complete picture of project impacts.

**Table 1.4 Timeline for Implementation of CCT and Accompanying Impact Evaluation**

| Timing | Activity |
| --- | --- |
| November 2007–September 2008 | Program Design (completion of Operational Manual, set up of MIS, preparation of guidelines, forms, and materials for training activities) |
| September–November 2008 | Sensitization at regional, district, ward, and community levels |
| October–November 2008 | Targeting activities (field data collection, data entry, and community validation of beneficiaries) |
| October–November 2008 | Training of district officers and community management committees on the targeting process |
| January–May 2009 | Baseline survey |
| September–October 2009 | Enrollment of beneficiaries |
| January 2010 | First payments made to beneficiary households |
| November 2010–February 2011 | Community scorecard exercise |
| July–September 2011 | Midline survey and first round of focus group interviews |
| August–October 2012 | Endline survey |
| July–August 2013 | Second round of focus group interviews |

*Source:* World Bank data.
*Note:* Activities shaded in gray are part of the evaluation; activities in white are part of implementation. CCT = conditional cash transfer; MIS = Management Information System.

## Implementation Timeline

Table 1.4 below shows the combined chronology of both the program and the evaluation.

## Notes

1. Much of the available evidence is summarized in evidence is summarized in a 2012 book on the rise of transfer programs in Sub-Saharan Africa (Garcia and Moore 2012).

2. Social funds are multisectoral programs that provide financing (usually grants) for small-scale public investments targeted at meeting the needs of the poor and of vulnerable communities, and at contributing to social capital and development at the local level (World Bank 2009).

3. The term "proxy means test" is used to describe a situation where information on household or individual characteristics correlated with welfare levels is used in a formal algorithm to proxy household income, welfare, or need (Grosh and Baker 1995).

4. The food poverty line in rural Tanzania, based on minimum caloric requirement for 28 days is T Sh 6,631 or approximately US$6 (2006 prices) (Gassmann and Behrendt 2006).

5. Tanzania's Local Government Development Capital Grant (LGDCG) system provides financing to local governments for local capital improvements, conditioned on LGAs meeting minimum requirements which ensure that the funds transferred to them are properly used (allowing them to be certified as LGDCG-compliant).

6. See, for instance, the impact of this kind of score card on improving educational outcomes in Uganda (Svensson and Bjorkman 2009).

7. Ideally, one would test the effectiveness of each of these separately: however, due to the lack of a strong central administration to manage a CCT program in Tanzania, all participating communities used the CDD model.

8. With a total of 80 participating communities (40 treatment and 40 control) and a standardized effect size of 0.20, it was expected to need to interview 20 households per community in order to achieve 80 percent power. Twenty-five households per community were then interviewed since not every household would have vulnerable children: some few households would only have vulnerable elderly. This calculation assumed 95 percent confidence levels for statistical significance and an intracluster correlation of 0.05. Evaluations of conditional cash transfer programs elsewhere have found effects of this size. For effects of this magnitude on health and education outcomes in a Nicaraguan CCT, see Rawlings and Rubio (2005), Table 6. For Mexico's PROGRESA program (now called *Oportunidades*), see effect sizes on child height in Behrman and Hoddinott (2001). Also see effect sizes on longer-term schooling outcomes in Behrman, Sengupta and Todd (2005).

# CHAPTER 2

# Results of the Baseline Survey

For the baseline survey, 1,764 households were selected based on a targeting exercise. Of these, 487 were located in Chamwino, 771 in Bagamoyo, and 506 in Kibaha. Baseline households are a subsample of total program (and control) households. All baseline households in the program communities were intended to be included in the program, but the program later decided to include more households with children. The result is that the baseline survey samples about 75 percent of the elderly beneficiaries and 50 percent of the child beneficiaries. The survey, however, represents a representative sample for both children and elderly.

## Vulnerable Groups

In this intervention, vulnerable children are defined as having one or both parents deceased, being abandoned, having chronically sick parents, or being chronically sick themselves. As shown in figure 2.1, only 29 percent of household members aged 18 and under in the baseline sample live with both parents, and 4 percent are orphans. Many children, although their parents are still alive, do not live with them. In particular, only 37 percent of the children in the sample live with their fathers. Working-age adults (aged 18–59) comprise only around one quarter of the members of survey households.

For the purposes of this study, vulnerable elderly are those who have no caregivers, are in poor health, or are very poor. Indeed, just over half of elderly household members in the sample have been too sick to perform their normal activities for 4 or more days in the past month. Almost one quarter are permanently physically disabled, and under 15 percent can do vigorous activities without difficulty.

The households included in the sample have also suffered from many severe shocks in the past five years. Figure 2.2 depicts the 10 most common shocks suffered by sample households in the five years previous to the baseline survey. A majority of the households experienced agricultural shocks including drought, floods, crop disease, pests, or animal damage. Almost a third of households had a household member that suffered from a chronic or severe illness or accident.

**Figure 2.1  Parental Status for Children in the Sample**

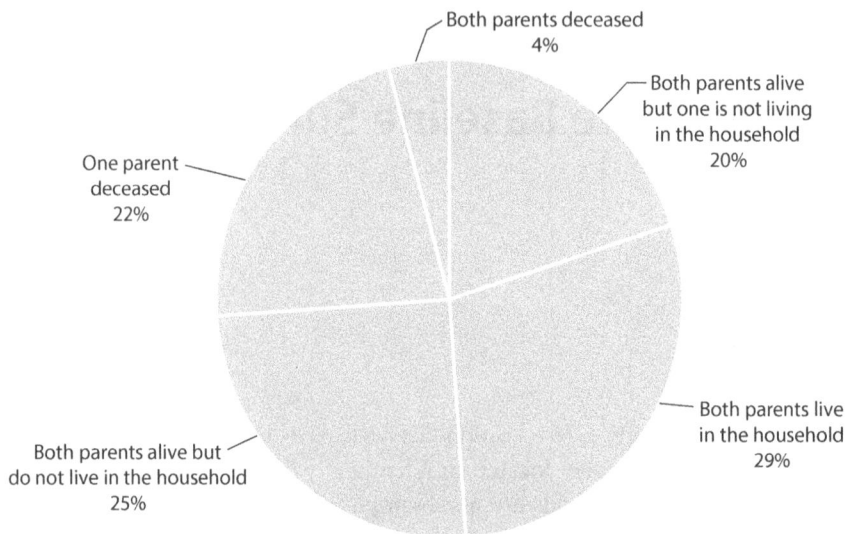

Both parents deceased
4%

Both parents alive
but one is not living
in the household
20%

One parent
deceased
22%

Both parents live
in the household
29%

Both parents alive but
do not live in the household
25%

*Source:* World Bank data.

**Figure 2.2  Most Common Shocks Suffered by Sample Households in the Past 5 Years**

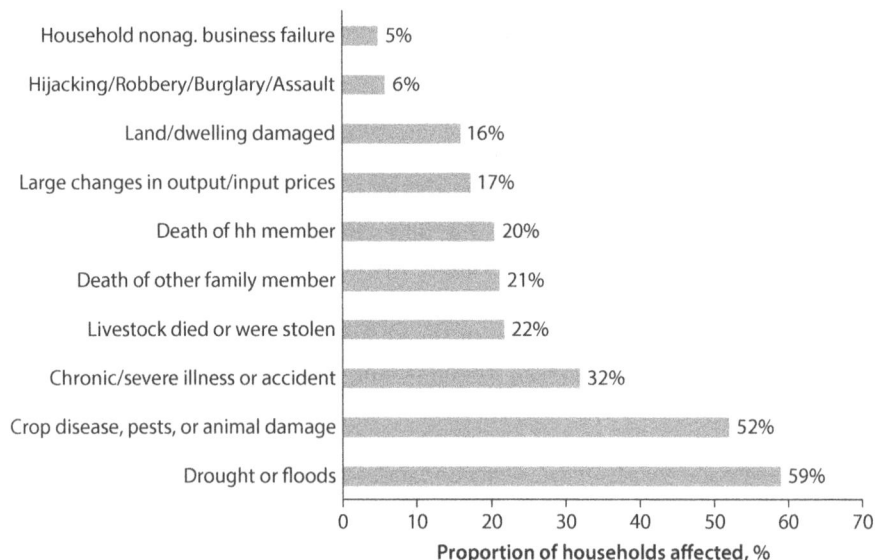

| | |
|---|---|
| Household nonag. business failure | 5% |
| Hijacking/Robbery/Burglary/Assault | 6% |
| Land/dwelling damaged | 16% |
| Large changes in output/input prices | 17% |
| Death of hh member | 20% |
| Death of other family member | 21% |
| Livestock died or were stolen | 22% |
| Chronic/severe illness or accident | 32% |
| Crop disease, pests, or animal damage | 52% |
| Drought or floods | 59% |

Proportion of households affected, %

*Source:* World Bank data.

## Household Characteristics

### Household Composition

In every district included in this survey, the average number of elderly people and children in each household far outweighs the average number of working-age adults (figure 2.3). Indeed, in over 40 percent of households, there is no working-age adult present. Of those working-age adults that are present, almost

**Figure 2.3 Household Composition by Age**

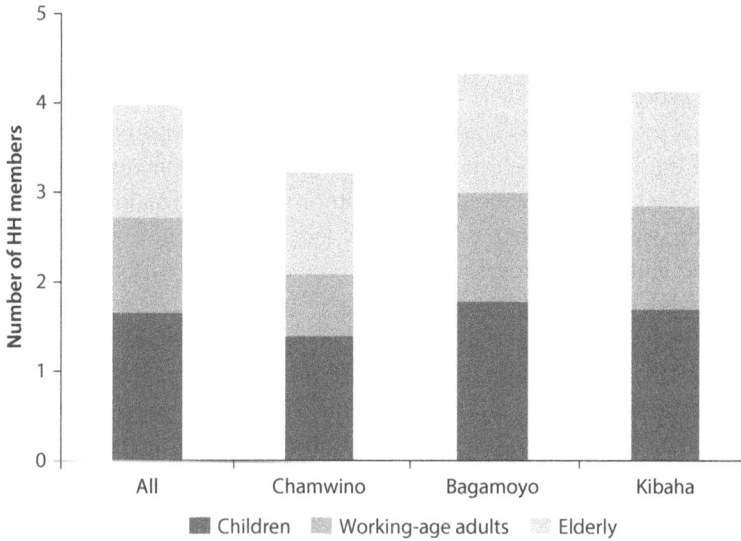

*Source:* World Bank data.

**Figure 2.4 Distribution of Children's Ages**

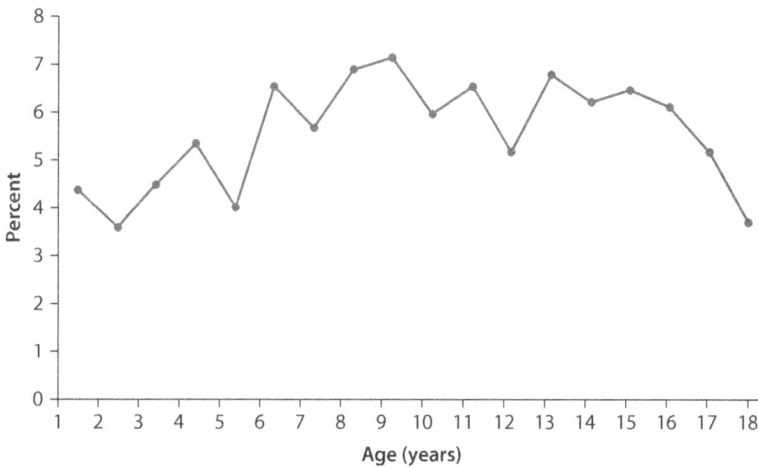

*Source:* World Bank data.

10 percent have a permanent disability. This indicates that this survey is effectively targeting the appropriate, vulnerable population.

There are no children in 38 percent of households and no elderly in approximately 12 percent of households. There are only 35 households that have no elderly or children (less than 2 percent of total households).

There are only five child-headed households, but 83 percent of the households are headed by an elderly person. Of the children in the sample, there seem to be fewer very young children (4 and under) and older children (over 15) than children aged 5–14 (see figure 2.4).

A majority of households in this sample are headed by men, particularly in Bagamoyo and Kibaha. Chamwino, in contrast, has a fairly equal distribution of male- and female-headed households (figure 2.5).

### Socioeconomic Indicators

A vast majority of the sample does not live in houses made of improved materials. Almost all of the houses have mud floors, and most have roofs made of mud or thatch (figure 2.6). Only 6 percent have an improved floor (mainly concrete but also including wood and tiles), while 94 percent of households have a mud floor. Indeed, over half of the households live in mud structures with a mud floor and walls with either a thatch or mud roof.

Households almost always use a pit latrine (71 percent) or have no sanitary facilities at all (28 percent) (figure 2.7). Only around 31 percent have access to piped water, and almost 40 percent of these households have untreated piped water. Over half of households (55 percent) obtain water from unimproved sources including uncovered wells, unprotected springs, rivers, lakes, and ponds.

**Figure 2.5  Percentage of Households That Are Female-Headed, by District**

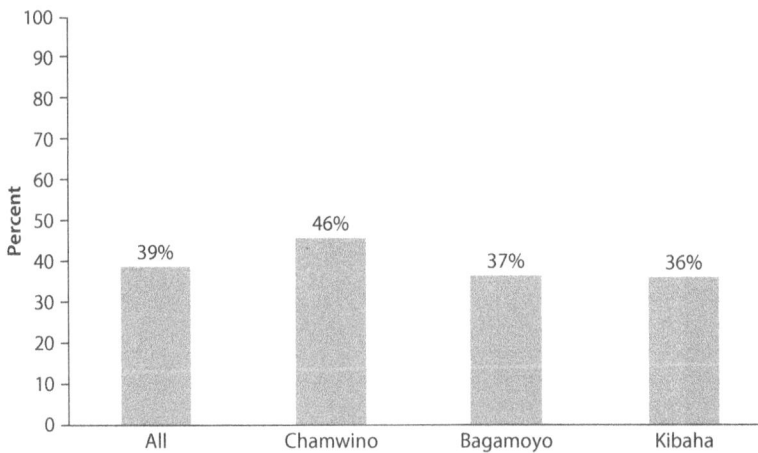

*Source:* World Bank data.

**Figure 2.6  Housing Construction Materials**

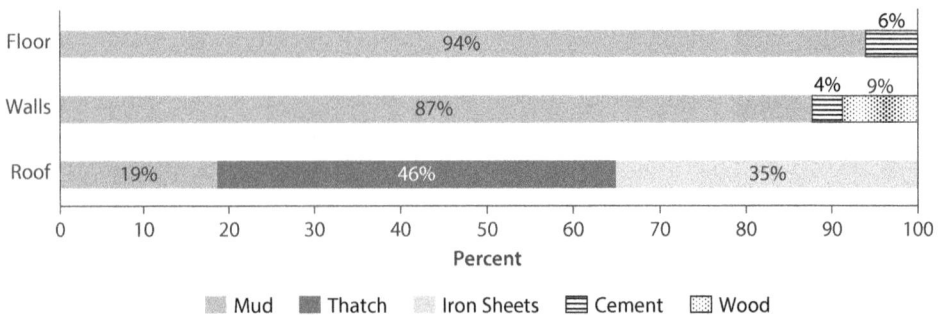

*Source:* World Bank data.

**Figure 2.7  Sanitary Facilities of Households**

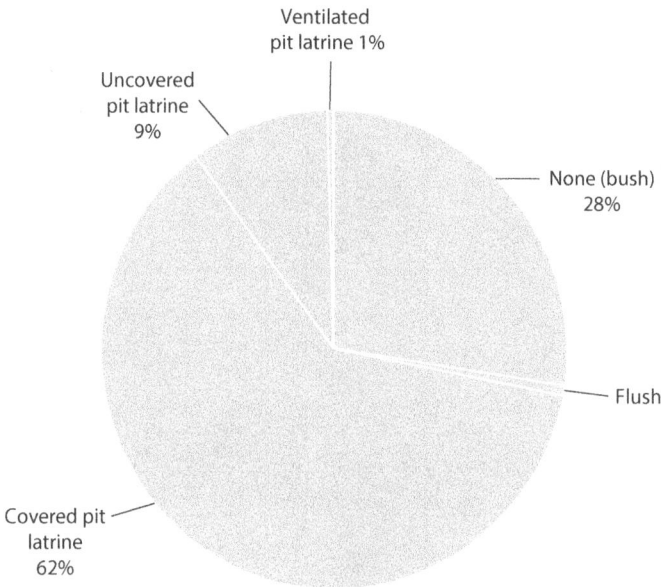

*Source:* World Bank data.

**Figure 2.8  Source of Water for Households**

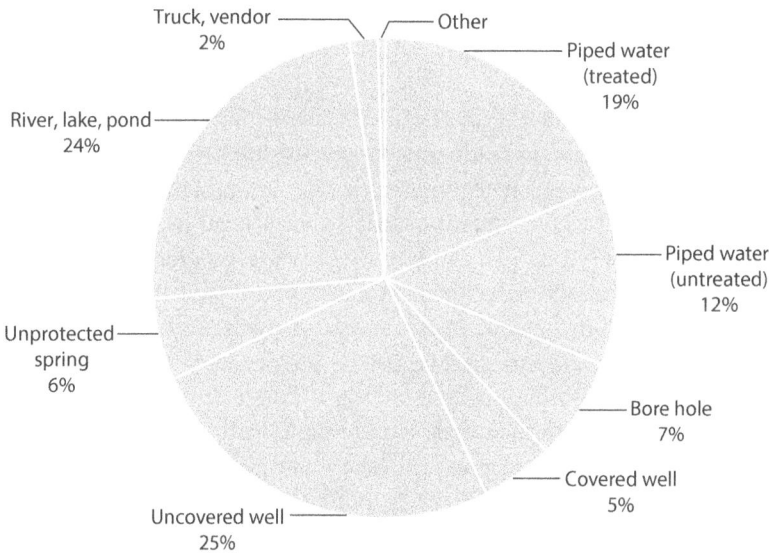

*Source:* World Bank data.

Rivers, lakes, and ponds alone are the source of water for almost a quarter of sampled households (figure 2.8).

Around 99 percent of households lack access to electricity; and 97 percent of all households use firewood (22 percent) or kerosene or paraffin (75 percent) for lighting (figure 2.9).

**Figure 2.9  Sources of Home Lighting**

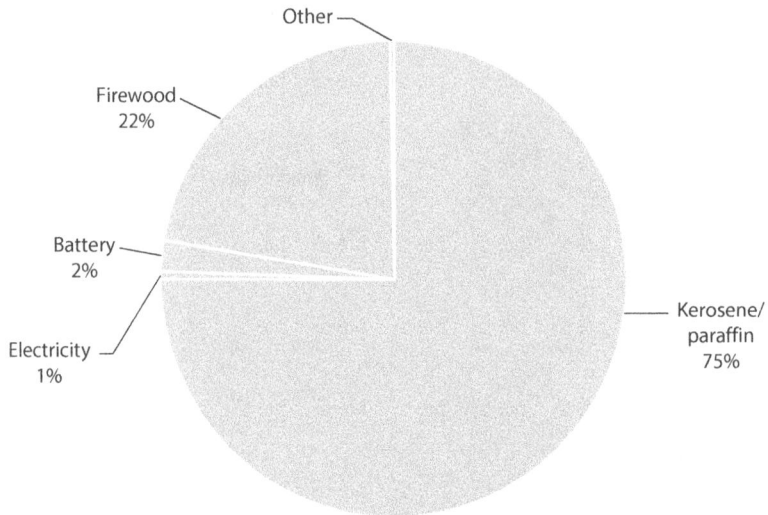

Source: World Bank data.

Almost all households own their own house or it is provided for free (only 29 households in the entire sample pay any kind of rent), and 85 percent claim to own some agricultural land. However, only one household reports having a title deed to this land. The average household owns 4.86 acres, while no household owns more than 80 acres.

## Education

Overall, fewer than half of the individuals in the sample report that they can read and write. Figure 2.10 breaks down the literacy rate among sample households in each district by age. Only 23 percent of elderly are literate (according to self-reports), which is much lower than the rate for younger generations. Over half of younger adults and children are literate. However, this is not the case in Chamwino, where only 40 percent of adults under the age of 60 are literate. Overall, 54 percent of men and 35 percent of women surveyed are literate, although the gender gap has disappeared among children, with female children even more likely to be literate than male children in Chamwino and Bagamoyo.

Current enrollment numbers (figure 2.11) show that females seem to enroll in school at least as often as males up to age 14, but at higher ages there is a gender gap in enrollment. This gap begins at age 15. Even though enrollment rates are relatively high, a significant proportion of children miss school regularly.

Figure 2.12 depicts the percentage of household members that were ever enrolled in school by age and gender. While among older generations men are significantly more likely to have ever been enrolled in school than women, this is not the case for children under the age of 15.

Of those enrolled in school, 25 percent have missed school in the past week, with the most common reasons being that the child was sick or that school was

**Figure 2.10  Literacy by District and Age**

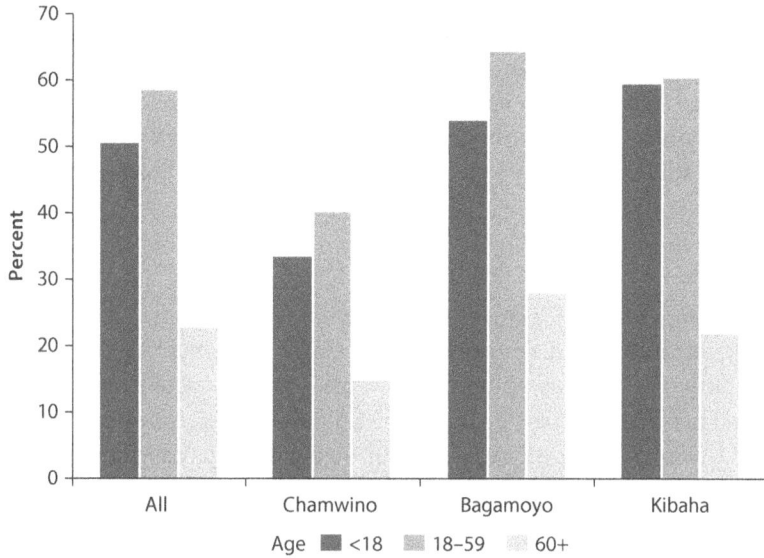

*Source:* World Bank data.

**Figure 2.11  Percent of Children Currently Enrolled in School**

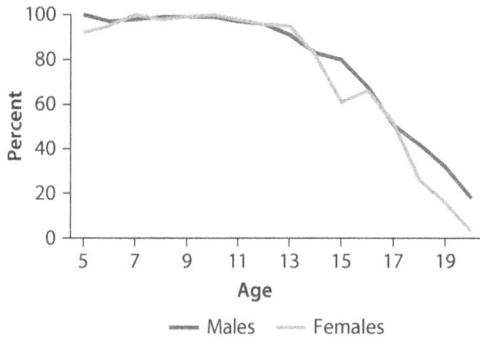

*Source:* World Bank data.

**Figure 2.12  Percentage of Study Participants Attended School Ever**

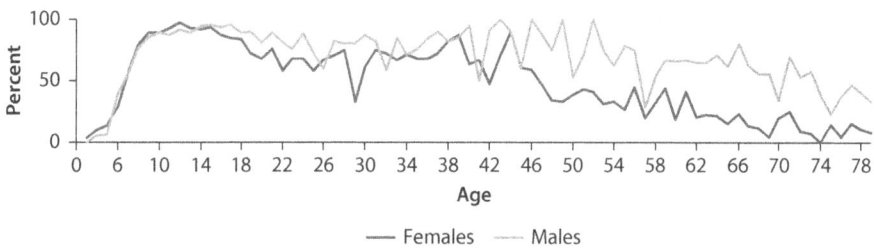

*Source:* World Bank data.

Community-Based Conditional Cash Transfers in Tanzania  •  http://dx.doi.org/10.1596/978-1-4648-0141-9

closed for a break. Additionally, classes were cancelled for 17 percent of respondents in the past week. Over 15 percent of children have repeated a grade.

The vast majority of enrolled students in the baseline survey attend government schools, with only 32 students enrolled in community, religious, and private schools, combined. The average expenditure for each school-enrolled member of a household is T Sh 25,608 (almost US$20 at the time of the survey) in the past year. Almost all students possess exercise books and school uniforms, although only 4 percent own textbooks.

## Health

In the past year, more than 40 percent of all individuals in the sample had visited a health clinic for their own diagnosis. For those suffering from a health problem in the last month, the most common type of health facility visited was a public dispensary, followed by a pharmacy or chemist. While 21 percent said that they received free treatment, 64 percent used their own cash to pay for health visits. The average cost for those who had to pay for treatment of a health problem in the past month was around T Sh 5,000 (US$3.85 at the time of the survey).

Overall, almost 30 percent of members of sample households reported being sick or injured in the past month. This includes 20 percent of children, 25 percent of working-age adults, and almost 40 percent of the elderly. Figure 2.13 gives a distribution of reported illnesses. Over 10 percent of individuals in sample households were permanently disabled, with blindness being the most common disability (almost half of disabled individuals), followed by being crippled, mentally disabled, and deaf.

Most adults in the baseline sample are able to do most daily activities fairly easily; however, many elderly struggle with basic tasks such as walking uphill.

## Economic Activity

The vast majority of adults in sample households spend most of their time doing agricultural work. In over 90 percent of households there is at least one member performing agricultural work. For those adults that do not spend most of their time in agriculture, almost all are either sick or incapacitated, otherwise self-employed, or (if a woman) performing other unpaid family work (figure 2.14).

In Chamwino, maize, sorghum, millet, and groundnuts are the most common crops grown. Almost 50 percent of households grow maize as their main crop, while 34 percent grow sorghum. Almost all production of these two crops is only or mainly for food. Groundnuts are an important second and third crop, and are much more likely to be grown for sale than is maize or sorghum. While 40 percent of households do not have a third main crop, only around 10 percent do not have a second main crop.

The most popular main crops in Bagamoyo are maize and cassava, and the other most important crops are paddy, sorghum, and pulses. Over half of the households surveyed grow maize as their main crop, while around 30 percent grow cassava. More than 90 percent of households grow at least two crops. Almost all maize-growing households report that it is used either exclusively or

**Figure 2.13  Among Individuals Suffering Some Injury or Illness in the Past Month, Share Who Suffered From Each of the Following**

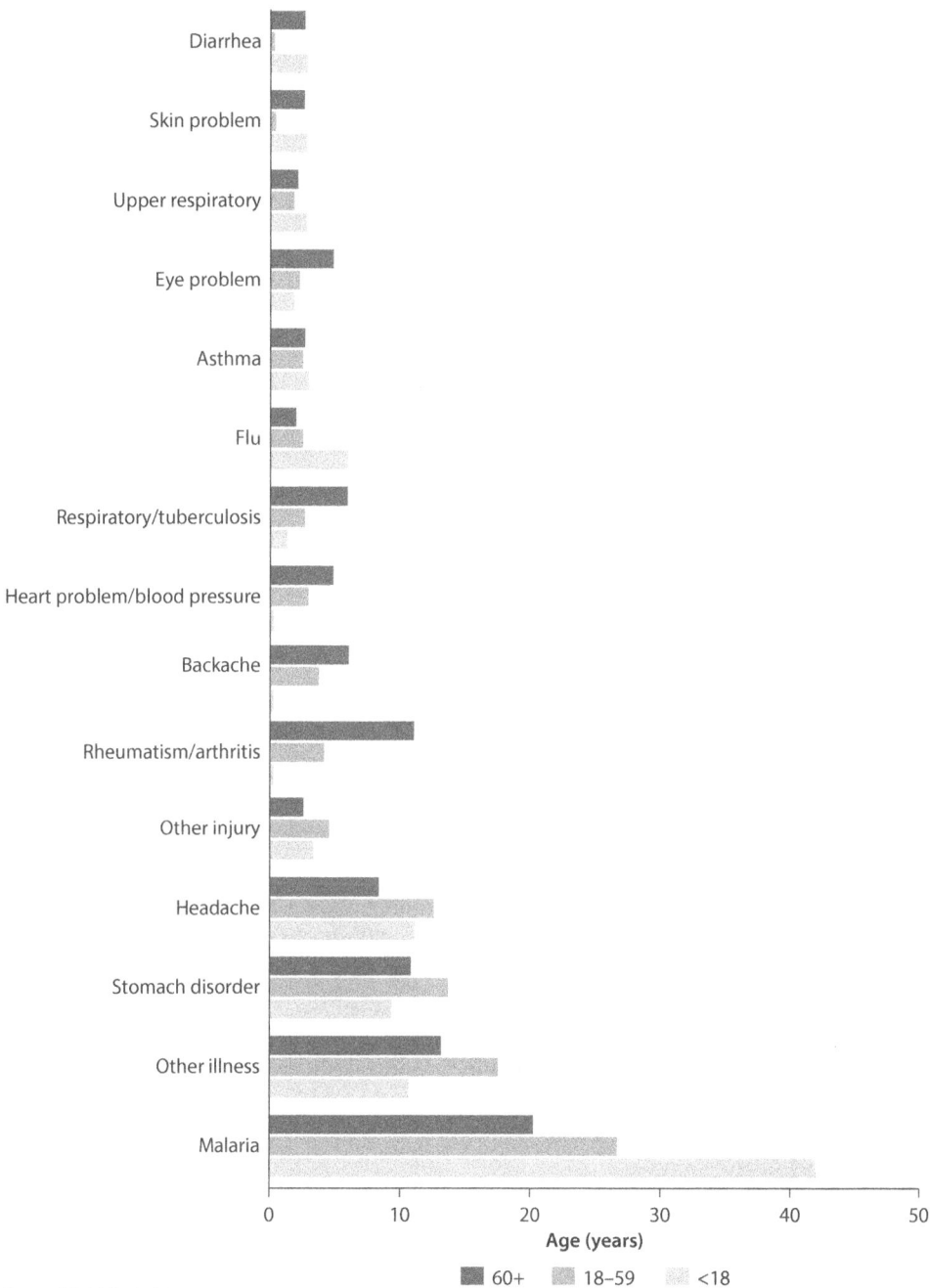

*Source:* World Bank data.

mainly for food, as is cassava. Higher proportions of sorghum, paddy, and pulses are grown for sale.

Unlike in the other districts, cassava is the most important main crop in Kibaha (almost 40 percent of households), followed by maize (37 percent), paddy

**Figure 2.14  Adult Time Use, by Gender**

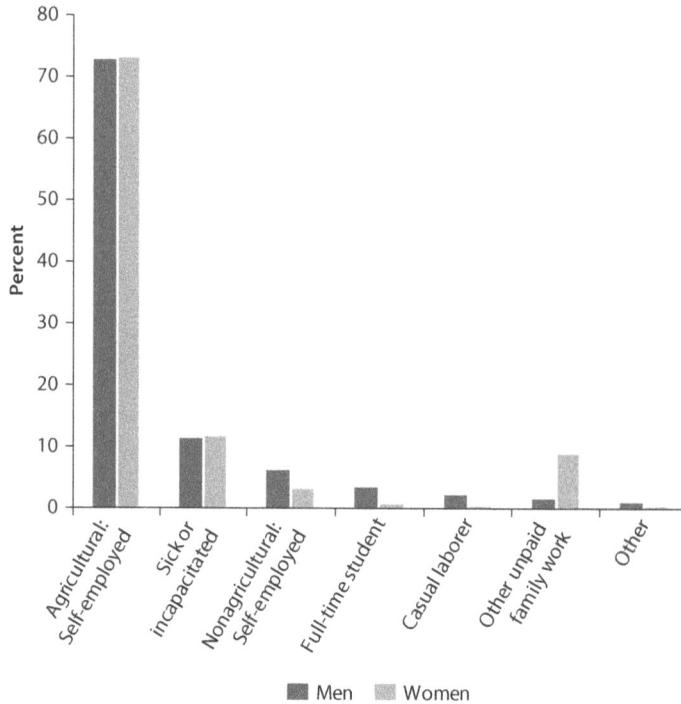

*Source:* World Bank data.

(12 percent), cashew nuts (6 percent), and sorghum (5 percent). These are also the most common second crops, with the addition of pulses, the most common third crop. The third crops in Kibaha are more diverse than in other districts, and are grown by a higher proportion of households (almost 80 percent). In addition to those already listed, okra and tomatoes are also grown by around 5 percent of households. Cashew nuts, tomatoes, and okra are grown for sale by over half of the households that grow them. Of the other crops mentioned, only sorghum and paddy are grown for sale by more than a handful of households (figure 2.15).

While most crops are grown for food, a majority of households in the survey reported the sale of food and cash crops as their main source of income (figure 2.16). Sale of cash crops is also the most commonly reported second most important source of income.

## Child Activities

Three quarters of children 7–17 years of age in the sample households spend most of their time studying (figure 2.17). The other quarter mainly work in agriculture or perform other unpaid family work. In contrast to adults and elderly, only 2 percent of children are sick or incapacitated.

While 75 percent of children are full-time students, some of these students also spend time working to earn income for the family. Only 2 percent of children participate in extra paid classes outside of school. In the sample, 36 percent of children under 18 work on a family income-generating activity. However, less

**Figure 2.15 Purpose of Most Important Crops**

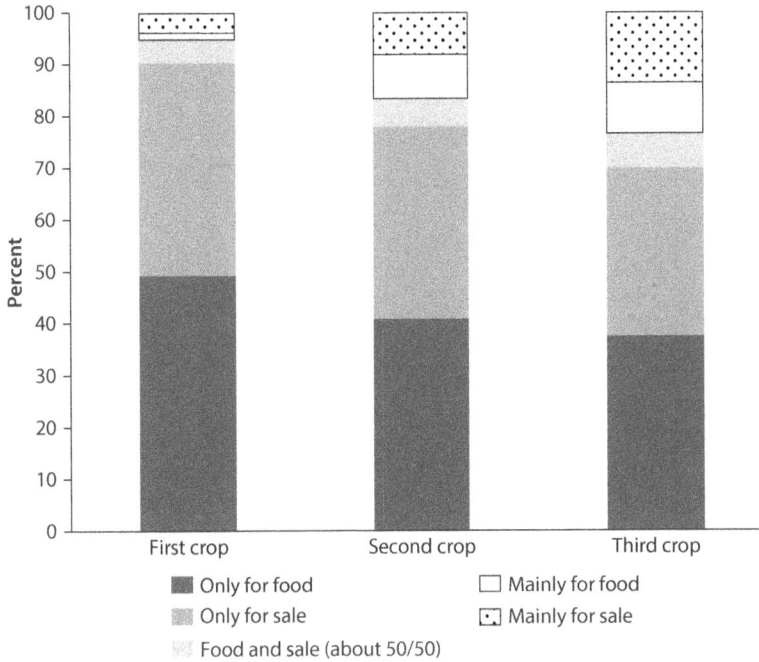

Source: World Bank data.

**Figure 2.16 Main Source of Income**

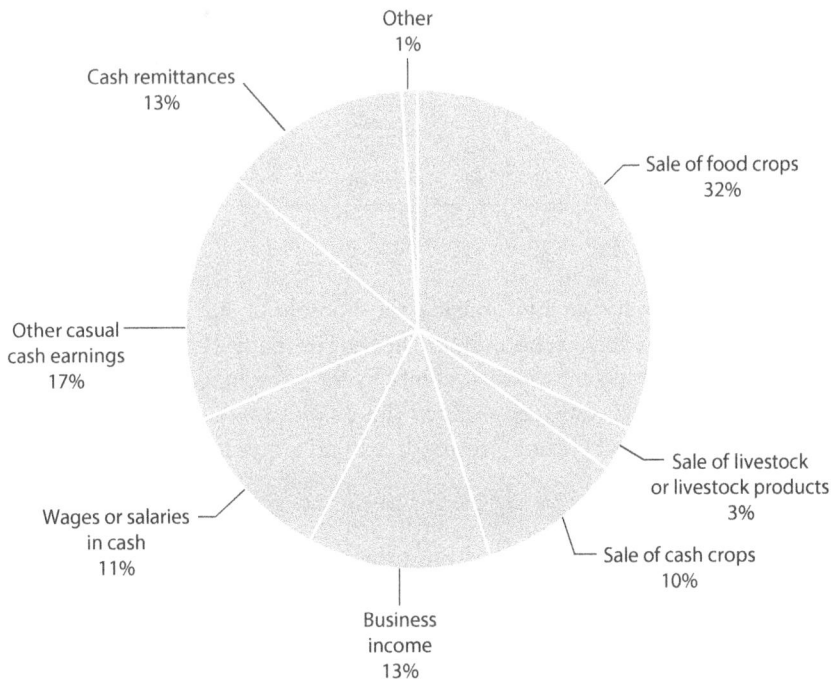

Source: World Bank data.

**Figure 2.17  Child Time Use**

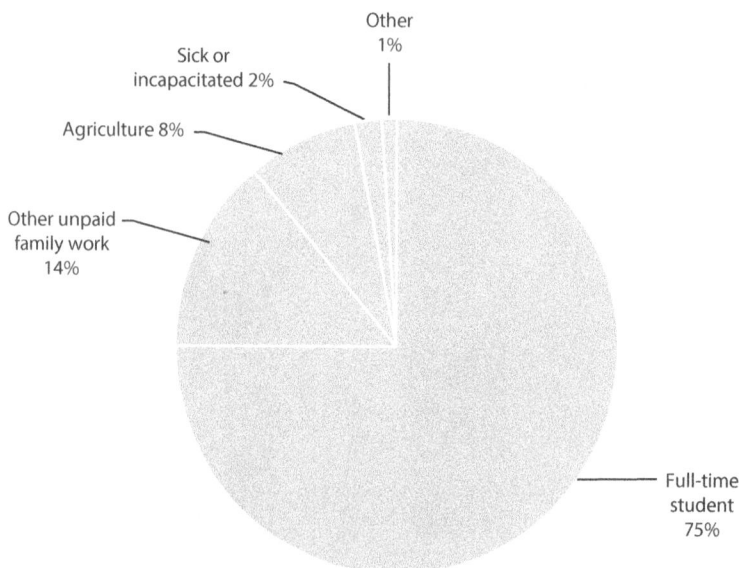

*Source:* World Bank data.
*Note:* Data summarized for children 7–17 years of age.

**Table 2.1  Children's Activities**

| Children (ages 5–18 years) who performed the specified activity in the past week: | | Yes | No | Don't Know | Total |
|---|---|---|---|---|---|
| Fetching water | 57% | 1,366 | 1,013 | 0 | 2,379 |
| Taking care of elderly | 28% | 675 | 1,704 | 0 | 2,379 |
| Cutting firewood | 28% | 665 | 1,714 | 0 | 2,379 |
| Cooking | 26% | 616 | 1,763 | 0 | 2,379 |
| Taking care of children | 16% | 388 | 1,990 | 1 | 2,379 |
| Cleaning toilet | 13% | 308 | 2,071 | 0 | 2,379 |
| Receiving after-school instruction | 2% | 50 | 2,328 | 1 | 2,379 |

*Source:* World Bank data.

than 5 percent work for anyone outside the household. As seen in table 2.1, children also perform various household chores. For many, this is in addition to attending school. The most common activity by far is fetching water. Over twice as many children fetch water as perform the second most common activities: taking care of elderly and cutting firewood. Around a quarter of children cook.

## Consumption and Assets

Figure 2.18 provides an overview of the proportion of households purchasing certain non-food items, and the average annual expenditure on these items for those that do purchase them. In February of 2009, T Sh 1,300 equaled one U.S. dollar. The most widely purchased item among the sample was matches, lighters,

**Figure 2.18  Non-food Purchases: Annual Expenditures and Share of Households Purchasing Specified Item**

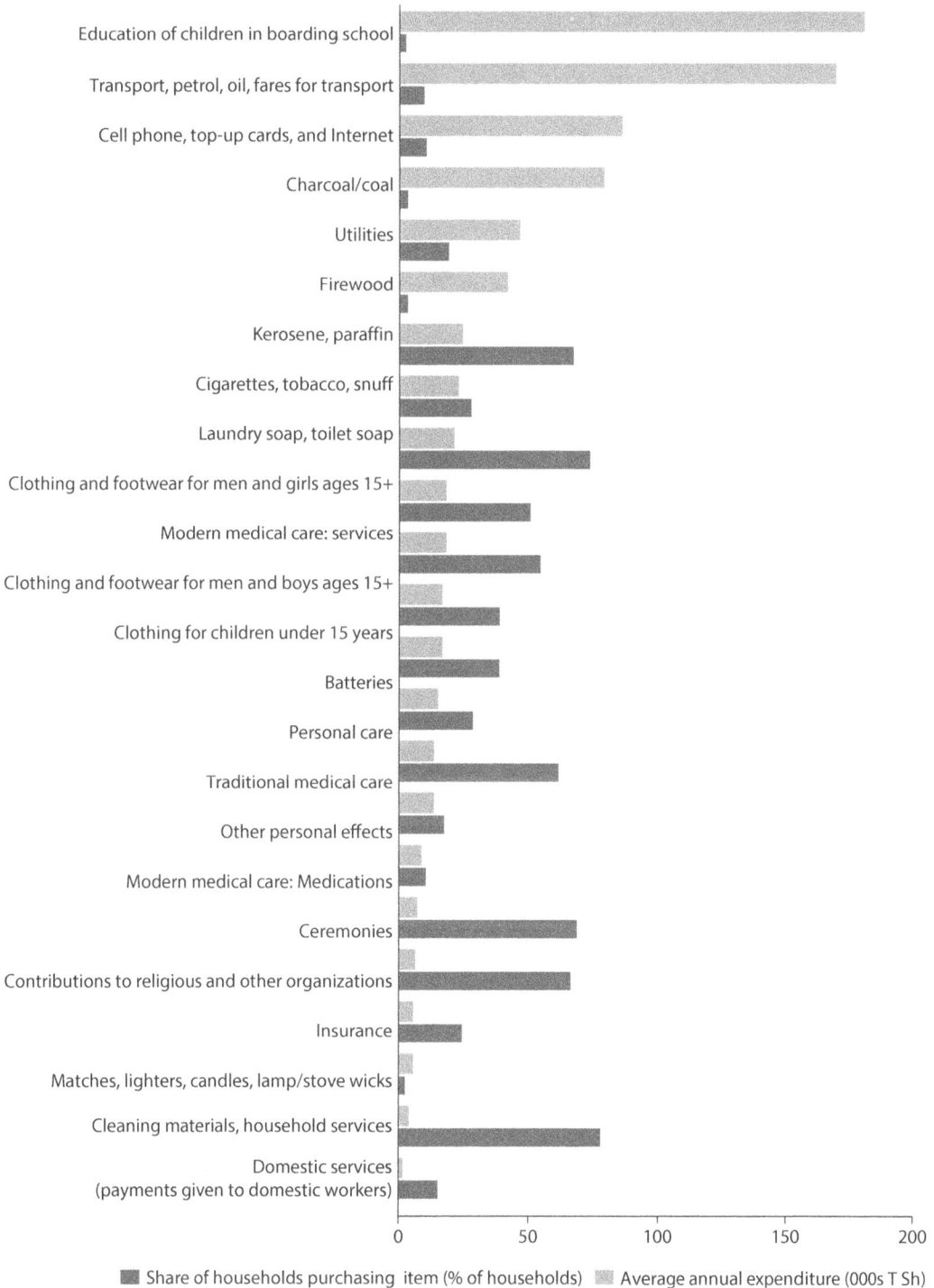

Share of households purchasing item (% of households)    Average annual expenditure (000s T Sh)

*Source:* World Bank data.
*Note:* T Sh = Tanzanian shilling.

candles, and lamp/stove wicks (almost 80 percent), followed by laundry/toilet soap, medications, kerosene or paraffin, and ceremonies.

Few households in the sample own livestock other than chickens; almost half of households own chickens. Goats and ducks or turkeys were the next most popular types of livestock, owned by around 4 percent of households.

As shown in figure 2.19, few of the households in the sample own many durable assets. The only asset owned by most households is a mattress or bed, followed by a radio, which only a third of households possess. Less than 1 percent of households own a television, and only one household owns a car or truck. The lack of assets among sample households indicates that the survey is effectively targeting a vulnerable population.

Out of 3,012 children in the survey, 1,272 (42 percent) own shoes and 1,902 (63 percent) own slippers. Shoes and slippers are important not only for protecting the feet from injury and infection, but also for preventing infections from worms and other parasites.

## Transfers

Very few households in the baseline sample gave out gifts worth more than T Sh 5,000 (US$3.85 at the time of the survey) in the past year, while a considerably higher proportion received goods or cash from friends or other sources worth T Sh 5,000 or more (Table 2.2). Only 6 percent of households gave away goods or cash worth more than T Sh 5,000, with the average amount for those that gave away that much cash (42 households) being around T Sh 17,000. For the 68 households that donated food, the average value was around T Sh 15,000, while the average value for in-kind transfers (only 22 households) was T Sh 42,872.

Less than half of the households in the sample received transfers (of cash, food, or other goods) worth at least T Sh 5,000. Of those receiving at least T Sh 5,000 in cash (25 percent of total households), the average amount received from individuals was around T Sh 30,000. Very few households reported receiving cash from the

**Figure 2.19  Percent of Households Owning Specified Asset**

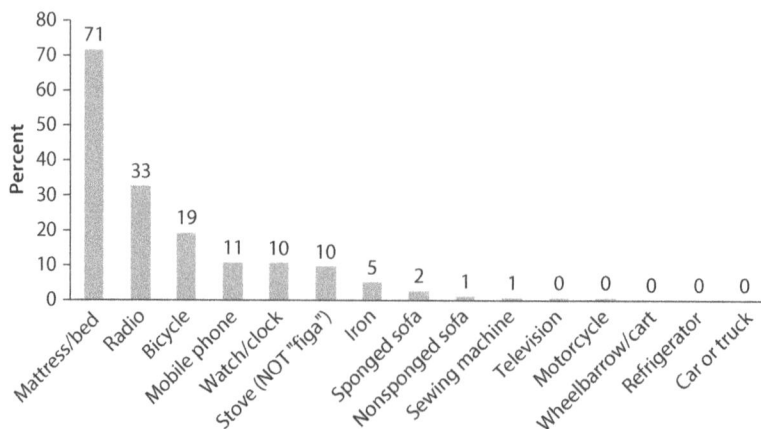

**Table 2.2 Household Transfers**

| Households receiving at least T Sh 5,000 from: | |
|---|---|
| Individuals | 40.4% |
| Government/TASAF | 3.8% |
| NGO/religious organization | 4.9% |

*Source:* World Bank data.
*Note:* NGO = nongovernmental organization; TASAF = Tanzania Social Action Fund; T Sh = Tanzanian shilling.

government, nongovernmental organizations (NGOs), or religious organizations (less than 1 percent). About 24 percent of total households received an average value of T Sh 33,500 (approximately US$26 at the time of the survey) worth of food from individuals (less than 2 percent received food transfers from NGOs or government), and T an average value of Sh 20,000 worth of other in-kind goods. Around 4 percent of households received an average value of in-kind goods of 14,325 (around US$10) from NGOs or religious organizations. Thus, potential receipts from the conditional cash transfer (CCT) program ($72 annually for each eligible elderly person and US$36 annually for each eligible child) would represent a manifold increase in transfer income for the average sampled household.

## Savings and Credit

Very few of the households in this sample have a bank account (less than 2 percent) or other savings (slightly over 1 percent). However, 29 percent of households attempted to borrow from an outside source in the past year. Of these, 64 percent were successful while 36 percent were turned down. Almost all of these loans or attempted loans were in the informal sector, with most from friends, neighbors, or relatives. The average value of an outstanding loan is a little over T Sh 50,000. While most of the loans obtained were used for subsistence needs or medical costs, the reasons that households did not attempt to borrow are more diverse (figure 2.20 and figure 2.21).

## Community

While few people believe that the quality of services in their community is excellent, on the whole they are fairly satisfied with the schools and health facilities (figure 2.22). Only 15 percent believe that the schools are average or poor, and around 30 percent think the same about the health facilities.

Few individuals in the sample participate in community institutions. Only 7 percent respond that any household member was a member of a self-help group in the past year. Of the 13 percent of respondents that say that there is a parent association (a group of parents organized to carry out improvements at the school) in their community, only 9 percent (slightly over 1 percent of all respondents) have a household member that participates in this association. Even more striking is the fact that there are 60 percent of respondents who say there is a community health committee in their community, but less than 3 percent say they participate in this committee. However, there is some community participation among the sample, as 36 percent say that they have contributed labor to a community development project.

**Figure 2.20  Reason Did not Attempt to Borrow**

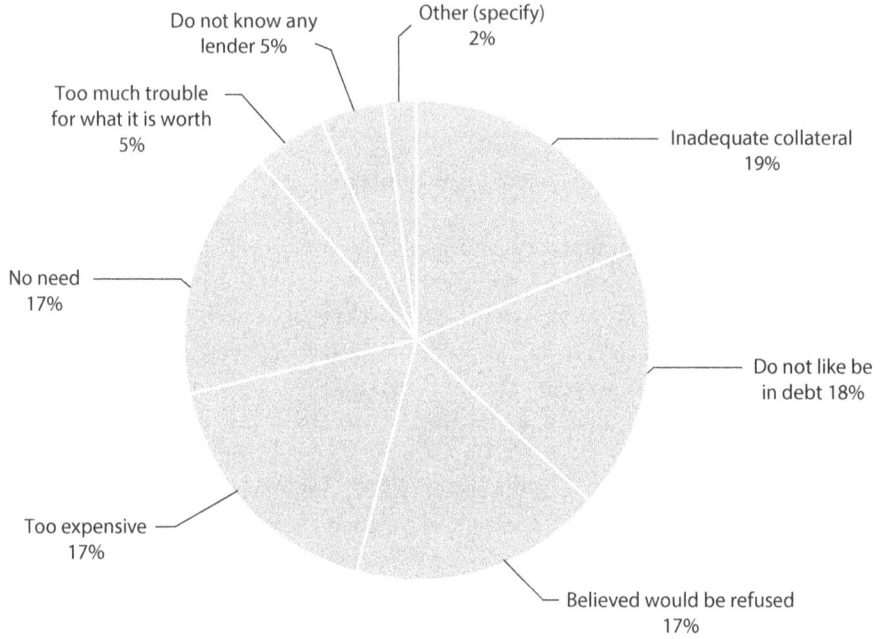

*Source:* World Bank data.

**Figure 2.21  Reason for Loan**

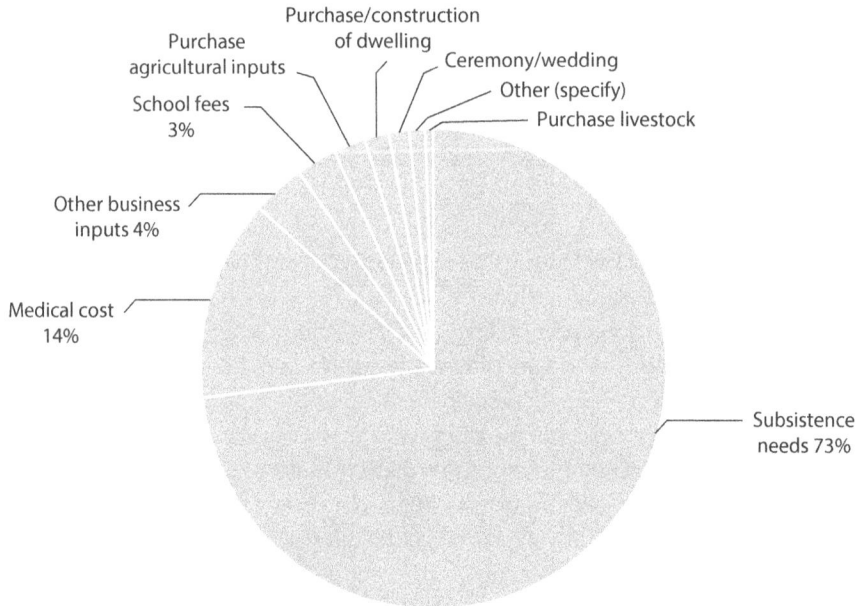

*Source:* World Bank data.

**Figure 2.22 Quality of Schools and Health Facilities**

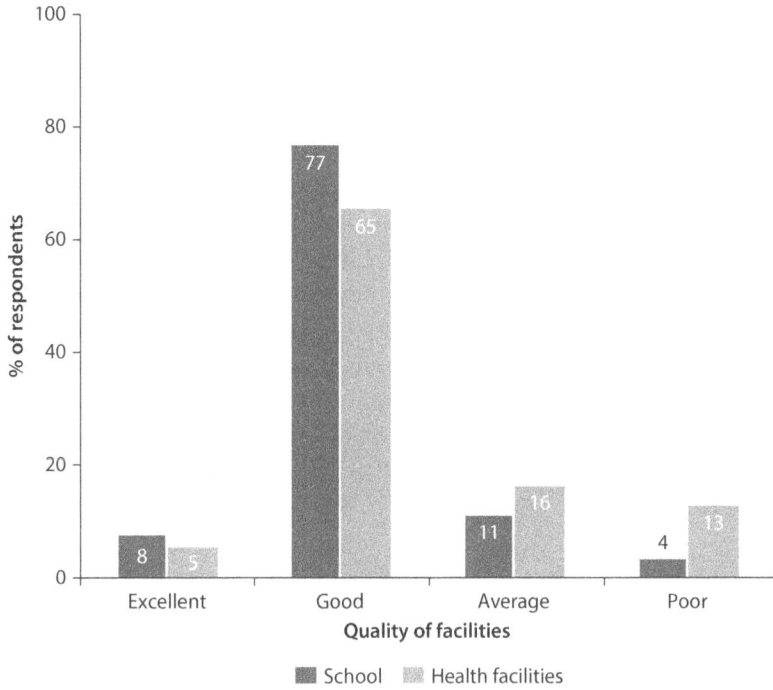

*Source:* World Bank data.

**Figure 2.23 Community Trust**

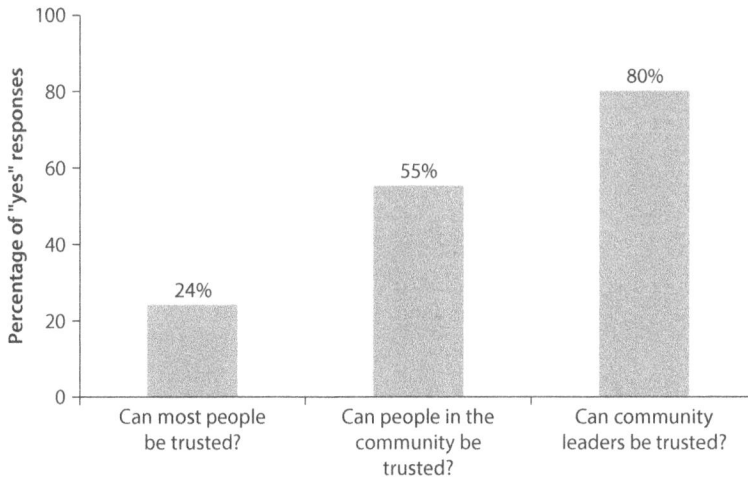

*Source:* World Bank data.

The majority of households report trusting members of their communities and their community leaders. However, they believe it is necessary to be careful around people in general. Only a quarter of respondents believed that they could trust most people (figure 2.23).

Community-Based Conditional Cash Transfers in Tanzania • http://dx.doi.org/10.1596/978-1-4648-0141-9

## Balance across Treatment and Comparison Groups

In this section, we demonstrate that households in treatment and control communities were similar across a variety of characteristics at the time of the baseline survey. The tables in this section show balance on a number of demographic, education, and health indicators.

For the most part, the difference between treatment and control communities is statistically insignificant at conventional levels (figure 2.24). For example, household size is nearly identical at slightly under four members per household in both groups. The difference between treatment and control community households is also not statistically significant for the following sets of variables: Financial (whether the household has a bank account or has borrowed in the past year); physical (whether the household has piped water); educational (household head literacy rates, children now in school, owning a school uniform); health (number of clinic visits, number of disabled household members, whether individuals were sick in the past month); and community interactions (contributing labor to community development projects, trust in community leaders).

In those few cases where there are statistically significant differences between households in treatment and control communities, they tend to suggest that—if anything—households in treatment communities were slightly worse off. For example, the households in treatment communities are less likely to have houses with improved floors or electricity than are those in the control group.

**Figure 2.24  Summary of Baseline Comparison**

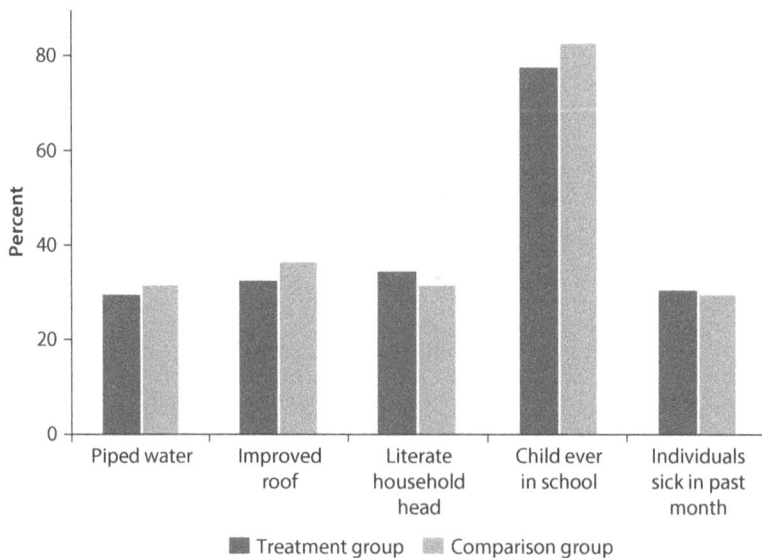

*Source:* World Bank data.

## Household Characteristics

In Table 2.3 below, we compare households in treatment and control communities across a range of household characteristics. There is not a significant difference between the average number of children, number of adults aged 18–59 years, or household size, indicating that households in both types of communities are similar in household membership. The main exception to this is the significant difference in the number of elderly, with control communities having a very slightly higher average number of elderly per household. However, this difference in the number of elderly is relatively small (an average of 0.1 additional elderly in control households, or one additional elderly across ten control households).

Financially, in terms of likelihood of having a bank account or having borrowed in the past year, the households in both types of communities are not significantly different. In terms of housing, households in treatment communities seem to be slightly worse off than households in control communities: They are less likely to have improved floors or to have electricity. Overall, treatment households and control households look quite similar.

## Education

Across a range of educational outcomes, there are no statistically significant differences between treatment and control communities. The means for the two groups are shown in Table 2.4.

**Table 2.3 Comparison of Household Characteristics between Treatment and Control Communities**

| Characteristic | Mean for HHs in treatment Villages | Mean for HHs in control villages | Difference | Significant? |
|---|---|---|---|---|
| Number of children | 1.69 | 1.61 | 0.08 | No |
| Number of elderly | 1.19 | 1.32 | −0.13 | 1% |
| Number of adults 18–59 years | 1.08 | 1.04 | 0.04 | No |
| Household size | 3.96 | 3.97 | −0.01 | No |
| Bank account (% HHs) | 1.6 | 2.1 | −0.5 | No |
| Borrowed past year (% HHs) | 19.3 | 18.2 | −1.1 | No |
| Improved roof (% HHs) | 33.0 | 37.2 | −4.3 | 10% |
| Improved floor (% HHs) | 3.0 | 8.7 | −5.7 | 1% |
| Improved toilet (% HHs) | 69.1 | 75.7 | −6.6 | 1% |
| Piped water (% HHs) | 30.2 | 31.6 | −1.4 | No |
| Electricity (% HHs) | 0.0 | 1.3 | −1.3 | 1% |
| Acres farmed | 2.12 | 1.87 | 0.24 | 10% |

Source: World Bank data.
Note: HH = household.
*Significance is reported at 1%, 5%, and 10% levels. Standard errors are clustered at the village level.

**Table 2.4  Comparison of Education Characteristics between Treatment and Control Communities**

| Characteristic | Mean for HHs in treatment villages | Mean for HHs in control villages | Difference | Significant?* |
|---|---|---|---|---|
| Literate HH head (% HHs) | 34.55 | 32.08 | 2.46 | No |
| Child ever in school (% children) | 78.36 | 83.23 | −4.87 | 5% |
| Child (6–17) now in school (% children) | 86.98 | 89.23 | −2.25 | No |
| Repeated a grade (% children in school) | 27.38 | 26.08 | 1.30 | No |
| Taken a national exam (% children in school) | 98.09 | 98.10 | −0.01 | No |
| Missed school in past week (% children in school) | 29.85 | 22.21 | 7.63 | 1% |
| Own exercise books (% children in school) | 94.48 | 95.56 | −1.08 | No |
| Own textbooks (% children in school) | 2.89 | 4.93 | −2.04 | 10% |
| Own school uniform (% children in school) | 90.89 | 93.43 | −2.54 | No |

*Source:* World Bank data.
*Note:* *Significance is reported at 1%, 5%, and 10% levels. Standard errors are clustered at the village level.
HH = household.

Library in the primary school of a treatment community in Chamwino district.

## Health

There are no significant differences between households in the treatment and control communities across a range of health indicators (Table 2.5). Households in both groups have approximately the same number of disabled people, health clinic visits for both elderly and children, and likelihood of being sick at the time of the baseline survey.

**Table 2.5  Comparison of Health Characteristics between Treatment and Control Communities**

| Characteristic | Mean for HHs in treatment villages | Mean for HHs in control villages | Difference | Significant?* |
|---|---|---|---|---|
| Disabled (# people in HH) | 0.42 | 0.44 | −0.02 | No |
| Hospitalized (# people in HH in last month) | 0.05 | 0.04 | 0.01 | No |
| Elderly health clinic visits (average #) | 2.74 | 2.63 | 0.10 | No |
| Child health clinic visits (average #) | 3.11 | 2.95 | 0.16 | No |
| Sick past month (% individuals) | 31.3% | 29.5% | 1.8% | No |
| Taken medication (% individuals with health problem) | 87.9% | 90.1% | −2.3% | No |
| Ill past year (% individuals) | 65.3% | 63.8% | 1.4% | No |
| Elderly with some vigor (% elderly) | 37.7% | 34.8% | −2.9% | No |

Source: World Bank data.
Note: *Significance is reported at 1%, 5%, and 10% levels. Standard errors are clustered at the village level.
HH = household.

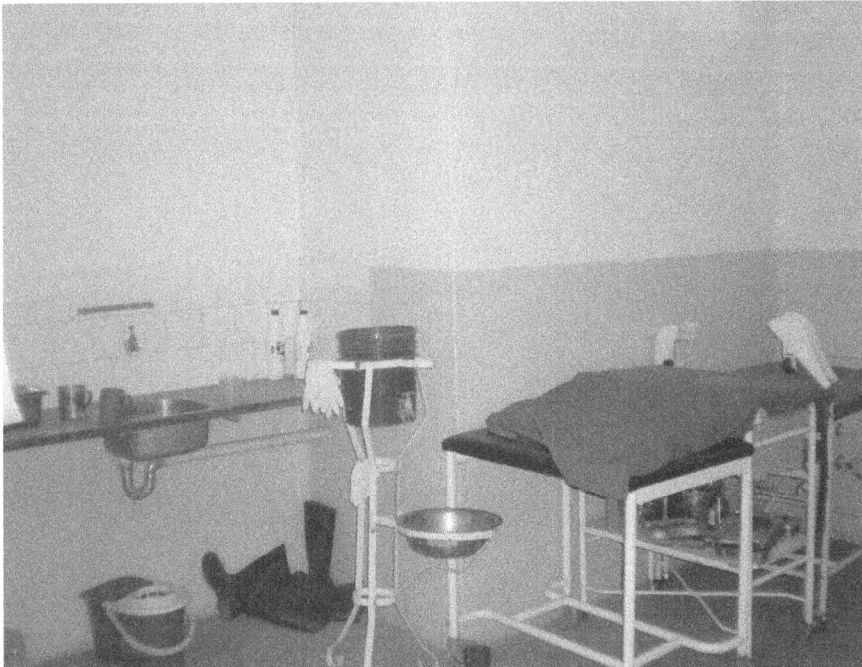

Health clinic in a control community in Chamwino district, serving several communities.

## Community Participation and Trust

Community participation and trust levels across treatment and control communities are broadly similar at the baseline (Table 2.6). There is no significant difference between the two groups in the likelihood to trust most people or community leaders. Only for the question of whether the respondent can trust people in the community was the difference between treatment and control communities on trust questions statistically significant, and even then only at the 10 percent level. Both groups are equally likely to have contributed labor to a community development project.

**Table 2.6  Comparison of Community Trust between Treatment and Control Communities**

| Characteristic | Mean for HHs in treatment villages | Mean for HHs in control villages | Difference | Significant?* |
|---|---|---|---|---|
| Contributed labor to a community development project (% HHs) | 36.25 | 35.27 | 0.98 | No |
| Can trust most people (% respondents) | 25.71 | 22.77 | 2.95 | No |
| Can trust people in community (% respondents) | 58.68 | 52.58 | 6.10 | 5% |
| Can trust community leaders (% respondents) | 80.87 | 80.07 | 0.80 | No |

*Source:* World Bank data.
*Note:* *Significance is reported at 1%, 5%, and 10% levels. Standard errors are clustered at the village level. HH = household.

# CHAPTER 3

# Evaluation Strategy

We use information collected at baseline, midline, and endline to estimate the causal effects of the conditional cash transfer (CCT) program using a strategy known as difference-in-differences. The results of the previous section indicate that, while households in treatment and control communities are largely similar, there are differences in a few variables between the groups at the baseline. This highlights the importance of an empirical strategy that takes initial conditions from the baseline into account. Rather than simply comparing whether households in treatment communities are better off than households in control communities during the follow-up surveys (which would bias against finding actual impacts), a difference-in-differences strategy examines whether treatment community households saw more improvement between baseline and follow-up than did control community households.

For example, imagine that children in treatment households were absent from school almost 30 percent of the time at baseline, whereas children in control households were only absent from school 22 percent of the time at baseline (see table 3.1). If, at midline, we measured that school absenteeism for children in treatment households in fact fell from 30 percent to 18 percent (a drop of 12 percentage points), we would compare that with the change for children in control households, say from 22 percent to 15 percent (a drop of 7 percentage points). The change in control households shows how much treatment households would have changed between baseline and midline in the absence of treatment, due to other factors (for example, improving economic conditions or a season with fewer negative shocks). To ascertain the actual effect of the treatment, we look at the difference in the change (or difference) between the treatment and the control groups. In this example, even though absenteeism fell by 12 percentage points among treatment households, the fact that it fell by 7 percentage points among comparison households suggests that only 5 percentage points of the drop (12 percentage points minus 7 percentage points) are due to the program. The other 7 percentage points of the drop are due to other factors that affect both treatment and control households and have nothing to do with the program; as such, we do not count them as an effect of the program.

**Table 3.1  Difference in Differences Example (%)**

|            | Treatment | Control | Difference |
|------------|-----------|---------|------------|
| Before     | 30        | 22      | 8          |
| After      | 18        | 15      | 3          |
| Difference | 12        | 7       | 5          |

In our estimation, we use fixed effects, which function similarly. Essentially, fixed effects remove what is fixed and unchanging in households over time, and therefore not caused by the treatment. We also use standard tests for statistical significance, so that we can be confident that a given estimate is different from zero. (The 5 percent age points in the example above could be driven by random errors in estimation; our regression estimates of standard errors tell us how confident we can be that absenteeism was actually reduced by 5 percentage points.) Our dataset includes information from 1,764 households surveyed at the baseline, 1,826 surveyed at midline (including split-offs), and 1,784 households surveyed at endline (including split-offs), for a total of 5,374 observations of households. In these households, we have data on 6,918 individuals at baseline, 7,027 individuals at midline, and 6,857 individuals at endline, for a total of 20,802 observations of individuals.

We analyze both individual-level outcomes and household-level outcomes. When we analyze household-level outcomes, we use the household-level dataset, where an observation is a household-year. When we analyze individual-level outcomes, we use the individual-level dataset, where an observation is a person-year. We carry out two types of analysis: One uses data from baseline and midline (on 3,590 households and 13,945 individuals) and the other uses data from baseline and endline (on 3,548 households and 13,775 individuals). For each of these analyses, we estimate the following empirical specification:

$$Outcome = \beta_1 + \beta_2(After) + \beta_3(Treatment \times After) + \Gamma(Fixed\ Effects) + \varepsilon$$

where *Outcome* is any of a number of important outcome measures (some at the household level and some at the individual level), *Treatment* indicates whether a household received treatment (it takes the same value in both periods), and *After* indicates that the observation comes from the follow-up survey (midline or endline) as opposed to the baseline survey. *Fixed Effects* is a set of dummy variables for each household (when we study household-level outcomes) or for each individual (when we study individual-level outcomes). These ensure that we take into account all of the characteristics of a household or of an individual that are unchanging over time (including those we cannot measure), in case treatment is somehow correlated with these characteristics. We essentially compare changes over time in one household (or individual) that receives treatment to changes over time in other households (or individuals) that do not receive treatment, as in the difference-in-differences example above. Note that a stand-alone dummy variable for *Treatment* would be collinear with our fixed effects, and so is not included; as a result, we only see *Treatment × After*, and not *Treatment* alone. The impact in which we are interested is $\beta_3$. This coefficient tells us the effect of receiving treatment at the time of the follow-up survey.

We use two definitions of "receiving treatment." First, we consider treatment to mean living in a treatment community and thus having been selected for treatment. This analysis is referred to as an "intent to treat" (ITT) estimate, since all surveyed households in treatment communities were initially intended to be beneficiaries of the program. Because our baseline survey occurred before the randomization of communities into treatment and control and before the beneficiary lists were finalized, some households we surveyed from treatment communities were not ultimately treated. In an ITT analysis, inference is based on the initial treatment intent (which is random), not on whether treatment was actually received (which may be for nonrandom reasons). Thus, in this first definition (ITT), *treatment* refers to having been initially assigned to treatment (whether or not the household ultimately received treatment). Note that at midline, some of the surveyed households in treatment communities had not received treatment (82 households) and a few of the surveyed households in control communities had received treatment (6 households). The former is likely due to households having been dropped from consideration during the verification process that occurred between baseline and midline. The latter is likely due to households residing near the border of two communities—one treatment and one control.

Second—and precisely to deal with the discrepancies described above—we consider treatment to mean actually receiving transfers as part of the CCT program. This analysis explores the "effects of treatment on the treated" (ETT), since we analyze impacts only on those who were ultimately given transfers.[1] Of course, there may be nonrandom reasons that someone in a treatment community does not receive treatment. For example, relatively less poor households might be the most likely to be cut from the program during the verification process. If less poor households are also the least likely to benefit from the program (because their incomes are already sufficiently high to afford education and health dispensary visits), then excluding them from the analysis might lead to overestimation of the program's benefits. Our ETT analysis circumvents this problem by instrumenting for receipt of treatment with being initially assigned to treatment (which is random). Essentially, we exploit that part of being treated that is driven by being randomly (and thus exogenously, in econometric terms) assigned to treatment. We ignore that part of being treated that is driven by household and community characteristics that might also affect the outcomes we study.

We slightly favor the ETT analysis because it circumvents the problems of intended beneficiaries not receiving treatment. Furthermore, it allows us to understand how the CCT program affects those who actually receive transfers (which is of prime interest to policymakers), rather than how it affects those in program communities (who usually but not always received transfers). In the text, we therefore focus on the results from the ETT analysis.

## Note

1.  We defined receiving treatment conservatively, such that if a household that had been receiving transfers split, all split-off households were considered as receiving treatment, regardless of whether they actually reported continuing to receive transfers. Thus, 22 split-off households that reported not receiving transfers were considered treatment households, because they may have received some transfers before splitting off from the original household.

# CHAPTER 4

# Impact Evaluation Results at the Midline

The households described in the previous section—treatment and control households—were surveyed a second time during July-September 2011, after beneficiaries had received transfers for 18–21 months. We were unable to gather data on 9 percent of original households at the midline survey. However, the likelihood of not being interviewed is uncorrelated with being a treatment village. A detailed analysis of attrition is discussed in appendix A.

We collected data on the same questions studied as a part of the baseline survey. From households in treatment communities, we additionally gathered data on their experience with receiving conditional cash transfers (CCTs)—including their interactions with the community management committee (CMC), how many payments they had received, how they collect payments, whether payments had been reduced for noncompliance, and so on. These data allow us to examine how households' behavior and welfare has changed over time, and importantly whether behavior and welfare changed differently among treatment vs. control households. Our aim is to assess whether at the midline, treatment households are better off than control households on any of a variety of dimensions. This would be evidence that this CCT is a viable way of improving livelihoods.

The midline survey is important for learning about the immediate, short-term effects of this CCT. However, an initial caveat is in order: 18–21 months of receiving transfers may not be a sufficiently long period for a comprehensive evaluation of this CCT. For example, households may be slow to adjust certain behaviors, and some effects may take more time to become visible. An endline survey—carried out between August and October 2012, after households had received transfers for 31–34 months—permits a better understanding of how enduring are these short-term impacts, and to learn about longer-term impacts. An analysis of both quantitative and qualitative findings at endline can be found in Chapter 7.

Next, we describe the estimated effects of the program on a variety of different household-level and individual-level variables. We analyze various factors in several broad categories: health-seeking behavior, health outcomes, child anthro-pometrics, education outcomes, expenditures, food consumption, children's activities and assets, savings and credit, community trust, community participa-tion and perception of public service quality, transfers paid out and received, and livestock, land, and other durable assets. We show that some effects are small or insignificant, while others are large and highly significant. These findings are details below.

## Health-Seeking Behavior

We first analyze how participation in the community-based conditional cash transfer (CB-CCT) (that is, treatment) affects health-seeking behavior of treated households' members. There are several ways to seek health: by obtaining pre-ventative health care, by going to a clinic when ill, by taking appropriate medi-cines and treatments in order to decrease the length of illness, and by paying for health insurance for one's self and one's family. Taking actions to avoid illness or appropriately treat illness when it does strike is incredibly important for health. Being healthy allows individuals to be more productive, and is therefore key to economic development, as well as household well-being overall. Participation in health insurance is also an incredibly important investment—especially given the substantial government subsidy and cost sharing that accompanies public health fund health insurance in Tanzania (Tanzanian German Programme to Support Health n.d.).[1]

In table 4.1, we present robust evidence that treatment is associated with significant increases in seeking treatment from a health center. This is true overall and across various age groups.

First, we see that treatment is associated with significantly more visits to health clinics by all people. At baseline, the average individual in the sample visited a health clinic 2.8 times per year. However, treatment is associated with 1.2 additional visits per year (column 1)—a 43 percent increase over the baseline mean number of visits. The effects of treatment (in number of visits but not in percentage terms) are even larger in magnitude among children ages 0–2 at baseline—a subpopulation specifically targeted by the health care conditions. Column (2) shows that treated children aged 0–1 at the baseline, who visited a health clinic 8.5 times per year at baseline, have an additional 2.3 visits per year due to treatment (a 27 percent increase over the baseline mean). column (3) shows that treated children aged 0–2 at the baseline, who attended a health clinic 10 times per year at baseline, have an additional 1.9 visits per year due to treatment (a 19 percent increase over the baseline mean number of visits). Treatment leads to an additional 1.1 visits per year among elderly (age 60+ at baseline) members of treatment households (column 4), which represents a large, 41 percent increase over the baseline average number of visits—2.8 per year—for this age group.

The CCT has effectively changed how individuals behave with respect to their health; more health-seeking behavior is occurring among both young

**Table 4.1 Effects of CCT on Health Center Visits by Age Group at the Midline**

| | Average number of health facility visits in the past year, by baseline age | | | |
|---|---|---|---|---|
| | (1) | (2) | (3) | (4) |
| | All | Age 0–1 year | Age 0–2 years | Age 60+years |
| Baseline mean | 2.80 | 8.52 | 10.00 | 2.78 |
| **Panel A: Effect of treatment on the treated** | | | | |
| Treatment (ETT) × After | 1.21 | 2.28 | 1.87 | 1.14 |
| | (0.33)*** | (1.14)** | (1.08)* | (0.36)*** |
| After | −1.37 | −2.81 | −2.95 | −1.21 |
| | (0.19)*** | (0.56)*** | (0.58)*** | (0.22)*** |
| **Panel B: Intention to treat** | | | | |
| Treatment (ITT) × After | 1.14 | 1.98 | 1.64 | 1.08 |
| | (0.67)* | (1.58) | (1.66) | (0.52)** |
| After | −1.37 | −2.81 | −2.95 | −1.20 |
| | (0.40)*** | (0.87)*** | (0.98)*** | (0.32)*** |
| R-squared (ITT) | 0.87 | 0.64 | 0.73 | 0.63 |
| Observations | 9,477 | 391 | 547 | 4,029 |

*Source:* World Bank data.
*Notes:* Clustered standard errors in parentheses. CCT = conditional cash transfer; ETT = effect of treatment on the treated; ITT = intention to treat.
Significance level: * = 10 percent, ** = 5 percent, *** = 1 percent.

children and the elderly. If visits to health care clinics improve health, well-being, or productivity, and if individuals were underinvesting in their health before the CCT, then the CCT may be generating large improvements in these areas.

In table 4.2, we analyze the type of care individuals seek when they are ill. We find that treated individuals are 15 percentage points more likely to visit a dispensary or hospital for their largest health problem (column 1), which is a result that is statistically significant at the 5 percent level. This result seems to be driven primarily by elderly individuals. As column (2) shows, treatment does not have a statistically significant impact on the propensity of those aged 0–18 to visit a dispensary or hospital for treatment of their main health problem (possibly because health problems are less severe among this age group). Indeed, column (3) shows that the effects are even more pronounced for elderly beneficiaries, who are 20 percentage points more likely to visit a dispensary or hospital for their largest health problem than are nonbeneficiaries (also significant at the 5 percent level).

Treatment does not have a statistically significant effect on the likelihood of beneficiaries of any age group to take medication for their largest health problem, although the coefficients suggest a positive correlation between treatment and the propensity to treat health problems with medicine. This latter result, however, is hard to interpret. If people are less severely sick when they do get sick, they may simply require less medicine. If being in a treatment community and seeking medical care more frequently leads to less severe illness, then it may lead to less use of medicine. However, being in a treatment community also has

**Table 4.2  Effects of CCT on Type of Health Treatment Sought, by Age Group at the Midline**

| | Those sick in past 4 weeks who... | | | | | |
| | Visited a dispensary/hospital for treatment | | | Took medication for treatment of main health problems | | |
| | (1) All | (2) Age 0–18 years | (3) Age 60+ years | (4) All | (5) Age 0–18 years | (6) Age 60+ years |
|---|---|---|---|---|---|---|
| Baseline mean | 0.52 | 0.60 | 0.46 | 0.90 | 0.92 | 0.89 |
| **Panel A: Effect of treatment on the treated** | | | | | | |
| Treatment (ETT) × After | 0.15 | 0.03 | 0.20 | 0.08 | 0.08 | 0.07 |
| | (0.07)** | (0.12) | (0.08)** | (0.05) | (0.09) | (0.06) |
| After | 0.01 | −0.00 | 0.04 | −0.10 | −0.09 | −0.09 |
| | (0.04) | (0.08) | (0.06) | (0.03)*** | (0.06) | (0.04)** |
| **Panel B: Intention to treat** | | | | | | |
| Treatment (ITT) × After | 0.15 | 0.03 | 0.19 | 0.07 | 0.07 | 0.07 |
| | (0.16) | (0.33) | (0.18) | (0.12) | (0.24) | (0.13) |
| After | 0.01 | −0.00 | 0.04 | −0.10 | −0.09 | −0.09 |
| | (0.11) | (0.24) | (0.13) | (0.09) | (0.18) | (0.10) |
| R-squared (ITT) | 0.86 | 0.91 | 0.82 | 0.84 | 0.90 | 0.78 |
| Observations | 3,744 | 1,002 | 1,645 | 3,751 | 1,003 | 1,650 |

Source: World Bank data.
Notes: Clustered standard errors in parentheses. CCT = conditional cash transfer; ETT = effect of treatment on the treated; ITT = intention to treat.
Significance level: * = 10 percent, ** = 5 percent, *** = 1 percent.

an income effect that makes medicine more affordable. This may contribute to the observed, null effect of being in a treatment community on use of medicine to treat one's main health problem.

One component of health behavior on which participation in the CCT program seems to have very strong and significant effects is on the likelihood of beneficiaries to use health insurance to finance medical care (table 4.3). Across all ages, treatment is associated with an 18 percentage point increase in the likelihood of financing medical care for their last health problem with health insurance, compared with control households. This result is statistically significant at the 1 percent level. This is a huge effect; at baseline, only 2.6 percent of households financed medical care with health insurance. This means that being in a treatment households is associated with 6.9 times more use of medical insurance.

Treatment affects the propensity to finance medical care with health insurance among subgroups of various ages. The largest effects are reported among young children. Treated children aged 0–1 at baseline are 42 percentage points more likely to have their treatment financed by health insurance than are similarly aged children in control households. Children aged 0–4 are 36 percentage points more likely to be insured, and children aged 0–18 are 34 percentage points more likely. Elderly members of beneficiary households are 15 percentage points

**Table 4.3 Effects of CCT on Likelihood of Using Health Insurance to Finance Treatment at the Midline**

| | Those sick in past 4 weeks who financed treatment with health insurance | | | | |
|---|---|---|---|---|---|
| | (1) | (2) | (3) | (4) | (5) |
| | All | Age 0–1 year | Age 0–4 years | Age 0–18 years | Age 60+ years |
| Baseline mean | 0.026 | 0.027 | 0.029 | 0.032 | 0.026 |
| *Panel A: Effect of treatment on the treated* | | | | | |
| Treatment (ETT) × After | 0.18 | 0.42 | 0.36 | 0.34 | 0.15 |
| | (0.06)*** | (0.12)*** | (0.11)*** | (0.09)*** | (0.05)*** |
| After | 0.04 | 0.00 | 0.06 | 0.03 | 0.02 |
| | (0.02)** | (0.00) | (0.06) | (0.05) | (0.01)* |
| *Panel B: Intention to treat* | | | | | |
| Treatment (ITT) × After | 0.17 | 0.38 | 0.35 | 0.31 | 0.14 |
| | (0.15) | (0.30) | (0.31) | (0.29) | (0.11) |
| After | 0.04 | −0.00 | 0.06 | 0.03 | 0.03 |
| | (0.05) | (.) | (0.17) | (0.14) | (0.03) |
| *R*-squared (ITT) | 0.88 | 0.79 | 0.85 | 0.89 | 0.84 |
| Observations | 3,324 | 115 | 269 | 907 | 1,433 |

*Source:* World Bank data.
*Notes:* Clustered standard errors in parentheses. CCT = conditional cash transfer; ETT = effect of treatment on the treated; ITT = intention to treat.
Significance level: * = 10 percent, ** = 5 percent, *** = 1 percent.

more likely to finance medical care with health insurance. Once again, all of these effects are statistically significant at the 1 percent level. Given the baseline average rates of financing medical care with health insurance among each age group, being in a treatment community is associated with sizeable increases in insurance coverage. As a direct result of receiving treatment, 0–1-year-olds are 16 times more likely to be insured, 0–4-year-olds are 12 times more likely, 0–18-year-olds are 11 times more likely, and those age 60+ years are six times more likely. This is a large change in how medical care is financed.

## Health Outcomes

We next analyze how participation in the community-based CCT affects health outcomes for members of treated households. One of the goals of this program has been to improve health by incentivizing health-seeking behavior and health-improving purchases and investments.

In table 4.4, we show that treatment is not associated with statistically significantly lower rates of illness during the 4 weeks previous to the interview—either overall or among specific subpopulations (children aged 0–4, children aged 0–18, and those over age 60). Similarly, we do not find any effects of treatment on the number days in the last 4 weeks for which the individual has been too sick to perform their normal daily activities.

Community-Based Conditional Cash Transfers in Tanzania • http://dx.doi.org/10.1596/978-1-4648-0141-9

**Table 4.4  Effects of CCT on Household Health Outcomes at the Midline**

| | If reported being sick in the past 4 weeks | | | | Number of days too sick for normal activities in the past 4 weeks | | | |
|---|---|---|---|---|---|---|---|---|
| | *(1)* *All* | *(2)* *Age 0–4 years* | *(3)* *Age 0–18 years* | *(4)* *Age 60+ years* | *(5)* *All* | *(6)* *Age 0–4 years* | *(7)* *Age 0–18 years* | *(8)* *Age 60+ years* |
| Baseline mean | 0.27 | 0.75 | 0.60 | 0.46 | 1.63 | 1.04 | 0.81 | 2.79 |
| *Panel A: Effect of treatment on the treated* | | | | | | | | |
| Treatment (ETT) × After | 0.01 | 0.00 | −0.03 | 0.05 | −0.24 | −0.07 | −0.15 | −0.21 |
| | (0.03) | (0.06) | (0.04) | (0.04) | (0.25) | (0.30) | (0.18) | (0.51) |
| After | −0.00 | −0.06 | −0.01 | 0.03 | 0.17 | −0.23 | −0.09 | 0.66 |
| | (0.02) | (0.03)** | (0.02) | (0.03) | (0.17) | (0.17) | (0.14) | (0.32)** |
| *Panel B: Intention to treat* | | | | | | | | |
| Treatment (ITT) × After | 0.01 | 0.00 | −0.03 | 0.04 | −0.22 | −0.07 | −0.14 | −0.20 |
| | (0.04) | (0.08) | (0.05) | (0.06) | (0.38) | (0.42) | (0.26) | (0.73) |
| After | −0.00 | −0.06 | −0.01 | 0.03 | 0.17 | −0.23 | −0.09 | 0.66 |
| | (0.03) | (0.05) | (0.04) | (0.04) | (0.28) | (0.26) | (0.21) | (0.48) |
| *R*-squared (ITT) | 0.66 | 0.62 | 0.61 | 0.59 | 0.66 | 0.63 | 0.61 | 0.62 |
| Observations | 13,923 | 1,106 | 5,221 | 4,032 | 13,922 | 1,106 | 5,221 | 4,031 |

*Source:* World Bank data.
*Notes:* Clustered standard errors in parentheses. CCT = conditional cash transfer; ETT = effect of treatment on the treated; ITT = intention to treat.
Significance level: * = 10 percent, ** = 5 percent, *** = 1 percent.

## Child Anthropometrics

Aside from illness in the last 4 weeks, an important question is whether treatment by the CCT program has had any impact on measureable aspects of child health. To get at this question, we show the effects of the program on child anthropometrics for children aged 0–4 years in table 4.5. In these specifications, we utilize child fixed effects; we thus control for any child-specific characteristics that might influence outcomes, and isolate the effects of treatment.

Assignment to treatment is not strongly associated with changes in children's anthropometric outcomes. Between baseline and midline, changes in weight, middle-upper-arm circumference, and oedema status (also known as edema or dropsy) are similar for children in treatment and in control communities (columns 2–4). There is some indication that treatment is associated with a growth in height that is 3.3 centimeters higher than the growth in height experienced by similar children in control communities (column 1); this result is statistically significant at the 10 percent level. However, when we include age group fixed effects[2] instead of child fixed effects, there is no longer any effect on height. This calls into question the robustness of any apparent impacts on height. It suggests little evidence of any anthropometric effects of the program.

We further investigated whether the community-based CCT has an impact on child Z-scores. The Z-score, or standard deviation classification system, is one way by which a child can be compared to a reference population. Essentially, Z-scores

**Table 4.5 Effects of CCT on Anthropometric Outcomes for Children Age 0–4 Years at the Midline (Absolute Levels)**

| | (1) | (2) | (3) | (4) |
|---|---|---|---|---|
| | Height (cm) | Weight (kg) | Middle-upper-arm circumference (cm) | Dummy—Child has edema |
| Baseline mean | 87.31 | 12.16 | 155.81 | 0.23 |
| *Panel A: Effect of treatment on the treated* | | | | |
| Treatment (ETT) × After | 3.30 | 0.02 | −3.31 | 0.14 |
| | (1.84)* | (0.39) | (2.87) | (0.13) |
| After | 16.35 | 4.87 | 10.46 | −0.32 |
| | (0.98)*** | (0.28)*** | (1.86)*** | (0.06)*** |
| *Panel B: Intention to treat* | | | | |
| Treatment (ITT) × After | 2.70 | 0.02 | −2.83 | 0.11 |
| | (4.28) | (0.95) | (7.55) | (0.31) |
| After | 16.35 | 4.87 | 10.46 | −0.32 |
| | (2.89)*** | (0.80)*** | (5.74)* | (0.19) |
| R-squared (ITT) | 0.97 | 0.98 | 0.95 | 0.90 |
| Observations | 208 | 240 | 190 | 208 |
| Number of individuals | 104 | 120 | 95 | 104 |

*Source:* World Bank data.
*Notes:* Clustered standard errors in parentheses. CCT = conditional cash transfer; ETT = effect of treatment on the treated; ITT = intention to treat.
Significance level: * = 10 percent, ** = 5 percent, *** = 1 percent.

**Table 4.6 Effects of CCT on Anthropometric Outcomes for Children Age 0–4 Years at the Midline (Z-Scores)**

| | (1) | (2) | (3) | (4) |
|---|---|---|---|---|
| | Length/height-for-age Z-score | Weight-for-age Z-score | Weight-for-length/ height Z-score | BMI-for-age Z-score |
| Baseline mean | −1.45 | −0.82 | 0.86 | 0.43 |
| *Panel A: Effect of treatment on the treated* | | | | |
| Treatment (ETT) × After | 0.86 | −0.29 | −0.03 | −1.55 |
| | (1.55) | (1.25) | (0.45) | (1.47) |
| After | 0.16 | 0.92 | 0.49 | 0.61 |
| | (0.67) | (0.79) | (0.22) | (0.21)*** |
| Observations | 204 | 152 | 126 | 128 |
| Number of individuals | 102 | 76 | 63 | 64 |

*Source:* World Bank data.
*Notes:* Clustered standard errors in parentheses. BMI = body mass index; CCT = conditional cash transfer; ETT = effect of treatment on the treated.
Significance level: * = 10 percent, ** = 5 percent, *** = 1 percent.

can tell us by how many standard deviations children differ from a healthy reference population on several dimensions. We calculated anthropometric Z-scores using the 2006 World Health Organization (WHO) child growth standards. We focus on four Z-scores in particular, all of which we computed for children aged

0–4: length/height-for-age, weight-for-height, body mass index (BMI)-for-age, and weight-for-age. The results appear in table 4.6. It is immediately apparent that treatment has no statistically significant effect on any of the four measures.[3]

## Education Outcomes

We also examined whether participation in the community-based CCT affects education outcomes. In table 4.7, we first show that treatment is associated with higher literacy among children aged 0–18 years (column 1). While at baseline, an average of 52 percent of children ages 0–18 years were literate, treatment made children 4 percentage points more likely to be literate. This is an 8 percent increase in the literacy rate, and the result is statistically significant at the 10 percent level. Furthermore, treatment also leads to a higher likelihood of 0–18 year olds having attended school at some point (column 2), and a greater likelihood of their being currently enrolled in school (column 3). While 69 percent of children aged 0–18 years at baseline had attended school at some point, treatment made them 7 percentage points more likely to have done so—a 10 percent increase over the mean rate. Also, while 59 percent of children aged 0–18 years were currently enrolled in school at baseline, treatment made children 6 percentage points more likely to be in school—a 10 percent increase over the baseline mean rate.

**Table 4.7  Effects of CCT on Household Education Outcomes at the Midline**

| | Age 0–18 years | | | | | Age 7–14 years | Age 15–18 years |
|---|---|---|---|---|---|---|---|
| | (1) | (2) | (3) | (4) | (5) | (6) | (7) |
| | Literate | Ever attended school | Currently in school | Missed school last week if enrolled-own fault | Took national exam-Standard IV+ | Completed Standard IV or higher | Completed Standard VII or higher |
| Baseline mean | 0.52 | 0.69 | 0.59 | 0.12 | 0.14 | 0.36 | 0.51 |
| *Panel A: Effect of treatment on the treated* | | | | | | | |
| Treatment (ETT) × After | 0.04 | 0.07 | 0.06 | 0.03 | 0.01 | 0.06 | 0.13 |
| | (0.02)* | (0.02)*** | (0.03)* | (0.03) | (0.02) | (0.03)* | (0.07)* |
| After | 0.18 | 0.13 | 0.02 | −0.03 | 0.01 | 0.29 | 0.26 |
| | (0.01)*** | (0.01)*** | (0.02) | (0.02) | (0.01) | (0.02)*** | (0.05)*** |
| *Panel B: Intention to treat* | | | | | | | |
| Treatment (ITT) × After | 0.04 | 0.06 | 0.06 | 0.02 | 0.00 | 0.06 | 0.12 |
| | (0.03) | (0.04)* | (0.05) | (0.05) | (0.03) | (0.05) | (0.11) |
| After | 0.18 | 0.13 | 0.02 | −0.03 | 0.01 | 0.29 | 0.26 |
| | (0.02)*** | (0.02)*** | (0.03) | (0.03) | (0.02) | (0.04)*** | (0.08)*** |
| *R*-squared (ITT) | 0.84 | 0.83 | 0.74 | 0.70 | 0.73 | 0.81 | 0.80 |
| Observations | 4,823 | 4,823 | 4,822 | 2,897 | 1,796 | 2,320 | 787 |

*Source:* World Bank data.
*Notes:* Clustered standard errors in parentheses. CCT = conditional cash transfer; ETT = effect of treatment on the treated; ITT = intention to treat.
Significance level: * = 10 percent, ** = 5 percent, *** = 1 percent.

Nonetheless, treatment does not have a statistically significant impact on the likelihood that enrolled children aged 0–18 missed school in the last week due to personal reasons (that is, not due to school closure, teacher absence, or some other factor outside their control) (column 4). It also does not affect the propensity for students aged 0–18 to have taken a national exam (column 5).

Treatment also seems to have a large impact on grade progression. Primary school begins at age seven and continues for seven years. The seven grades of primary school are Standard I through Standard VII. We find evidence that treatment has a large impact on whether children aged 7–14 years have completed Standard IV (lower primary school) or higher education, and on whether children aged 15–18 years have completed Standard VII or higher education. At baseline, an average of 36 percent of children aged 7–14 had completed Standard IV. Treatment is associated with a 6 percentage point increase in the rate of completion of Standard IV or higher education, which is about a 17 percent increase over the baseline mean incidence of Standard IV completion. This result is statistically significant at the 10 percent level.

Similarly, at baseline, an average of 51 percent of children aged 15–18 years had completed Standard IV. Again, this is completion of primary school education, which is a prerequisite for passing on to secondary education. Treatment is associated with a 13 percentage point increase in the rate of completion of Standard VII (primary school) or higher education, which is about a 25 percent increase in the baseline mean incidence of Standard VII completion. This result is also statistically significant at the 10 percent level. Thus, treatment appears to have a positive and important impact on educational attainment and grade progression.

Schoolyard in a treatment community in Kibaha district.

Community-Based Conditional Cash Transfers in Tanzania • http://dx.doi.org/10.1596/978-1-4648-0141-9

That the CCT has dramatically boosted whether a child has ever attended school, as well as whether they are currently enrolled in school, but not whether the child recently attended school suggests that the program is enrolling new students but is not encouraging students to spend more time in school than they already do. It could be the case that the conditions for remaining in the transfer program (80 percent attendance rates) are nonbinding (that is, students were already attending at that rate or higher), as only 12 percent of parents at baseline reported their child as having missed school at least once in the past week.

## Expenditures

We also examined whether participation in the community-based CCT changes the amount and composition of annual expenditures on various items. In table 4.8, we show that treatment leads to statistically significantly higher expenditures on children's clothing (significant at the 1 percent level), expenditures on clothing for women and girls over age 15 (significant at the 10 percent level), and expenditure on formal insurance (significant at the 1 percent level). In particular, treatment households annually spend T Sh 3,985 more on children's clothing (column 2), T Sh 3,511 more on clothing and footwear for women and girls over age 15 (column 4), and T Sh 1,268 more on insurance (column 10).

We do not find statistically significant evidence that treatment households spend less on cigarettes, tobacco, and snuff, though the coefficient on treatment is negative (column 1). We also do not find statistically significant evidence that treatment households spend more on modern medical care services or medication (columns 7–8) or on education for children in boarding school (column 9), though the coefficient on treatment for each of these expenditure categories is positive. Treatment has almost no effect—statistically or economically—on expenditures on clothing for men and boys over age 15 (column 3). The coefficient on treatment for this expenditure category (T Sh 242) is very small. Similarly, the coefficient on expenditure on weddings, parties, funerals, and dowries is also small (424) compared to the significant coefficients described above, and is statistically insignificant at conventional levels (column 6). Overall, these results suggest that the program encouraged spending on women and children, and potentially had effects on health and education spending.

## Food Consumption

In addition to non-food expenditures, we also evaluated how participation in the CCT program affects weekly food consumption. We found no significant impact on the consumption of almost any key food item. Table 4.9 shows the effects of treatment on both the purchased value and the home-produced value of six of the most common food consumption items: Super Sembe maize flour, husked rice, sugar, Dona maize flour, dried beans, and other flour. In the case of two of these goods—sugar and dried beans—we consider only the value purchased and

**Table 4.8  Effects of CCT on Household Non-Food Expenditures at the Midline**

| | (1) | (2) | (3) | (4) | (5) | (6) | (7) | (8) | (9) | (10) |
|---|---|---|---|---|---|---|---|---|---|---|
| | | | | Average annual expenditure on the following goods | | | | | | |
| | Cigarettes tobacco, snuff | Children's clothing (all HHs in sample) | Clothing/foot-wear for men and boys >15 years of age | Clothing/foot-wear for women and girls >15 years of age | Other personal effects | Wedding parties/ funerals/ dowries | Modern medical care services | Modern medical care: medication | Education for children in boarding school | Insurance (car, medical, life) |
| Baseline mean | 6,347 | 6,389 | 6,407 | 9,252 | 1,983 | 4,045 | 10,066 | 5,081 | 5,817 | 181 |
| *Panel A: Effect of treatment on the treated* | | | | | | | | | | |
| Treatment (ETT) × After | −2,143 | 3,985 | −242 | 3,511 | 695 | 424 | 1,749 | 1,684 | 2,538 | 1,268 |
| | (2,038) | (1,481)*** | (1,451) | (1,986)* | (414)* | (987) | (2,840) | (1,107) | (3,852) | (267)*** |
| After | 203 | 71 | 39,441 | −733 | −770 | −432 | −3,918 | −2,683 | −3,875 | 173 |
| | (1,249) | (916) | (1,047) | (1,308) | (346)** | (823) | (2,216)* | (907)*** | (3,362) | (51)*** |
| *Panel B: Intention to treat* | | | | | | | | | | |
| Treatment (ITT) × After | −1,998 | 3,715 | −226 | 3,274 | 648 | 395 | 1,631 | 1,570 | 2,367 | 1,182 |
| | (2,733) | (1,991)* | (1,951) | (2,669) | (557) | (1,328) | (3,816) | (1,487) | (5,179) | (360)*** |
| After | 194 | 88 | 1,010 | −719 | −767 | −430 | −3,911 | −2,677 | −3,865 | 178 |
| | (1,793) | (1,316) | (1,504) | (1,876) | (496) | (1,181) | (3,182) | (1,302)** | (4,826) | (74)** |
| R-squared | 0.55 | 0.60 | 0.57 | 0.56 | 0.62 | 0.52 | 0.54 | 0.55 | 0.54 | 0.58 |
| Observations | 3,436 | 3,436 | 3,436 | 3,436 | 3,436 | 3,436 | 3436 | 3,436 | 3,436 | 3,436 |
| Number of households | 1,611 | 1,611 | 1,611 | 1,611 | 1,611 | 1,611 | 1,611 | 1,611 | 1,611 | 1,611 |

*Source:* World Bank data.

*Notes:* Clustered standard errors in parentheses. CCT = conditional cash transfer; ETT = effect of treatment on the treated; ITT = intention to treat; HHs = households.

Significance level: * = 10 percent, ** = 5 percent, *** = 1 percent.

**Table 4.9  Effects of CCT on Household Food Consumption at the Midline**

| | (1) | (2) | (3) | (4) | (5) | (6) | (7) | (8) | (9) | (10) |
|---|---|---|---|---|---|---|---|---|---|---|
| | | | | | Value of food consumption in the past week | | | | | |
| | Maize (flour) super/Sembe - purchased | Maize (flour) super/Sembe - produced | Maize (flour) Dona - purchased | Maize (flour) Dona - produced | Other flour (Millet, cassava, sorghum, barley) purchased | Other flour (Millet, cassava, sorghum, barley) - produced | Rice (husked) purchased | Rice (husked) - produced | Dried beans - purchased | Sugar - purchased |
| Baseline mean | 3,600 | 216 | 700 | 371 | 166 | 424 | 263 | 61 | 551 | 580 |
| *Panel A: Effect of treatment on the treated* | | | | | | | | | | |
| Treatment (ETT) × After | 65.59 | 699.62 | −46.67 | −109.15 | −70.02 | −526.83 | −159.64 | −413.08 | −72.41 | 120.56 |
| | (626.34) | (711.19) | (235.26) | (204.86) | (88.43) | (278)* | (353.73) | (463) | (174.5) | (151) |
| After | −2,095.5 | 1,937.35 | −442.65 | 351.76 | −9.26 | 455.01 | 1,159.71 | 1,368 | 603.40 | 860.49 |
| | (397.39)*** | (500.38)*** | (139.19)*** | (108.36)*** | (55.28) | (252.68)* | (280.17)*** | (318)*** | (124)*** | (98)*** |
| *Panel B: Intention to treat* | | | | | | | | | | |
| Treatment (ITT) × After | 61.16 | 652.32 | −43.52 | −101.77 | −65.29 | −491.21 | −148.84 | −385 | 112.41 | −67.52 |
| | (842.01) | (956.69) | (316.30) | (275.40) | (119) | (373.97) | (475.27) | (623) | (203) | (234) |
| After | −2,095.2 | 1,940.22 | −442.84 | 351.31 | −9.54 | 452.85 | 1,159.05 | 1,366 | 860.98 | 603.10 |
| | (570.48)*** | (717.84)*** | (199.79)** | (155.62)** | (79.25) | (362.91) | (402.06)*** | (456)*** | (141)*** | (178)*** |
| R-squared (ITT) | 0.64 | 0.56 | 0.52 | 0.56 | 0.60 | 0.65 | 0.55 | 0.54 | 0.61 | 0.60 |
| Observations | 3,436 | 3,436 | 3,436 | 3,436 | 3,436 | 3,436 | 3,436 | 3,436 | 3,436 | 3,436 |

*Source:* World Bank data.

*Notes:* Clustered standard errors in parentheses. CCT = conditional cash transfer; ETT = effect of treatment on the treated; ITT = intention to treat.

Significance level: * = 10 percent; ** = 5 percent; *** = 1 percent.

not the value produced at home, since home production of these two goods is negligible. For the other four, we consider both the purchased and the home produced values. This results in 10 items, which jointly account for over half of total food consumption value in our study villages.

When we examine the effects of treatment on these items, the only statistically significant coefficient is a reduction in "other flour" production (T Sh 527 less in the last week), which is statistically significant at the 10 percent level. Thus, consumption of these food items seems to be generally unaffected by the CCT program.

We also examined the effects of treatment on the full set of food items for which data were collected at both baseline and midline. This included 35 food items obtained by three different procurement methods (home produced, purchased, and gift), for a total of 105 potential effects studied. Few results were statistically significant (only 14 out of 105), and even fewer were of relatively large magnitude (the two largest, statistically significant effects were an increase of T Sh 256 in the value of home produced peas, lentils, and other pulses, and an increase of T Sh 122 spent on tomatoes—both significant at the 5 percent level). This indicates that the CCT program likely did not have much direct impact on the individual items consumed by the beneficiary households. It also suggests that the caloric intake by household members did not change much as a result of the program— although it is possible that calories were divided in a different way among household members as a result of the program.

## Children's Activities and Assets

We examined whether participation in the community-based CCT changes the type of activities children perform, and whether it affects ownership of two assets associated with health improvements: children's shoes and children's slippers (also known as flip-flops or sandals). In table 4.10, we show that treatment makes children 46 percent less likely to have cleaned the toilet in the last week. While 13 percent of children cleaned the toilet each week on average at baseline, treated children are 6 percentage points less likely to do so (column 3). This result is statistically significant at the 5 percent level. While treatment is negatively correlated with cutting wood, cooking, and child care, these effects are small and not statistically significant at conventional levels (columns 2, 4, and 5). Treatment is positively correlated with fetching water and caring for the elderly (columns 1 and 6), but these effects are likewise economically small in magnitude and are also statistically insignificant. The lack of statistical significance in all cases except cleaning the toilet implies that treatment and control households were not appreciably different in terms of their children's propensity to perform these tasks.

Conversely, treatment does have a large and strongly significant impact on whether children own shoes. In particular, treated children are 48 percent more likely to own a pair of shoes. This is because, while 42 percent of children, on average, owned shoes at baseline, treatment is associated with a 20 percentage point increase in shoe ownership (column 7). This effect is significant at the

**Table 4.10  Effects of CCT on Children's Activities and Assets at the Midline**

| | (1) | (2) | (3) | (4) | (5) | (6) | (7) | (8) |
|---|---|---|---|---|---|---|---|---|
| | *Did the child do the following activities last week?* | | | | | | *Doe the child have...* | |
| | *Fetch water* | *Cut wood* | *Clean toilet* | *Cook* | *Provide child care* | *Provide elderly care* | *Shoes?* | *Slippers?* |
| Baseline mean | 0.57 | 0.28 | 0.13 | 0.26 | 0.16 | 0.28 | 0.42 | 0.63 |
| *Panel A: Effect of treatment on the treated* | | | | | | | | |
| Treatment (ETT) × After | 0.01 | −0.04 | −0.06 | −0.02 | −0.01 | 0.02 | 0.20 | 0.06 |
| | (0.03) | (0.05) | (0.03)** | (0.04) | (0.04) | (0.05) | (0.05)*** | (0.04) |
| After | 0.23 | 0.34 | 0.11 | 0.26 | −0.02 | −0.11 | 0.13 | 0.19 |
| | (0.03)*** | (0.03)*** | (0.01)*** | (0.03)*** | (0.03) | (0.04)*** | (0.03)*** | (0.02)*** |
| *Panel B: Intention to treat* | | | | | | | | |
| Treatment (ITT) × After | 0.01 | −0.04 | −0.06 | −0.02 | −0.01 | 0.02 | 0.18 | 0.05 |
| | (0.08) | (0.08) | (0.05) | (0.06) | (0.07) | (0.08) | (0.07)** | (0.06) |
| After | 0.23 | 0.33 | 0.11 | 0.26 | −0.02 | −0.11 | 0.13 | 0.19 |
| | (0.06)*** | (0.06)*** | (0.03)*** | (0.05)*** | (0.05) | (0.06)* | (0.05)*** | (0.04)*** |
| *R*-squared (ITT) | 0.75 | 0.74 | 0.70 | 0.80 | 0.70 | 0.70 | 0.76 | 0.72 |
| Observations | 5,007 | 5,007 | 5,007 | 5,007 | 5,006 | 5,007 | 6,180 | 6,180 |

*Source:* World Bank data.
*Notes:* Clustered standard errors in parentheses. CCT = conditional cash transfer; ETT = effect of treatment on the treated; ITT = intention to treat.
Significance level: * = 10 percent, ** = 5 percent, *** = 1 percent.

1 percent level. This is a large and important effect given the recognized health benefits of wearing shoes—which include the prevention of worms, cuts, and other infections, among other health benefits. Also, owning shoes may encourage school attendance. We do not find a statistically significant impact of treatment on owning slippers, though the sign of the coefficients is positive. As shoes are a higher-quality substitute for slippers, it is encouraging that the CCT has a greater and more significant positive effect on shoe than on slipper ownership.

## Savings and Credit

We also examined whether participation in the community-based CCT (that is, treatment) changes household savings and credit decisions. In table 4.11, we show that treatment makes households about twice as likely to have nonbank savings (column 2). Only 12 percent of households have nonbank savings overall during the baseline, and treatment is associated with a 25 percent increase (3 percentage points) in the rate of nonbank savings. This result is statistically significant at the 10 percent level. The coefficient on bank savings is actually negative, suggesting that households may be saving more overall and also transferring their savings from banks to the home, though the coefficient on treatment is statistically insignificant in the case of bank savings (column 1). Treatment does not have a statistically significant effect on the propensity to take out a loan (column 3).

**Table 4.11  Effects of CCT on Household Savings and Credit at the Midline**

| | (1) | (2) | (3) |
|---|---|---|---|
| | Does someone in the household have a bank account? | Does someone in the household have nonbank savings? | Has someone in the household taken out a loan in the last year? |
| Baseline mean | 0.02 | 0.12 | 0.20 |
| *Panel A: Effect of treatment on the treated* | | | |
| Treatment (ETT) × After | −0.01 | 0.03 | 0.04 |
| | (0.01) | (0.02)* | (0.03) |
| After | 0.01 | 0.02 | 0.01 |
| | (0.01) | (0.01)** | (0.02) |
| *Panel B: Intention to treat* | | | |
| Treatment (ITT) × After | −0.01 | 0.03 | 0.04 |
| | (0.01) | (0.02) | (0.04) |
| After | 0.01 | 0.02 | 0.01 |
| | (0.01) | (0.01) | (0.03) |
| *R*-squared (ITT) | 0.65 | 0.55 | 0.61 |
| Observations | 3,435 | 3,433 | 3,435 |

*Source:* World Bank data.
*Notes:* Clustered standard errors in parentheses. CCT = conditional cash transfer; ETT = effect of treatment on the treated; ITT = intention to treat.
Significance level: * = 10 percent, ** = 5 percent, *** = 1 percent.

## Community Trust

Next, we examined whether participation in the community-based CCT changes household members' reported trust of people overall, people in their community, and leaders of their community. An important component of this CCT program is its community-based nature, relying heavily on communities to deliver the program. Indeed, this feature distinguishes it from CCT programs in other countries that are almost always carried out by the central government (although usually with some community role). There may be reasons to believe that the collaboration involved in carrying out this community based CCT leads to higher levels of communal trust.

In table 4.12, we show that treatment makes household members less likely to trust people overall (column 1), but more likely to trust community leaders (column 3). While on average 24 percent of people reported trusting people overall at baseline, members of treated households are 7 percentage points less likely to report trusting people overall (a 29 percent decline in such trust). Also, while on average 80 percent of people reported trusting their community leaders at baseline, members of treated households are 6 percentage points more likely to trust community leaders (about an 8 percent increase in this type of trust). Both of these results are significant at the 10 percent level. Treated households also report lower trust of members of the community, on average, but these results are not statistically significant.

Community-Based Conditional Cash Transfers in Tanzania • http://dx.doi.org/10.1596/978-1-4648-0141-9

**Table 4.12  Effects of CCT on Household Members' Trust of Their  Community at the Midline**

|  | *(1)* | *(2)* | *(3)* |
|---|---|---|---|
|  | *Can most people be trusted?* | *Can people in the community be trusted?* | *Can community leaders be trusted?* |
| Baseline mean | 0.24 | 0.56 | 0.80 |
| *Panel A: Effect of treatment on the treated* | | | |
| Treatment (ETT) × After | −0.07 | −0.04 | 0.06 |
|  | (0.04)* | (0.03) | (0.03)* |
| After | 0.31 | 0.20 | −0.03 |
|  | (0.03)*** | (0.02)*** | (0.02) |
| *Panel B: Intention to treat* | | | |
| Treatment (ITT) × After | −0.06 | −0.04 | 0.05 |
|  | (0.05) | (0.04) | (0.04) |
| After | 0.31 | 0.20 | −0.03 |
|  | (0.04)*** | (0.03)*** | (0.03) |
| *R*-squared (ITT) | 0.59 | 0.60 | 0.56 |
| Observations | 3,421 | 3,419 | 3,424 |

*Source:* World Bank data.
*Notes:* Clustered standard errors in parentheses. CCT = conditional cash transfer; ETT = effect of treatment on the treated; ITT = intention to treat.
Significance level: * = 10 percent, ** = 5 percent, *** = 1 percent.

These findings suggest that the CCT has indeed changed the way people feel about their communities and their leaders. Greater trust of leaders is likely built by the fact that leaders have more resources to distribute, and treated households are the principal beneficiaries of those additional resources. That is, beneficiary households now have more money because their community management committee is giving it directly to them. On the other hand, the program targets only a subset of the community, which understandably creates some feelings of inequity. Treated households now have neighbors that are aware they have more resources, and who may feel they have a claim to some portion of them. This may serve to break down traditional solidarity networks, where households depended largely on one another for gifts and loans in the absence of a targeted CCT. As a result, the CCT may have generated a lack of trust in other people, which we are seeing in the data.

## Community Participation and Perception of Public Service Quality

Next, we examined whether participation in the community-based CCT changes several general measures of community participation and perception of public service quality. These include household members' propensity to participate in community development projects, their perceptions of public service quality, and whether their community has a parents' association or a community health committee. At design, it was expected that these additional resources might lead the most vulnerable households to be more engaged in community projects.

As table 4.13 shows, treatment is not associated with statistically significant increases in participation in community development projects (column 1), though the coefficient suggests a slight positive correlation between treatment and participation in such projects. Importantly, there is no evidence that any distrust in community members that comes from treatment (table 4.12) is associated with a lower propensity to participate in community development projects. If anything, treatment encourages such participation (though the result is not statistically significant at conventional levels).

We also importantly see that treatment is associated with significantly more positive ratings of schooling and health facilities in the community. On average during the baseline, 85 percent of people consider schooling quality to be good or excellent, and 71 percent consider health facilities to be good or excellent. However, respondents that received treatment are 10 percentage points more likely to give a good-or-excellent rating to schooling (column 2), and 13 percentage points more likely to give a good-or-excellent rating to health facilities (column 3).

Also, respondents who received treatment are 13 percentage points more likely to say that *both* schooling *and* health facilities are of good-or-excellent quality (something that only 65 percent of respondents say, on average during the baseline survey) (column 4). All three of these results are significant at the 5 percent level of significance or higher. They suggest a large, causal impact of participation in the CB-CCT on public perception of local public service quality. This may be related to health centers and schools independently taking initiative

**Table 4.13 CCT Effects on Community Participation and Perceptions of Public Service Quality at the Midline**

|  | (1) | (2) | (3) | (4) | (5) | (6) |
|---|---|---|---|---|---|---|
|  | Household contributed labor to CD project | Rates schooling good or excellent | Rates health facilities good or excellent | Rates schooling and health facilities good or excellent | Community has parents' association | Community has health committee |
| Baseline mean | 0.36 | 0.85 | 0.71 | 0.65 | 0.11 | 0.57 |
| *Panel A: Effect of treatment on the treated* | | | | | | |
| Treatment | 0.02 | 0.10 | 0.13 | 0.13 | 0.03 | 0.15 |
| (ETT) × After | (0.05) | (0.05)** | (0.05)*** | (0.06)** | (0.04) | (0.06)** |
| After | −0.13 | −0.17 | −0.13 | −0.15 | 0.05 | −0.06 |
|  | (0.03)*** | (0.03)*** | (0.03)*** | (0.04)*** | (0.02)** | (0.05) |
| *Panel B: Intention to treat* | | | | | | |
| Treatment | 0.02 | 0.10 | 0.13 | 0.12 | 0.03 | 0.14 |
| (ITT) × After | (0.06) | (0.06) | (0.07)* | (0.08) | (0.05) | (0.08)* |
| After | −0.13 | −0.17 | −0.13 | −0.15 | 0.05 | −0.06 |
|  | (0.04)*** | (0.04)*** | (0.05)*** | (0.05)*** | (0.04) | (0.06) |
| R-squared (ITT) | 0.59 | 0.55 | 0.57 | 0.55 | 0.53 | 0.58 |
| Observations | 3,435 | 3,434 | 3,435 | 3,434 | 3,435 | 3,435 |

*Source:* World Bank data.
*Notes:* Clustered standard errors in parentheses. CCT = conditional cash transfer; ETT = effect of treatment on the treated; ITT = intention to treat.
Significance level: * = 10 percent, ** = 5 percent, *** = 1 percent.

Community-Based Conditional Cash Transfers in Tanzania • http://dx.doi.org/10.1596/978-1-4648-0141-9

to improve their services with the demonstrated interest by outside actors shown through the conditions of the program, or the conditions of the program could lead beneficiaries to focus more on these services, use them more (as is clearly true with health services and to some degree with education services), and have a positive experience with them.

Finally, we see that treatment communities are much more likely to have a community health committee as a direct result of treatment (column 6)—though they are no more likely to have a parents' association (column 5). While 57 percent of households live in communities with a community health committee, on average, treated households are 15 percentage points more likely to have one. This result is statistically significant at the 5 percent level. It suggests that the CB-CCT has had a significant impact on how citizens organize and voice concerns related to local public service delivery.

## Transfers Paid Out and Received

Participation in the community-based CCT might very well affect what treatment households are able to receive from other sources. On the one hand, we might think that getting transfers from Tanzania Social Action Fund (TASAF) would deter individuals and possibly nongovernmental organization (NGOs) and religious organizations from giving transfers of any kind to CB-CCT beneficiary households. These individuals and organizations may perceive beneficiary households as "less needy" as a result of their receipt of transfers from TASAF, and accordingly reduce their transfers. On the other hand, beneficiary households might increase the amount of money they pay out to other households, as a result of receiving treatment. They now feel richer and therefore may pay out more money to nonbeneficiary households—whether out of altruism, or given an existing risk-pooling arrangement with neighbors.

Table 4.14 shows that treatment has a large and statistically significant impact on transfers received during the previous year. Treatment households are 92 percentage points more likely to receive a transfer of at least T Sh 5,000 from the government or TASAF (column 1)—an unsurprising result given those treatment households by definition receive a transfer above T Sh 5,000. However, being a treatment household is negatively correlated with having received a transfer from an NGO or religious organization (column 2) and with having received a transfer from an individual (column 3), although these effects are not statistically significant.

Columns 4–6 reveal that while treatment does not have a statistically significant effect on *whether* households receive a transfer from an individual or an NGO/ religious organization, it has a large effect on the *size* of transfers received. Treatment is associated with about T Sh 111,000 more per year from the government and TASAF (column 4), but with almost T Sh 1,000 less from NGOs and faith-based organizations (FBOs) (column 5), and with T Sh 14,000 less from individuals (column 6). This implies that more than 13 percent of the transfer gains received from TASAF and the government are mitigated by reduced

**Table 4.14  Effects of CCT on Transfers Received, by Source, and Paid Out at the Midline**

| | (1) | (2) | (3) | (4) | (5) | (6) | (7) |
|---|---|---|---|---|---|---|---|
| | Household received at least T Sh 5,000 from group, last 12 months | | | Value of all transfers received (cash, food, and other in-kind) from group, last 12 months | | | Value of all transfers given out, last 12 months |
| | Government/ TASAF | NGO or FBOs | Individuals | Government/ TASAF (T Sh) | NGO or FBOs (T Sh) | Individuals (T Sh) | |
| Baseline mean | 0.04 | 0.05 | 0.40 | 648 | 1,038 | 20,229 | 1,523 |
| *Panel A: Effect of treatment on the treated* | | | | | | | |
| Treatment | 0.92 | −0.01 | −0.02 | 111,235 | −940.74 | −13,754 | 683.96 |
| (ETT) × After | (0.02)*** | (0.02) | (0.04) | (5,318)*** | (748.96) | (6,347)** | (734.97) |
| After | −0.01 | −0.01 | 0.13 | −197.03 | 624.66 | 25,538.96 | 404.74 |
| | (0.01) | (0.02) | (0.03)*** | (449.58) | (636.90) | (5,415)*** | (620.84) |
| *Panel B: Intention to treat* | | | | | | | |
| Treatment | 0.86 | −0.01 | −0.02 | 103,713 | −877 | −12,824 | 638 |
| (ITT) × After | (0.03)*** | (0.03) | (0.05) | (7,444)*** | (1,008) | (8,532) | (989.04) |
| After | −0.00 | −0.01 | 0.13 | 259 | 621 | 25,483 | 408 |
| | (0.02) | (0.02) | (0.04)*** | (762) | (914) | (7,778)*** | (892) |
| *R*-squared (ITT) | 0.86 | 0.55 | 0.60 | 0.70 | 0.53 | 0.58 | 0.62 |
| Observations | 3,435 | 3,435 | 3,435 | 3,435 | 3,435 | 3,435 | 3,435 |

*Source:* World Bank data.

*Notes:* Clustered standard errors in parentheses. CCT = conditional cash transfer; ETT = effect of treatment on the treated; FBO = faith-based organization; ITT = intention to treat; NGO = nongovernmental organization; TASAF = Tanzania Social Action Fund; T Sh = Tanzanian shilling.

Significance level: * = 10 percent, ** = 5 percent, *** = 1 percent.

transfers from other sources. The reduction in transfers from NGOs and religious organizations is clearly much smaller than the reduction in transfers from individuals. This suggests that most of this money is staying in the communities and simply benefiting nonbeneficiary households in the form of spillovers.

Table 4.15 sheds some light on the types of transfers that cash transfers from TASAF are crowding out. Columns 1–3 show how receiving treatment affects transfers from individuals; it is associated with almost T Sh 9,000 fewer in cash and T Sh 5,000 fewer in food. These amounts represent 119 percent and 63 percent of their respective mean baseline values, and are therefore very sizeable impacts. There is no statistically significant effect on other types of in-kind transfers. This suggests that losses in transfer revenue from individuals due to being in a treatment household come mostly from the receipt of fewer cash transfers, but also from less food support.

Columns 4 shows, unsurprisingly, that treatment leads to significantly higher cash transfers (an additional T Sh 111,000 per year). Columns 5 and 6 indicate there is no effect on the (very small, on average) food and other in-kind transfers received from TASAF or the government. Columns 7–9 show that the losses of NGO transfers due to being treated are economically small overall, and only statistically significant in the case of food donations by NGOs (treated households receive about T Sh 600 less).

**Table 4.15 Effects of CCT on Transfers Received at the Midline, by Source and Transfer Type**

| | (1) | (2) | (3) | (4) | (5) | (6) | (7) | (8) | (9) |
|---|---|---|---|---|---|---|---|---|---|
| | Value of all transfers of this type received from individuals, last 12 months | | | Value of all transfers of this type received from government/TASAF, last 12 months | | | Value of all transfers of this type received from NGO/religious organizations, last 12 months | | |
| | Cash (T Sh) | Food (T Sh) | Other in-kind (T Sh) | Cash (T Sh) | Food (T Sh) | Other in-kind (T Sh) | Cash (T Sh) | Food (T Sh) | Other in-kind (T Sh) |
| Baseline mean | 7,569 | 8,148 | 4,657 | 139 | 179 | 331 | 275 | 201 | 562 |
| *Panel A: Effect of treatment on the treated* | | | | | | | | | |
| Treatment (ETT) × After | −8,971 (3,586)** | −5,144 (3,027)* | 64.93 (1,765) | 111,762 (5,220)*** | −90 (277) | −438 (404) | −367 (555) | −576 (288)** | 3.34 (311) |
| After | 14,522 (3,092)*** | 7,868 (2,448)*** | 2,845 (1,413)** | −475 (326.17) | 138 (195) | 140 (342) | 399 (501) | 379 (242) | −153 (195) |
| *Panel B: Intention to treat* | | | | | | | | | |
| Treatment (ITT) × After | −8,360 (4,827)* | −4,792 (4,076) | 61 (2,376) | 104,205 (7,294)*** | −83 (373) | −408 (542) | −343 (745) | −537 (387) | 3.12 (418) |
| After | 14,485 (4,447)*** | 7,846 (3,523)** | 2,845 (2,031) | −17.01 (73) | 137 (279) | 138 (490) | 398 (720) | 376 (346) | −153 (280) |
| R-squared (ITT) | 0.57 | 0.60 | 0.54 | 0.71 | 0.38 | 0.35 | 0.51 | 0.51 | 0.53 |
| Observations | 3,426 | 3,419 | 3,423 | 3,435 | 3,434 | 3,435 | 3,434 | 3,435 | 3,434 |

*Source:* World Bank data.
*Notes:* Clustered standard errors in parentheses. CCT = conditional cash transfer; ETT = effect of treatment on the treated; ITT = intention to treat; NGO = nongovernmental organization; TASAF = Tanzania Social Action Fund; T Sh = Tanzanian shilling.
Significance level: * = 10 percent, ** = 5 percent, *** = 1 percent.

## Livestock, Land, and Other Durable Assets

Table 4.16 illustrates the effects of the CB-CCT on ownership of land and major durable assets.[4] It is immediately apparent that while being selected into treatment is positively correlated with owning each of the assets considered in the table—land, a sewing machine, a stove, a radio, and a mobile phone—these effects are generally not statistically significant.

Only in the case of bicycles is treatment associated with greater ownership of the asset: 19 percent of people owned a bicycle on average during the baseline survey, and those that received treatment were 6 percentage points more likely to own one. It may be the case that households are acquiring newer or updated versions of assets they already owned (such that expenditures on assets does not show up in the form of greater asset ownership). Alternately, it could be that land and household durable assets such as these are simply not the types of expenditures stimulated by a year and a half of small, bimonthly transfers, especially in the absence of savings instruments or inducements.

Table 4.17, however, shows that treatment households tend to acquire some new livestock assets. Following treatment, households tend to purchase additional indigenous goats (including kids) and local chickens (excluding chicks) when compared to similar households in the control group. Column 4 indicates

**Table 4.16 Effects of CCT on Land and Durable Asset Ownership at the Midline**

|  | (1) | (2) | (3) | (4) | (5) | (6) |
|---|---|---|---|---|---|---|
|  | Acres of land | Sewing machine | Stove | Radio | Mobile phone | Bicycle |
| Baseline mean | 4.15 | 0.006 | 0.10 | 0.33 | 0.11 | 0.19 |
| *Panel A: Effect of treatment on the treated* |  |  |  |  |  |  |
| Treatment (ETT) × After | 0.30 | 0.01 | 0.03 | 0.04 | 0.02 | 0.06 |
|  | (0.42) | (0.01) | (0.02) | (0.03) | (0.03) | (0.03)** |
| After | −0.15 | 0.01 | 0.02 | 0.01 | 0.12 | −0.01 |
|  | (0.21) | (0.00)* | (0.02) | (0.02) | (0.02)*** | (0.02) |
| *Panel B: Intention to treat* |  |  |  |  |  |  |
| Treatment (ITT) × After | 0.28 | 0.01 | 0.03 | 0.03 | 0.02 | 0.06 |
|  | (0.57) | (0.01) | (0.03) | (0.04) | (0.04) | (0.04) |
| After | −0.15 | 0.01 | 0.02 | 0.01 | 0.12 | −0.00 |
|  | (0.31) | (0.01) | (0.02) | (0.03) | (0.03)*** | (0.03) |
| R-squared (ITT) | 0.64 | 0.60 | 0.65 | 0.68 | 0.66 | 0.68 |
| Observations | 3,431 | 3,436 | 3,436 | 3,436 | 3,436 | 3,436 |

*Source:* World Bank data.
*Notes:* Clustered standard errors in parentheses. CCT = conditional cash transfer; ETT = effect of treatment on the treated; ITT = intention to treat.
Significance level: * = 10 percent, ** = 5 percent, *** = 1 percent.

**Table 4.17 Effects of CCT on Livestock Ownership at the Midline**

|  | (1) | (2) | (3) | (4) | (5) | (6) | (7) | (8) | (9) |
|---|---|---|---|---|---|---|---|---|---|
|  | Dairy cows (incl calves) | Indigenous cows (incl calves) | Dairy goats (incl kids) | Indigenous goats (incl kids) | Local chickens (excl chicks) | Foreign chickens (excl chicks) | Sheep | Pigs | Turkeys and ducks |
| Baseline mean | 0.80 | 0.005 | 0.25 | 2.37 | 0.10 | 0.21 | 0.19 | 0.14 | 0.80 |
| Mean of outcome variable | 0.002 | 0.100 | 0.014 | 0.361 | 2.46 | 0.166 | 0.040 | 0.019 | 0.148 |
| *Panel A: Effect of treatment on the treated* |  |  |  |  |  |  |  |  |  |
| Treatment (ETT) × After | −0.00 | −0.02 | 0.03 | 0.43 | 0.99 | 0.24 | 0.02 | 0.01 | −0.005 |
|  | (0.01) | (0.08) | (0.03) | (0.14)*** | (0.33)*** | (0.23) | (0.05) | (0.03) | (0.05) |
| After | 0.00 | 0.05 | 0.01 | 0.03 | −0.35 | 0.01 | 0.03 | −0.00 | 0.03 |
|  | (0.00) | (0.02)** | (0.01) | (0.05) | (0.19)* | (0.01) | (0.04) | (0.02) | (0.03) |
| *Panel B: Intention to treat* |  |  |  |  |  |  |  |  |  |
| Treatment (ITT) × After | −0.00 | −0.02 | 0.03 | 0.40 | 0.93 | 0.23 | 0.02 | 0.01 | −0.005 |
|  | (0.01) | (0.11) | (0.04) | (0.19)** | (0.44)** | (0.32) | (0.07) | (0.04) | (0.07) |
| After | 0.00 | 0.05 | 0.01 | 0.03 | −0.35 | 0.02 | 0.03 | −0.00 | 0.03 |
|  | (0.01) | (0.03) | (0.02) | (0.07) | (0.28) | (0.02) | (0.05) | (0.03) | (0.04) |
| R-squared (ITT) | 0.50 | 0.60 | 0.50 | 0.67 | 0.66 | 0.79 | 0.59 | 0.54 | 0.71 |
| Observations | 3,435 | 3,435 | 3,435 | 3,435 | 3,434 | 3,435 | 3,435 | 3,435 | 3,435 |

*Source:* World Bank data.
*Notes:* Clustered standard errors in parentheses. CCT = conditional cash transfer; ETT = effect of treatment on the treated; ITT = intention to treat.
Significance level: * = 10 percent, ** = 5 percent, *** = 1 percent.

that treatment leads households to purchase an average of 0.43 additional goats (that is, more than two goats for every five treated households), while column 5 indicates that treatment leads households to purchase one additional local chicken. These are substantial effects given that the average household has 0.36 indigenous goats and 2.46 local chickens. Households may invest in these assets because they are seen more as investments rather than consumption goods.

## Notes

1.  Basic health services are provided at no costs provided that regular contributions are paid in the range of T Sh 10,000–15,000. The Tanzanian government matches the member contributions to 100 percent of the paid premium.

2.  Specifically, we use fixed effects for the six-month age range in which a child falls between the following age groups: 0–5, 6–11, 12–17, … , and 54–59 months old. Note that only children under age five were measured. Using age group fixed effects instead of child fixed effects allows us to use a larger sample of children, since we are not restricted to only estimating treatment effects using children measured at both baseline and midline (which is only a small set of all children measured, given that only children aged 0–5 at the time of a survey round were measured). Effectively, we compare children of a given age range at baseline to children in that same age range at midline. These results are available upon request.

3.  Because anthropometric data were only collected for children aged 0–4 at the time of a given survey, and given that the baseline and midline are over two years apart in time, only children aged 0–2 during the baseline also were weighed and measured at endline. Because our specifications use child fixed effects, we do not use all data on children's anthropometrics, but only the data of children that appear in both baseline and midline (that is the 0–2 children at baseline). Another possibility is to include household fixed effects rather than child fixed effects. Effectively, this strategy compares a child's anthropometric data to those of other children in his or her household. However, specifications which use household fixed effects yielded similarly statistically insignificant results.

4.  We exclude cars and motorcycles from the list of durable assets because less than 1 percent of the population has each of these assets.

# CHAPTER 5

# Results of the Community Score Card Exercise

An important qualitative data collection exercise was carried out after the base-line survey (January-May 2009) and after the beginning of transfer payments (January 2010), but before the midline survey (July-September 2011). For this qualitative work, a social accountability tool—the community score card (CSC)—was used to evaluate the effectiveness of the community-based conditional cash transfer (CB-CCT) program from several different angles, described below. This analysis was carried out by the Public Affairs Foundation (Public Affairs Foundation 2011), headed by Dr. Sita Sekhar, and the findings are summarized below.

This tool sought beneficiary and service provider feedback on the CCT program in general, and the quality of local health and education service delivery in particular. The CSC exercise was conducted in 20 treatment communities across the three pilot districts between November 2010 and February 2011. Feedback was sought through four CSC processes: an input tracking matrix, a self-assessment score card, a community score card, and an interface meeting. Through these processes, score cards were conducted on health services, education services, and the CCT (conditional) component of the program.

## Community Score Card Process

Data collection for the CSC exercise was collected by a Tanzanian firm (hereafter, the qualitative researchers) experienced in conducting quantitative and qualitative studies in the country and trained by Public Affairs Foundation senior staff. The team was comprised of a coordinator, a moderator, and a scribe. Two teams covered one community, one team each on health and education services.

To initiate fieldwork, the qualitative researchers held preliminary meetings with staff from the main local primary school and dispensary, members of the Village Council, and the Tanzania Social Action Fund (TASAF) to explain the CSC process. Meetings were also held with community representatives to create awareness of the CSC process and ensure their participation. All participants were informed about the date, time, and venue (usually schools) of the group discussions a few days before the CSC process took place.

The community score card process consisted of four steps:

1. *Input Tracking:* For this step, program staff attempted to see where the inputs into the CCT program were being used, and to match expenditures to inputs. In addition, it attempted to check how well targeting reached the expected vulnerable populations. It also looked at what infrastructure and other materials were available in school and health facilities.

2. *Community Performance Score Card:* In the community performance score card, the community directly provided feedback on the operation of the program. Separate focus groups on health and education for men and women first chose indicators they felt could be used to rate the success of the program, and then rated the quality of health and education services using these indicators. (As a result, different communities often used different sets of indicators to rate the quality of health and education services, complicating cross-community comparisons.) The participants in these focus groups were chosen using a list of program beneficiaries provided by the community management committees (CMCs) in the communities. For the education focus group, 20 children from the beneficiary list were selected randomly. Five to eight men and five to eight women whose children or grandchildren were selected accompanied these children and participated. The health focus group comprised five to eight men and five to eight women that either had children under five or were elderly beneficiaries of the CCT program.

3. *Self*-evaluation Score Card: The CMC that is administering the CCT and the schools and health centers participating in the program gave themselves a self-assessment of how they see the system performing (these could end up being similar to those chosen by other groups, but often providers rate themselves differently compared to beneficiaries).

4. *Interface Meeting:* During this meeting, providers (CMC, health staff, school teachers, and so on) and the community (men and women) were brought together to share their results, discuss findings, and come up with an action plan on how to make the process work better.

## Data Analysis

The Public Affairs Foundation produced separate reports on the CSCs generated in each of the 20 communities. These reports include separate CSCs on health, education, and the CCT program as a whole. They also describe information about the participants, indicators selected by beneficiaries and service providers to assess service performance, corresponding scores for the indicators, and observations of the qualitative researchers on the group dynamics during the group discussions.

As a first step in analyzing the data, the Public Affairs Foundation determined the common indicators selected by beneficiaries under the input tracking matrix, self-assessment score card, community score card, and interface meeting across the communities. In the second step, frequently reported indicators across the communities were presented. Additionally, a combined score was calculated for each indicator by simple addition (see the report produced by the Public Affairs Foundation for more information on this process and these results). The communities were compared according to the scores given for a particular indicator.

For the third step, individual indicators identified by the beneficiaries were grouped into broader indicators of significance such as quality, infrastructure, access, and so on. Based on the qualitative information gathered during the score card process, additional indicators were also identified and presented. These data were analyzed and presented in a format similar to that discussed above for the different stages of the CSC process: specifically, input tracking, self-assessment, community performance score card, and interface meeting.

Data pertaining to action plans were presented for only those communities that reported a score of three or less for the selected indicators. Data were analyzed and presented in a matrix describing the indicator, the proposed action by the stakeholder, the responsible authority or department for implementation of the proposed action, and the probable date of commencement of the action.

Observations recorded during the CSC process and beneficiary remarks were categorized under four categories: (a) challenges faced in conducting the CSC exercise; (b) education/health service-specific suggestions; (c) CCT program-specific suggestions; and (d) beneficiary reflections on the CCT program.

## Main Findings

### Education

The community scorecards found that there was a serious lack of infrastructure and materials in almost all communities, with none having infrastructure of the quality to which they felt entitled. Over half of the schools reported a problem with water access, and students had to share study materials in many schools. Men were more concerned about these infrastructure indicators than were women, who instead emphasized quality indicators (such as the number of teachers) more heavily.

Table 5.1 shows the six education indicators most commonly chosen by communities to be evaluated. These relate to both general infrastructure quality and the impact of the CCT on education-related outcomes. This table shows the number of communities giving a score of 1 (lowest), 2, 3, 4, and 5 (highest) as their rating of their community's performance on that indicator. If a community did not rate one of these six areas, their community consensus score is listed as "no mention."

All communities in the score card exercise reported strong improvements in education indicators, such as enrollment and attendance, as a result of the CCT program. In fact, several communities reported that all beneficiary children had 100 percent attendance, and attendance for girls seemed to increase more than

**Table 5.1  Results of the Community Score Card Exercise—Education**

| | Number of communities | | | | | |
| | Infrastructure indicators | | Indicators of conditional cash transfer impact | | | |
| Consensus score | Availability of water | Availability of houses for teachers | Increase in attendance | Increase in uniforms | Increase in use of study material | Increase in enrollments |
|---|---|---|---|---|---|---|
| 5 | 0 | 0 | 5 | 4 | 3 | 5 |
| 4 | 0 | 0 | 12 | 12 | 7 | 13 |
| 3 | 3 | 0 | 3 | 3 | 8 | 1 |
| 2 | 1 | 9 | 0 | 0 | 2 | 0 |
| 1 | 14 | 7 | 0 | 0 | 0 | 0 |
| Not mentioned | 2 | 4 | 0 | 1 | 0 | 1 |

*Source:* World Bank data.

attendance for boys. In the self-assessment phase, educators noted that children seemed to have more educational supplies, such as uniforms and study materials.

The action plans developed during the interface meeting mainly focused on asking various actors, ranging from the community to the government and non-governmental organization (NGOs), to provide more assistance or materials, such as providing more study materials, teachers, and infrastructure. To improve the CCT program, they also called more generally for a new selection of a greater number of beneficiaries, as well as training for beneficiaries on more productive uses for the transfers.

### Health

Health facility infrastructure and service quality were ranked low in most of the communities as well (table 5.2). Table 5.2 shows the number of communities giving a score of 1 (lowest), 2, 3, 4, and 5 (highest) to each of eight different areas related to the quality of health care. If a community did not rate one of these eight areas, their score is again listed as "no mention." Half of the communities chose the availability of staff, medicines, water, toilets, and housing for staff as important indicators of inputs, although there was more variation in health indicators considered important than there was among education input indicators. Another major basic service quality issue mentioned by service providers in many communities was a lack of a transportation vehicles for emergencies. In general, the service providers ranked infrastructure indicators more highly than did other community members. Men generally seemed to rank infrastructure indicators more poorly than did women, who were more concerned with access indicators, such as the availability of nearby staff quarters.

Very few of the indicators of CCT impact received a low ranking, indicating that in general participants had positive opinions of the impact of the program. However, reduced illness and elderly health visits were ranked relatively lower than were decreased mortality and increased immunizations.

**Table 5.2 Results of the Community Score Card Exercise—Health**

| | Number of communities | | | | | | | |
| | Infrastructure indicators | | Indicators of conditional cash transfer impact | | | | | |
| Consensus score | Availability of medicine | Availability of water | Increased immunization of infants | Reduced infant mortality | Reduced maternal mortality | Increase in elderly health checkups | Reduced illness among infants | Reduced illness for elderly |
|---|---|---|---|---|---|---|---|---|
| 5 | 0 | 1 | 9 | 7 | 12 | 5 | 3 | 6 |
| 4 | 1 | 0 | 8 | 8 | 4 | 9 | 10 | 3 |
| 3 | 8 | 6 | 3 | 4 | 1 | 5 | 6 | 10 |
| 2 | 3 | 3 | 0 | 0 | 0 | 0 | 0 | 0 |
| 1 | 3 | 6 | 0 | 0 | 0 | 0 | 0 | 0 |
| No mention | 5 | 4 | 0 | 1 | 3 | 1 | 1 | 1 |

*Source:* World Bank data.

The action plan created during the health interface meeting called for similar interventions to those of the education meeting. Specifically, constructing new facilities and increasing the supply of materials were considered important actions for both groups. Participants also wanted to increase transparency in the selection of beneficiaries. The groups additionally called for measures to increase awareness in the community of beneficial health measures, such as attending health checkups and increasing knowledge about various illnesses.

Overall, these qualitative exercises greatly informed the midline analysis by identifying some interesting ways in which the CCT has helped or failed to help communities. It also provided an impetus for a survey of health care facilities and schools in the endline survey, to allow further exploration of these indicators using quantitative methods.

# CHAPTER 6

# Results of the Midline Focus Group Exercise

The midline focus group exercise was conducted in six communities at the time of the midline quantitative survey (July–September 2011) to obtain direct feedback on how the community-run conditional cash transfer (CCT) program has affected beneficiary communities. This section is adapted from the final report of Synovate, the firm contracted to carry out the focus groups.

The goal of this analysis was to examine household-level impacts, community dynamics, and the process of implementation of the CCT. The specific household-level subthemes investigated were the impacts on education and health, employment, time use, transfers and savings, decision making, and attitudes and preferences. In the community, the exercise looked at potential conflicts, traditional solidarity systems, quality and use of services, perceptions of service providers, and communitywide impacts. The two components of the program process investigated were the use of resources and the effectiveness and efficiency of program operations and activities. Overall, the midline focus groups revealed participant perceptions of broad improvements in education, health, and other areas of life as a result of the CCT.

Focus groups were conducted by Synovate in two communities in each of the three program districts. Focus groups were conducted with health care providers, Village Councils, community management committees (CMCs), educators, beneficiaries, and nonbeneficiaries. The beneficiaries and nonbeneficiaries were divided into male and female groups due to sensitive topics of discussion. Each of these categories of group discussions was held for all six selected communities, with the exception of Village Council focus groups which were held in only four communities.

The Tanzania Social Action Fund (TASAF) provided lists of beneficiaries, CMCs, health providers, and educators to recruit participants. The nonbeneficiary respondents were directly selected using a recruitment questionnaire designed to capture similar categories of families to those of the respondents (having a young or school-aged child or elderly person in the household). Each focus group had 8–10 members.

The focus groups identified a wide range of program impacts, both directly on beneficiaries and on the wider community; see Table 6.1 for sample responses. Among beneficiaries, food became much more available as a result of the program. Many elderly beneficiaries were able to purchase health insurance, and accordingly make more visits to health centers or dispensaries. An increase in health-seeking behavior for young children was also reported. Furthermore, beneficiary children were more likely to attend and perform well at school, were able to afford school supplies, and generally seemed to have higher self-esteem as a result of the program.

In addition to these effects on the directly targeted health and education behaviors of beneficiaries, other diverse impacts were also reported. These included home improvements and productive investments, among others.

In the larger community, participants reported that the management and quality of health and education services had improved, and that traditional solidarity systems had become even stronger. While there were some reports of conflict

**Table 6.1  Sample Responses from the Individual Focus Groups**

| Respondent group | Quotation |
| --- | --- |
| Health providers | "…..if they will not receive the money because they have not complied with program rules that will not be fair, they cannot afford the basic needs which they are supposed to get by using that money." |
| Educators | "Personally I believe the program has affected my professional in a good way. The project on my side has helped children progress well in their academics in terms of gaining education. Children have access to facilities such as books, uniforms, which have a positive impact in their school attendance. I think it has made our profession as a teacher respected because the project highly acknowledges the education sector." |
| Community management committees | "They are benefiting because they get medical insurance, there are some elders who are blind and others are too old to even do farm work so this money enables them to sustain their living." |
| Village councils | "The majority of people in our community are farmers, so once they receive the money then the work begins. They use the money to buy chicken feeds and for weeding their farms." |
| Male beneficiaries | "It has assisted us to pay our children school fees, uniforms school materials and the surplus we get help us to buy some other things like soap, food and domestic animals such as chicken and goats." |
| Female beneficiaries | "The number of school going children have increased from before, beliefs that hindered girl children from attending school have been done away with." |
| Male nonbeneficiaries | "Before the inception of the CB-CCT program sick persons' would be taken to a traditional medicine man for treatment, but now we have health insurance, we visit the health centers for treatment." |
| Female nonbeneficiaries | "Trouble emanates sometimes from those who are not selected, they felt that they also deserved to be included in the beneficiary list. Maybe it is because we do not understand the selection process; we fail to understand that the process is managed by certain principles and guidelines. We asked ourselves why them and not us." |

*Source:* World Bank data.
*Note:* CB-CCT = community-based conditional cash transfer.

related to the program, only one community reported significant problems related to jealousy of nonbeneficiaries. Nonbeneficiaries in many communities did suggest that the selection process could be improved by measures such as increasing transparency and ensuring that all of the most vulnerable community members are included. However, in general they were positive about the selection process and believed that it had been highly participatory.

Beneficiaries reported wide-ranging benefits, although they indicated that the transfer was not large enough. They stated that health care has become better and more accessible, but in some places there was an insufficient number of health staff. Beneficiaries did not report being directly involved in decision-making in schools and health facilities, but they did report occasionally participating indirectly through community meetings or committees. While some reported an improvement in child performance in school, others did not report such an impact. Many felt that schools did not have enough teachers, and reported that sometimes the facilities were up to three hours away, both of which impeded improvements in educational performance.

Overall, beneficiaries believed the CCT system is efficient, and did not seem concerned about corruption. Some reported using the transfers to conduct small business activities. While generally, beneficiaries were happy with the selection process, some believed it failed to select all needy, vulnerable community members, and others thought it should be revised due to changing circumstances. Most beneficiaries were aware of the conditions of the program, although awareness could still be improved. Perceptions of CMC performance were positive and CMC members were characterized as proactive.

Among nonbeneficiaries, most participants knew about the CCT program. They believed that the program had benefited the beneficiary households that previously could not afford good health care or education materials. However, they believed that in some instances, the benefits of this increased participation in the formal health and education sectors were mitigated by the low quality of the facilities. Yet they also reported that the management of these facilities had improved as a result of the program. A few nonbeneficiaries expressed jealously, and some reported that the selection was biased, although they also reported that the beneficiaries sometimes share their money with others.

The CMCs reported that the CCT is reaching the targeted individuals, and has enabled beneficiaries to improve schooling and health behaviors, as well as make general household improvements. However, the behavior of some school and health staff and the quality of some of the facilities is perceived to be somewhat lacking. CMCs report an increase in investment activities, particularly in farming and livestock, and say that some beneficiaries have also been able to save money for the future. In general, the communities have become more informed about the benefits of health visits, so that even elderly and young children not enrolled in the program attend clinics more often. The main challenges that the CMCs reported were accusations of favoritism, an inadequate allowance, and complaints from nonbeneficiaries. The CMCs, similar to other groups, also reported a strengthening of traditional community ties and a willingness to help each other. Some CMC members believed that they received enough training to adequately perform their duties, while others reported being unclear about their roles. Generally, CMC members believed that the selection process is fair, but that it sometimes creates tension and so community members need to be better educated about how it works.

The education service provider participants displayed a clear knowledge of the intended beneficiaries and purposes of the CCT program. They generally believed that the program had impacted their work positively. Many educators reported an increased workload due to the compliance requirements of the program. Some educators suggested a need to emphasize the temporary nature of the CCT so as not to encourage dependency, as well as some concern about vulnerable children not included in the program. Some educators felt directly involved and invested in the program, as they are responsible for ensuring compliance. Others felt that their role is fairly indirect, and said they do not receive responses to feedback they provide to CCT administrators with reporting forms.

The village council (VC) focus groups reported improvements in health and education services in their communities, as well as improved quality of life for beneficiary households. The VCs say that the transfers have increased beneficiaries' ability to afford school uniforms for their children and have thereby increased child self-esteem and social participation. There were some reports of increased longevity for the elderly due to the ability to afford health care, although treatment is still limited by a lack of medicines and laboratories. Community members reportedly visit health centers more often and traditional doctors less. While the VCs largely reported that the CCT is reaching the correct households, one community reported some irregularities. The VCs also reported some concern about the security of the transfer funds once they are withdrawn from the bank, as the CMCs do not have reliable transportation or an escort to prevent theft. Similar to the CMCs, the VCs face numerous complaints from nonbeneficiaries who would like to be part of the program. Some VCs have advised beneficiaries on how to invest the transfer money for more sustainable and productive use, and some investment in these types of activities is reported. Most communities reported strong community ties, although one community had experienced substantial tension due to the resentment of nonbeneficiaries. The VCs reported being strongly impressed with the performance of the CMCs, even though CMC members are not compensated and are not provided with a means of transportation.

The health providers reported an increased workload because more beneficiaries are using medical services and have also increased their health knowledge as a result of the CCT program. They stated that while most services in their facilities are adequate, they lack some medicines and there are insufficient medical personnel to serve all patients in a timely manner. The providers generally reported that the transfers have improved beneficiary health outcomes, but that the amount of support was not adequate to meet all basic needs. Although the health providers are responsible for reporting compliance, many did not feel comfortable reporting noncompliance, as they are worried that poor families will lose an already inadequate transfer. They reportedly often try to communicate directly with beneficiaries to encourage them to follow the rules of the program. Health providers also reported that the CCT program has increased beneficiary confidence and communication, and that it has changed social norms to encourage visits to modern healthcare facilities rather than traditional practitioners.

The main recommendations across all groups include adopting measures to encourage program sustainability by promoting income-generating investments, increasing awareness and knowledge of the program to promote a sense of community ownership, and facilitating continued good performance by the CMCs by providing them with a bicycle, increased compensation, and additional training. The focus group participants also suggested increasing the number of teachers and health personnel. The main recommendations to TASAF were to better integrate VCs, to include community input on the recruitment questionnaire for program beneficiaries, and to ensure that money is given to beneficiaries on time. Also, a secure means of transportation for CMC members to distribute cash and a greater emphasis on clinic visits for children under five could improve the effectiveness of the program.

# CHAPTER 7

# Impact Evaluation Results at Endline

The endline survey was conducted between August and October 2012, 31–34 months after the community-based conditional cash transfer (CB-CCT) program was launched in January 2010. An endline survey is especially useful because it provides insight into longer-term impacts of the conditional cash transfer (CCT) program. This shows which impacts endure, which disappear over time, and which take some time to appear—coming to the surface only at endline. We were unable to gather data on 13 percent of baseline households at the endline survey. However, the likelihood of not being interviewed is uncorrelated with being a treatment village. A more detailed analysis of attrition is discussed in appendix A.

While midline survey results used data from the baseline and midline, endline survey results use data from the baseline and endline. Similar to the midline, the endline results were analyzed using both effect of treatment on the treated (ETT) and intent to treat (ITT) regressions, as discussed in chapter 3.

By endline, we found that treatment led to fewer days reported sick as well as fewer health center visits. Treatment also led to greater school attendance, shoe ownership among children, purchases of health insurance, and trust in community leaders. However, treatment had almost no effect on savings and credit decisions, nor did it impact consumption (food, non-food, and durable items)—though it did lead to greater expenditure on productive assets like chickens and goats.

To lend greater insight into the particular individuals and households benefiting most from the CCT, we also carried out analysis focusing on heterogeneous treatment effects. These regressions help us observe not just whether the CCT helped people overall, but whether it helped particular groups more than others. We considered a number of different groups:

- Women vs. men (or girls vs. boys)
- The poorest half vs. the less poor half of households (on an asset index constructed using principal components analysis)
- Households in Kibaha vs. Bagamoyo vs. Chamwino districts.

For outcomes related to children's education, we ran heterogeneous treatment effect regressions for children who were in school vs. out of school at baseline. For household-level outcomes, we also ran heterogeneous treatment effect regressions for households in villages that had experienced a recent drought and those that had not.

Finally, we ran several regressions with data not collected or not analyzed at midline, such as household voting, participation in village council meetings, and participation in collective action opportunities.

## Health-Seeking Behavior and Health Outcomes

Starting with health-related outcomes, we find that participation in the CB-CCT (that is, treatment) affected health-seeking behaviors and outcomes at endline. Table 7.1 shows that treatment is associated with decreases in yearly health center visits at endline. While this is true for the entire treated population, the decreases are most notable among children aged 0–2 years.

In column (1), we see that treatment, as of endline, is associated with statistically significantly fewer visits to health centers for all ages. The average individual at baseline visited a health center 2.8 times a year. At endline, individuals across both groups were attending clinics about one fewer time per year, but treatment was associated with 0.41 fewer visits per year beyond that.

The effects of treatment are especially large among children age 0–2 years, a subpopulation subjected to relatively intensive health care conditions (columns 2

**Table 7.1  Effect of CCT on Health Center Visits, by Age Group at Endline**

|  | Average number of health facility visits in the past year, by baseline age | | | |
|---|---|---|---|---|
|  | *(1)* <br> All ages | *(2)* <br> Age 0–1 year | *(3)* <br> Age 0–2 years | *(4)* <br> Age 60+years |
| Baseline mean | 2.80 | 8.54 | 9.20 | 2.78 |
| *Panel A: Effect of treatment on the treated* | | | | |
| Treatment (ETT) × After | −0.41 | −3.07 | −3.00 | −0.39 |
|  | (0.22)* | (1.62)* | (1.23)** | (0.24) |
| After | −0.98 | −2.34 | −3.87 | −0.08 |
|  | (0.15)*** | (1.15)** | (0.92)*** | (0.17) |
| Observations | 12,629 | 507 | 721 | 5,343 |
| *R*-squared | 0.037 | 0.144 | 0.277 | 0.003 |
| *Panel B: Intention to treat* | | | | |
| Treatment (ITT) × After | −0.38 | −2.64 | −2.71 | −0.37 |
|  | (0.31) | −1.79 | (1.49)* | (0.30) |
| After | −0.98 | −2.34 | −3.87 | −0.08 |
|  | (0.23)*** | (1.51) | (1.24)*** | (0.22) |

*Source:* World Bank data.
*Note:* Clustered standard errors in parentheses. CCT = conditional cash transfer; ETT = effect of treatment on the treated; ITT = intention to treat.
Significance level: * = 10 percent, ** = 5 percent, *** = 1 percent.

and 3). Specifically, the conditions required children age 0–2 years to attend a health center six times per year, or roughly every other month. These children also reported going to statistically significantly fewer health center visits at endline. Column (2) shows that treated children aged 0–1 year went to a health center 8.54 times a year at baseline. By endline, however, these children went to 3.07 fewer visits than their counterparts in comparison villages, significant at the 10 percent level, in addition to the fact that all children (treatment and comparison) are attending the clinic around two fewer times. This result is different from those reported at midline (table 4.1, column 2), where treatment led children age 0–1 to visit a health clinic 2.28 more times a year (significant at the 5 percent level).

Treatment had a similar and statistically significant effect on children age 0–2. In column (3), we see that treated children age 0–2 years went to health centers 9.2 times a year at baseline. At endline, these children visited health centers 3 fewer times a year than their counterparts in comparison villages. Recall that at midline, treatment led children age 0–2 to visit a health clinic 1.87 more times a year—a finding that was significant at the 10 percent level (table 4.1, column 3).

One possible explanation for the decrease in health center visits among children age 0–2 is that the health center attendance conditionality was nonbinding. As previously mentioned, treated children age 0–2 years were required by the CCT to attend at least six health center visits a year. At baseline, however, the median child age 0–2 years already visited health centers 9.19 a year. Exploring

A health clinic in Chamwino district, 2012.

the baseline findings further, we see that the health visit conditions of the program were binding for only 32 percent of children age 0–2 years at baseline.

We observe no statistically significant difference at endline between treatment and comparison health center attendance rates for elderly individuals (age 60+ years). As with the other subpopulations, these findings differ from the midline results. In table 4.1, column (4), we noted that at the time of the midline survey, treated elderly individuals went to an average of 1.14 more health center visits a year (significant at the 1 percent level). As with the young, the elderly were still attending the clinic more often than the conditions require.

From table 7.1, we can conclude that treatment does not have sustained positive effects on health center visits. At midline we saw statistically significant increases in health center visits across all ages and subpopulations, but the endline results report statistically significant decreases among some subpopulations. Such differences may be due to various reasons: Over time, clinics may have become increasingly crowded in treatment communities, disincentivizing attendance; or households may have, as the conditions were better understood, used the conditions as a guideline for how often one should visit a clinic (that is, fewer times than the baseline mean number of visits). The most obvious explanation, perhaps, is simply improved health, which we explore further in the next section.

In table 7.2, we begin our exploration of the differences between how male and female household members responded to treatment at endline. These results were estimated using ETT regressions.

While treatment led both genders to visit health centers less frequently by endline, we find that the decreases are only statistically significant for females. Column (1) shows that at endline, treatment led women of all ages to go to an average of 0.46 fewer health facility visits per year (significant at the 10 percent level), while it had no significant effect on men.

Perhaps most strikingly, girls age 0–2 went to an average of 9.25 health facility visits a year at the baseline. However, by endline treatment led these girls to have 3.78 fewer visits per year (significant at the 5 percent level), as shown in (column 3). It should be noted, however, that the difference between the effect on boys and on girls age 0–2 years is not statistically significant—just as for gender differences among other age groups. Elderly women similar saw a decrease in health facility visits due to treatment—from a baseline mean of 2.86 to 0.58 fewer visits at endline as a result of treatment (significant at the 10 percent level).

Treatment is negatively correlated with illness for all subpopulations shown in table 7.3, though these impacts are only statistically significant overall and for the subpopulation of children age 0–4 years. Column (1) shows that overall, by endline treated individuals were 5 percentage points less likely to report being sick in the last 4 weeks—a reduction in illness that is significant at the 5 percent level. Column (5), however, shows no statistically significant overall impacts of treatment on the number of sick days reported in the last 4 weeks.

**Table 7.2 Heterogeneous Gender Treatment Effect on Health Center Visits, by Age Group at Endline**

| | Average number of health facility visits in the past year | | | |
|---|---|---|---|---|
| | (1) | (2) | (3) | (4) |
| | All ages | Age 0–1 year | Age 0–2 years | Age 60+ years |
| Baseline mean: female | 2.95 | 8.08 | 9.25 | 2.86 |
| Baseline mean: male | 2.62 | 8.9 | 9.15 | 2.69 |
| Effect on females | −0.46 | −3.07 | −3.78 | −0.58 |
| | (0.26)* | (1.91) | (1.52)** | (0.34)* |
| Effect on males | −0.36 | −2.71 | −2.33 | −0.15 |
| | (0.24) | (2.07) | (1.54) | (0.26) |
| Difference between effect on males and effect on females | 0.10 | 0.36 | 1.45 | 0.42 |
| | (0.24) | (2.30) | (1.81) | (0.39) |
| Number of observations | 12,629 | 507 | 721 | 5,343 |

*Source:* World Bank data.
*Notes:* Results reported in this table are based on effect of treatment on the treated (ETT) regressions. Clustered standard errors in parentheses.
Significance level: * = 10 percent, ** = 5 percent, *** = 1 percent.

**Table 7.3 Effects of CCT on Household Health Outcomes at Endline**

| | Reported being sick in past 4 weeks | | | | Number of days too sick for normal activities in past 4 weeks | | | |
|---|---|---|---|---|---|---|---|---|
| | (1) | (2) | (3) | (4) | (5) | (6) | (7) | (8) |
| | All ages | Age 0–4 years | Age 0–18 years | Age 60+ years | All ages | Age 0–4 years | Age 0–18 years | Age 60+ years |
| Baseline mean | 0.27 | 0.75 | 0.60 | 0.46 | 1.64 | 1.05 | 0.81 | 2.79 |
| *Panel A: Effect of treatment of the treated* | | | | | | | | |
| Treatment (ETT) x After | −0.05 | −0.11 | −0.03 | −0.02 | −0.33 | −0.77 | −0.14 | −0.27 |
| | (0.02)** | (0.06)* | (0.03) | (0.04) | (0.21) | (0.34)** | (0.17) | (0.44) |
| After | 0.08 | 0.06 | 0.02 | 0.13 | 0.97 | 0.40 | 0.21 | 2.06 |
| | (0.01)*** | (0.04) | (0.02) | (0.02)*** | (0.15)*** | (0.26) | (0.12)* | (0.30)*** |
| Observations | 18,192 | 1,437 | 6,684 | 5,345 | 18,192 | 1,437 | 6,684 | 5,345 |
| R-squared | 0.01 | 0.01 | 0.00 | 0.02 | 0.01 | 0.01 | 0.00 | 0.03 |
| *Panel B: Intention to treat* | | | | | | | | |
| Treatment (ITT) x After | −0.04 | −0.10 | −0.03 | −0.02 | −0.31 | −0.70 | −0.13 | −0.26 |
| | (0.03) | (0.07) | (0.04) | (0.04) | (0.27) | (0.41)* | (0.21) | (0.54) |
| After | 0.08 | 0.06 | 0.02 | 0.13 | 0.97 | 0.39 | 0.21 | 2.06 |
| | (0.02)*** | (0.05) | (0.02) | (0.03)*** | (0.20)*** | (0.34) | (0.16) | (0.38)*** |

*Source:* World Bank data.
*Note:* Clustered standard errors in parentheses. CCT = conditional cash transfer; ETT = effect of treatment on the treated; ITT = intention to treat.
Significance level: * = 10 percent, ** = 5 percent, *** = 1 percent.

Columns (2) and (6) indicate that at endline, treated children aged 0–4 were 11 percentage points less likely to report being sick in the last 4 weeks (significant at the 10 percent level) and had 0.77 fewer sick days in the last 4 weeks— that is, almost one full day that they were able to do normal activities (significant at the 5 percent level).

These results differ from the midline, where we observed no significant impact on the likelihood that treated individuals reported being sick in the past 4 weeks (table 4.4). This suggests that perhaps the health impacts of treatment may take longer than 18 months (the timing of the midline survey) to materialize. The significant effects from table 7.3 are summarized in figure 7.1.

The decreases in illness rates discussed may explain why we saw reductions in the number of average health facility visits by treated individuals at endline. In table 7.1, we noted that the subpopulation of children age 0–2 went to statistically significantly fewer health center visits. Unsurprisingly, these are similar to the subpopulations that also had statistically significant decreases in illnesses reported, as shown in table 7.3, columns (2) and (6).

Next, in table 7.4, we see that at endline both treated females and treated males were less likely to report being sick in the past 4 weeks. Column (1) shows that at endline, treated females overall were 6 percentage points less likely to report being sick in the last 4 weeks. This is a 21 percent decrease from their baseline mean and is significant at the 5 percent level. However, treated females did not report any statistically significant decreases in the number of days they were too sick to perform normal activities.

Treated males age 0–4 saw statistically significant decreases both in the average number of days they were sick in the last 4 weeks (0.18 fewer days) and in the number of days they were too sick to perform normal activities (0.8 fewer days). Both of these results are significant at the 5 percent level. Males age 0–18 reported 0.3 fewer days in the last 4 weeks for which they were too sick to perform normal activities (significant at the 10 percent level).

**Figure 7.1  Effect of CCT on Health Outcomes**

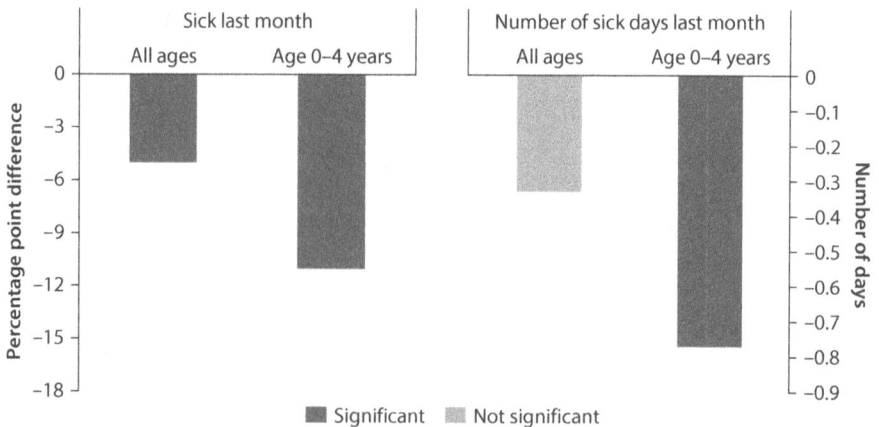

Source: World Bank data.
Note: CCT = conditional cash transfer.

**Table 7.4  Heterogeneous Gender Treatment Effects of CCT on Household Health Outcomes at Endline**

| | Reported being sick in past 4 weeks | | | | Number of days too sick for normal activities in past 4 weeks | | | |
|---|---|---|---|---|---|---|---|---|
| | *(1)* *All ages* | *(2)* *Age 0–4 years* | *(3)* *Age 0–18 years* | *(4)* *Age 60+ years* | *(5)* *All ages* | *(6)* *Age 0–4 years* | *(7)* *Age 0–18 years* | *(8)* *Age 60+ years* |
| Baseline mean: female | 0.29 | 0.71 | 0.59 | 0.44 | 1.71 | 1.00 | 0.81 | 2.79 |
| Baseline mean: male | 0.26 | 0.79 | 0.62 | 0.48 | 1.54 | 1.08 | 0.80 | 2.78 |
| Effect female | −0.06 | −0.04 | −0.01 | −0.02 | −0.34 | −0.71 | 0.05 | −0.22 |
| | (0.02)** | (0.09) | (0.04) | (0.05) | (0.30) | (0.50) | (0.24) | (0.64) |
| Effect male | −0.04 | −0.18 | −0.05 | −0.03 | −0.32 | −0.80 | −0.30 | −0.33 |
| | (0.03) | (0.08)** | (0.04) | (0.04) | (0.23) | (0.37)** | (0.18)* | (0.55) |
| Difference effect male and effect female | 0.02 | −0.13 | −0.04 | −0.01 | 0.02 | −0.10 | −0.36 | −0.12 |
| | (0.03) | (0.11) | (0.04) | (0.06) | (0.32) | (0.56) | (0.26) | (0.82) |
| Observations | 18,192 | 1,437 | 6,684 | 5,345 | 18,192 | 1,437 | 6,684 | 5,345 |

*Source:* World Bank data.
*Notes:* Results reported in this table are based on effect of treatment on the treated (ETT) regressions. Clustered standard errors in parentheses. CCT = conditional cash transfer.
Significance level: * = 10 percent, ** = 5 percent, *** = 1 percent.

An important dimension along which to divide sample households is those with fewer versus more assets—an important indicator of poverty. For our analysis, we divided the treated population into two asset groups. We first performed a principal components analysis that examined ownership of a large array of household items, and we extracted the first principal component of this analysis to serve as our index of asset wealth. Individuals in the poorest half of asset ownership at the baseline are referred to as the "poorest," while those in the top half of asset ownership at the baseline are referred to as the "less poor."

Among the poorest, treatment is associated with statistically significant decreases in illness rates at endline. There are not similar, statistically significant impacts on illness among the less poor (table 7.5). Overall, the poorest treated individuals at endline were 6 percentage points less likely to have been sick in the past 4 weeks (column 1). Similarly, these individuals reported being too sick for normal activities 0.53 fewer days at endline. Both of these results are significant at the 10 percent level.

The poorest children age 0–4 saw decreases in both measures of illness in the past 4 weeks. They were reported to be sick 0.99 fewer days (significant at the 10 percent level), and had a 17 percentage point decrease in illness (not significant). Figure 7.2 summarizes the significant results from table 7.5.

In table 7.6, we find that at endline treatment does not have a statistically significant effect on the likelihood that, once they get ill, beneficiaries of any age group visit a dispensary or hospital for treatment (columns 1–3). As column (4) indicates, treatment also does not have a statistically significant effect on the likelihood that beneficiaries overall take medication for their largest health problems.

**Table 7.5 Heterogeneous Poverty Treatment Effects of CCT on Household Health Outcomes at Endline**

| | Reported being sick in past 4 weeks | | | | Number of days too sick for normal activities in past 4 weeks | | | |
|---|---|---|---|---|---|---|---|---|
| | (1) All ages | (2) Age 0–4 years | (3) Age 0–18 years | (4) Age 60+ years | (5) All ages | (6) Age 0–4 years | (7) Age 0–18 years | (8) Age 60+ years |
| Baseline mean: poorest | 0.30 | 0.76 | 0.63 | 0.41 | 1.79 | 1.16 | 0.89 | 2.67 |
| Baseline mean: less poor | 0.26 | 0.75 | 0.58 | 0.51 | 1.50 | 0.95 | 0.73 | 2.92 |
| Effect poorest | −0.06 | −0.17 | −0.04 | −0.01 | −0.53 | −0.99 | −0.30 | −0.42 |
| | (0.03)* | (0.11) | (0.05) | (0.05) | (0.31)* | (0.52)* | (0.25) | (0.57) |
| Effect less poor | −0.04 | −0.07 | −0.02 | −0.05 | −0.25 | −0.63 | −0.03 | −0.24 |
| | 0.03 | (0.07) | (0.04) | (0.05) | (0.26) | (0.39) | (0.20) | (0.70) |
| Difference effect less poor and effect poor | 0.02 | 0.10 | 0.02 | −0.05 | 0.28 | 0.36 | 0.27 | 0.18 |
| | (0.04) | (0.13) | (0.05) | (0.07) | (0.37) | (0.59) | (0.29) | (0.93) |
| Observations | 18,192 | 1,437 | 6,684 | 5,345 | 18,192 | 1,437 | 6,684 | 5,345 |

*Source:* World Bank data.
*Note:* Results reported in this table are based on effect of treatment on the treated (ETT) regressions. Clustered standard errors in parentheses. CCT = conditional cash transfer.
Significance level: * = 10 percent, ** = 5 percent, *** = 1 percent.

**Figure 7.2 Health Impact for the Poorest Households**

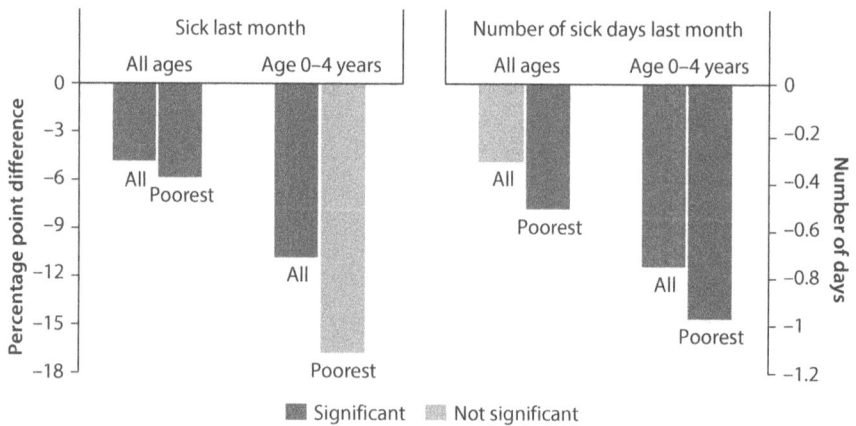

*Source:* World Bank data.

Beneficiaries age 0–18, however, are 11 percentage points less likely to take medication for treatment of their main health problem, a result that is significant at the 5 percent level (column 5). This finding is hard to interpret. One possibility is that children age 0–18 in the program are less severely sick when they do get sick, so they simply require less treatment. If being in a treatment community and seeking medical care more frequently leads to decrease in the severity of illness, than it may lead to less use of medicine.

**Table 7.6  Effects of CCT on Type of Health Treatment by Age Group at Endline**

| | Individuals sick in the past 4 weeks who... | | | | | |
| | Visited a dispensary/hospital for treatment | | | Took medication for treatment of their main health problems | | |
| | (1)<br>All ages | (2)<br>Age 0–18 years | (3)<br>Age 60+ years | (4)<br>All ages | (5)<br>Age 0–18 years | (6)<br>Age 60+ years |
|---|---|---|---|---|---|---|
| Baseline mean | 0.52 | 0.60 | 0.46 | 0.90 | 0.92 | 0.89 |
| *Panel A: Effect of treatment on the treated* | | | | | | |
| Treatment (ETT) × After | 0.04 | −0.03 | 0.03 | −0.01 | −0.11 | 0.00 |
| | (0.05) | (0.10) | (0.06) | (0.03) | (0.06)** | (0.03) |
| After | 0.10 | 0.06 | 0.13 | 0.06 | 0.11 | 0.04 |
| | (0.04)*** | (0.07) | (0.04)*** | (0.02)*** | (0.04)*** | (0.02)** |
| Observations | 2,935 | 532 | 1,688 | 2,963 | 542 | 1,702 |
| R-squared | 0.03 | 0.04 | 0.03 | 0.01 | 0.02 | 0.01 |
| *Panel B: Intention to treat* | | | | | | |
| Treatment (ITT) × After | 0.04 | −0.03 | 0.03 | −0.01 | −0.09 | 0.00 |
| | (0.08) | (0.19) | (0.09) | (0.05) | (0.10) | (0.05) |
| After | 0.10 | 0.06 | 0.13* | 0.06 | 0.11 | 0.04 |
| | (0.07) | (0.17) | (0.07) | (0.03) | (0.08) | (0.03) |

*Source:* World Bank data.
*Note:* Clustered standard errors in parentheses. CCT = conditional cash transfer; ETT = effect of treatment on the treated; ITT = intention to treat.
Significance level: * = 10 percent, ** = 5 percent, *** = 1 percent.

The CCT program had a very strong and significant effect on the likelihood that beneficiaries used health insurance to finance medical care at endline (table 7.7). In column (1) we see that treatment is associated with a 20 percentage point increase in the likelihood of financing medical care with health insurance. This result is statistically significant at the 1 percent level. This is a huge effect; on average, only 2.6 percent of people financed medical care with health insurance at baseline, and that number had increased only to 5.6 percent for comparison households by endline. This means that being in a treatment household is associated with five times greater likelihood of using medical insurance (figure 7.3)

Treatment is also associated with statistically significant increases in the likelihood that children age 0–18 and elderly age 60 and older use health insurance. In column (4) we see that children age 0–18 are now 28 percentage points more likely to finance treatment with health insurance than similarly aged children in comparison households. Column (5) shows that elderly members of beneficiary households are 17 percentage points more likely to use insurance at endline.

Recall that at the midline we found that treated individuals also had increased their likelihood of using health insurance. Thus, the endline findings reported in table 7.7 suggest that treatment has a sustained positive effect on using health insurance to finance treatment.

**Table 7.7  Effects of CCT on Likelihood of Using Health Insurance to Finance Treatment at Endline**

| | Those sick in past 4 weeks who financed treatment with health insurance | | | | |
|---|---|---|---|---|---|
| | (1) All ages | (2) Age 0–1 year | (3) Age 0–4 years | (4) Age 0–18 years | (5) Age 60+ years |
| Baseline mean | 0.026 | 0.027 | 0.029 | 0.032 | 0.026 |
| *Panel A: Effect of treatment on the treated* | | | | | |
| Treatment (ETT) × After | 0.20 | 0.23 | 0.19 | 0.28 | 0.17 |
| | (0.05)*** | (0.23) | (0.15) | (0.10)*** | (0.05)*** |
| After | 0.03 | 0.07 | 0.08 | 0.02 | 0.03 |
| | (0.01)** | (0.07) | (0.06) | (0.03) | (0.02)** |
| Observations | 2,525 | 86 | 173 | 474 | 1,426 |
| R-squared | 0.09 | 0.05 | 0.09 | 0.10 | 0.08 |
| *Panel B: Intention to treat* | | | | | |
| Treatment (ITT) × After | 0.18 | 0.14 | 0.15 | 0.23 | 0.16 |
| | (0.09)* | (0.28) | (0.24) | (0.19) | (0.08)** |
| After | 0.03 | 0.07 | 0.08 | 0.02 | 0.03 |
| | (0.03) | (0.13) | (0.12) | (0.06) | (0.03) |

*Source:* World Bank data.
*Note:* Clustered standard errors in parentheses. CCT = conditional cash transfer; ETT = effect of treatment on the treated; ITT = intention to treat.
Significance level: * = 10 percent, ** = 5 percent, *** = 1 percent.

**Figure 7.3  Effect of Treatment on Share of Households Financing Treatment with Health Insurance**

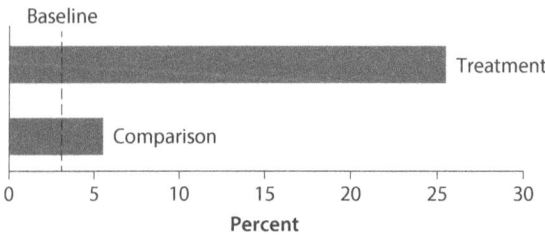

*Source:* World Bank data.

In table 7.8, we observe that both treated males and treated females increased their likelihood of using health insurance at endline. Column (1) shows that men overall saw a 23 percentage point increase, while women only realized a 17 percentage point increase. Both of these results are significant at the 1 percent level.

Both genders at age 0–18 and over age 60 also realized statistically significant increases in their likelihood to use health insurance at endline. From column (4)

**Table 7.8 Heterogeneous Gender Treatment Effects of CCT on Likelihood of Using Health Insurance at Endline**

| | Those sick in past 4 weeks who financed treatment with health insurance | | | | |
|---|---|---|---|---|---|
| | (1) All ages | (2) Age 0–1 year | (3) Age 0–4 years | (4) Age 0–18 years | (5) Age 60+ years |
| Baseline mean: female | 0.03 | 0.09 | 0.05 | 0.05 | 0.03 |
| Baseline mean: male | 0.02 | 0 | 0.01 | 0.02 | 0.02 |
| Effect female | 0.17 | 0.08 | 0.28 | 0.25 | 0.13 |
| | (0.05)*** | (0.43) | (0.20) | (0.12)** | (0.06)** |
| Effect male | 0.23 | 0.20 | 0.01 | 0.30 | 0.22 |
| | (0.07)*** | (0.15) | (0.19) | (0.14)** | (0.07)*** |
| Difference effect male and effect female | 0.06 | 0.12 | −0.28 | 0.05 | 0.08 |
| | (0.06) | (0.42) | (0.25) | (0.15) | (0.08) |
| Observations | 2,525 | 86 | 173 | 474 | 1,426 |

*Source:* World Bank data.
*Note:* Results reported in this table are based on effect of treatment on the treated (ETT) regressions. Clustered standard errors in parentheses. CCT = conditional cash transfer.
Significance level: * = 10 percent, ** = 5 percent, *** = 1 percent.

we see that males age 0–18 were 30 percentage points more likely to use health insurance while their female counterparts were 25 percentage points more likely to do so. Both results are significant at the 5 percent level.

In column (5) we find that elderly female household members are 13 percentage points more likely to use health insurance while elderly male household members are now 21 percentage points more likely to. Both of these findings are significant at the 1 percent level.

In table 7.9, column (1) we see that at endline, households in both asset groups responded to treatment in a similar and statistically significant fashion. The poorest households realized a 20 percentage point increase in their likelihood of using insurance, while the less poor households realized a 19 percentage point increase. Both results are significant at the 1 percent level.

While both groups overall had similar increases in their likelihood to use insurance, some differences appear in the subpopulation age groups. For example, in column (4) we see that at endline the poorest individuals age 0–18 had a 53 percentage point increase in their likelihood to use health insurance (significant at the 1 percent level), but their counterparts in the top half of asset ownership realized only a 20 percentage point increase (significant at the 10 percent). At the baseline, both less poor and poorest children age 0–18 had the same average insurance usage rate. This indicates that over time, treatment had a particularly large effect on the poorest children with regards to their likelihood to use health insurance. The difference in the effect for less poor and the poorest for children age 0–18 (very obvious in figure 7.4) is also statistically significant and

**Table 7.9  Heterogeneous Poverty Treatment Effects of CCT on Likelihood of Using Health Insurance to Finance Treatment at Endline**

| | Those sick in past 4 weeks who financed treatment with health insurance | | | | |
| --- | --- | --- | --- | --- | --- |
| | *(1)* *All ages* | *(2)* *Age 0–1 years* | *(3)* *Age 0–4 years* | *(4)* *Age 0–18 years* | *(5)* *Age 60+ years* |
| Baseline mean: poorest | 0.02 | 0.06 | 0.05 | 0.03 | 0.02 |
| Baseline mean: less poor | 0.03 | 0 | 0.01 | 0.03 | 0.03 |
| Effect poorest | 0.20 | 0.33 | −0.04 | 0.53 | 0.15 |
| | (0.06)*** | (0.27) | (0.28) | (0.15)*** | (0.06)** |
| Effect less poor | 0.19 | 0.21 | 0.26 | 0.20 | 0.18 |
| | (0.06)*** | (0.29) | (0.17) | (0.12)* | (0.05)** |
| Difference effect less poor and effect poorest | −0.01 | −0.13 | 0.30 | −0.33 | 0.02 |
| | (0.06) | (0.37) | (0.32) | (0.19)* | (0.07) |
| Observations | 2,525 | 86 | 173 | 474 | 1,426 |

*Source:* World Bank data.
*Note:* Results reported in this table are based on effect of treatment on the treated (ETT) regressions. Clustered standard errors in parentheses. CCT = conditional cash transfer.
Significance level: * = 10 percent, ** = 5 percent, *** = 1 percent.

**Figure 7.4  Effect of Conditional Cash Transfer on Financing Medical Treatment with Insurance, by Age**

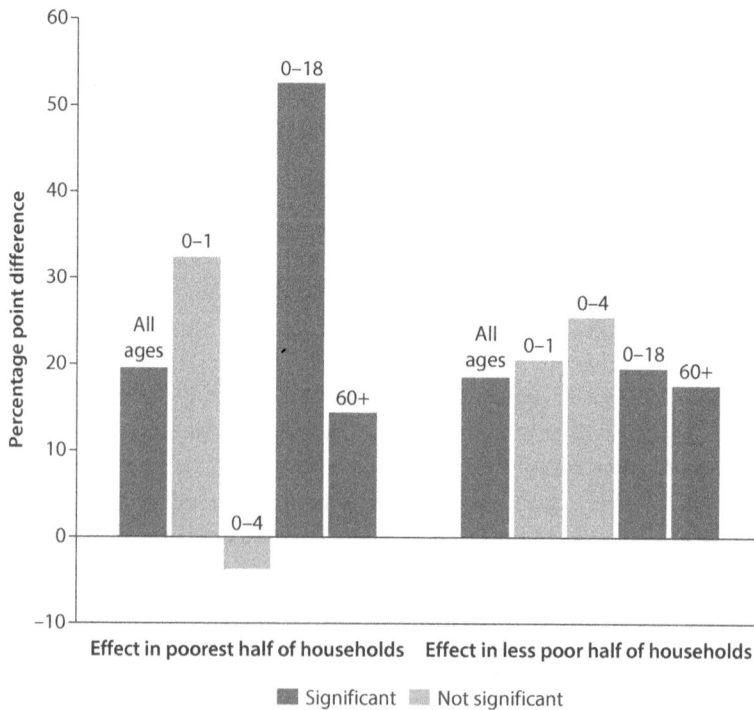

*Source:* World Bank data.

**Table 7.10 Heterogeneous Geography Treatment Effects of CCT on Likelihood of Using Health Insurance to Finance Treatment at Endline**

| | Those sick in past 4 weeks who financed treatment with health insurance | | | |
|---|---|---|---|---|
| | (1) | (2) | (3) | (4) |
| | All ages | Age 0–1 year | Age 0–4 years | Age 0–18 years |
| Baseline mean: Kibaha | 0.07 | 0.08 | 0.08 | 0.08 |
| Baseline mean: Bagamoyo | 0.01 | 0 | 0 | 0.01 |
| Baseline mean: Chamwino | 0.02 | 0 | 0.02 | 0.02 |
| Effect Kibaha | 0.38 | 0.16 | 0.36 | 0.38 |
| | (0.08)*** | (0.37) | (0.28) | (0.10)*** |
| Effect Bagamoyo | 0.18 | 0.50 | 0.35 | 0.18 |
| | (0.07)** | (0.43) | (0.22) | (0.07)*** |
| Effect Chamwino | 0.37 | 1.0 | 0.60 | 0.31 |
| | (0.13)*** | 0.00*** | (0.28)** | (0.10)*** |
| Difference effect Bagamoyo and effect Kibaha | −0.21 | 0.34 | −0.00 | −0.20 |
| | (0.10)** | (0.57) | (0.36) | (0.12)* |
| Difference effect Chamwino and effect Kibaha | −0.02 | 0.84 | 0.24 | −0.07 |
| | (0.15) | (0.37)** | (0.39) | (0.14) |
| Observations | 984 | 76 | 198 | 592 |

*Source:* World Bank data.

*Note:* Results reported in this table are based on effect of treatment on the treated (ETT) regressions. Clustered standard errors in parentheses. CCT = conditional cash transfer.

*** $p < .01$, ** $p < .05$, * $p < .1$.

negative. This underscores our finding that treatment had a much larger effect on the poorest households.

Table 7.10 reports the different treatment effects reported by the three pilot districts at endline. Column (1) shows that households in Kibaha realized a 38 percentage point increase in their likelihood of using health insurance (significant at the 1 percent level), households in Bagamoyo realized an 18 percentage point increase (significant at the 5 percent level), and households in Chamwino had a 37 percentage point increase in their likelihood to use health insurance (significant at the 1 percent level). While the percentage point increases in Kibaha and Chamwino are twice those of Bagamoyo, Bagamoyo had the largest increase relative to its baseline.

Children age 0–18 in all three districts also realized increases in their likelihood to use health insurance. All these results are significant at the 1 percent level. The statistically significant and positive coefficient on the difference between the effect in Chamwino and the effect in Kibaha underscores that treatment had a larger effect in Chamwino than in Kibaha.

Generally, although all three districts had large and significant increases in the likelihood that treated individuals used health insurance, Bagamoyo and Chamwino had the largest gains.

### Qualitative Findings

A major finding of the qualitative fieldwork in almost every village visited was that many of the beneficiaries and community leaders involved stressed the importance of the community health fund (CHF) for beneficiary households. The heads of the health facilities across the villages involved in the qualitative work said that most or nearly all beneficiary households were enrolled in the program. In a village in Kibaha, the head of the dispensary said that when Tanzania Social Action Fund (TASAF) transfers are distributed, she sends the dispensary staff to the distribution point to sign up any household that is not yet participating or needs to renew their membership while they feel relatively "rich." This type of proactive behavior by health facility staff may help explain the particularly large effect of the program on the likelihood of using insurance for poorer children and the elderly in our sample, since they are encouraged to join the CHF at a time when they have higher liquidity, and when their need to comply with conditions is relatively more salient. While this dispensary head and others mentioned that other (nonbeneficiary) community members do sign up for the program, they emphasized participation in the CHF more for beneficiaries. Similarly, the community management committee (CMC) in a village in Bagamoyo explained that it is important to "sensitize" the beneficiaries on how they should spend the money, and that they stress the importance of contributing to the CHF. This highlights community leader and service provider perceptions that the CHF is complementary to the CB-CCT program, and that greater use of health insurance should be encouraged.

Some of the beneficiaries mentioned that they visited the health center frequently as a result of becoming a member of the CHF, however even nonparticipants seemed to attend the clinic when they were sick. One reason that the quantitative evaluation may not have found an increase in clinic visits at endline due to the program may have been that most beneficiaries were already visiting the clinic more than required (9.2 times for 0–2-year-olds, well above the 6 times per year conditionality, and 2.78 times for elderly, also above the 1 time per year conditionality). One beneficiary in a focus group in Bagamoyo said that he went to the clinic almost every day, until the staff told him that he was healthy and so did not need to visit the clinic so often. Indeed, most of the elderly beneficiaries that participated in the qualitative fieldwork had been to the clinic within the past two months.

The qualitative findings can also help explain the muted impact of the program on the use of drugs to finance treatment. One beneficiary in a focus group in Bagamoyo district reported how she did not need to pay to go to the clinic because of the program, but that when she did go it often lacked necessary drugs. Since she then would have to buy the drugs somewhere else using her own money, she felt it was less useful to go to the dispensary. Indeed, the head of one health center in Kibaha stated in an in-depth interview that a lack of drugs is a major problem for her and that the process to replenish drugs is lengthy and complicated. She explained that she had put in a request for more drugs in April since the clinic had depleted its supply, and had not obtained the drugs until July. If a lack of drugs is a common problem across the program communities, this could also help explain why health clinic visits do not increase as a result of the CB-CCT program. Beneficiaries that are not able to obtain adequate treatment at the health facility may decide to stay home rather than be told to buy additional drugs that they cannot afford.

Takeaways:

- Cash transfers have positive health impacts. Participating households were less likely to report being sick and less likely to lose work time to illness.
- Encouraging communication between various programs can increase the impact. Coordinating across programs can lead to the kind of complementarity that is observed between the cash transfer distribution and the community health fund registration.

## Child Anthropometrics

In table 7.11, we show how the program affected anthropometrics for children aged 0–4. In these specifications, we use child fixed effects, thus we control for any child-specific characteristics that might influence outcomes, and isolate the effects of treatment.

As we see, assignment to treatment is not significantly associated with changes in children's anthropometric outcomes at endline. Between the baseline and endline, changes in height, weight, and middle-upper-arm circumference (MUAC) are similar for children in treatment and in control communities

**Table 7.11 Effects of CCT on Anthropometric Outcomes for Children Age 0–4 at Endline (Absolute Levels)**

|  | (1) | (2) | (3) |
|---|---|---|---|
|  | Height (cm) | Weight (kg) | MUAC (cm) |
| Baseline mean | 87.31 | 12.16 | 155.81 |
| *Panel A: Effect of treatment on the treated* | | | |
| Treatment (ETT) × After | 0.61 | 0.18 | 1.61 |
|  | (1.38) | (0.30) | (2.16) |
| After | 9.55 | 2.51 | 6.51 |
|  | (0.87)*** | (0.21)*** | (1.40)*** |
| Observations | 561 | 708 | 553 |
| R-squared | 0.27 | 0.30 | 0.17 |
| *Panel B: Intention to treat* | | | |
| Treatment (ITT) × After | 0.53 | 0.16 | 1.42 |
|  | (2.48) | (0.52) | (4.04) |
| After | 9.55 | 2.51 | 6.51 |
|  | (1.80)*** | (0.41)*** | (2.92)** |

*Source:* World Bank data.
*Note:* Clustered standard errors in parentheses. CCT = conditional cash transfer; ETT = effect of treatment on the treated; ITT = intention to treat; MUAC = middle-upper-arm circumference.
Significance level: * = 10 percent, ** = 5 percent, *** = 1 percent.

(columns 1–3), although we do observe a pattern of positive differences for treatment children, that is, we can rule out any strong, negative effects.

Recall that in our discussion of table 4.5, we showed that treatment was associated with a growth in height that was significantly higher than the growth experienced by similar children in control communities at midline (column 1). The results reported were significant at the 10 percent level. Table 7.11, column (1), suggests that if treatment continues to have a positive effect on height at endline, the result is no longer significant.

### Qualitative Findings

Health providers in in-depth interviews and focus groups did not report any measurable differences between beneficiary and nonbeneficiary children in terms of health or growth. However, educators in focus groups in Bagamoyo did state that children are now getting more to eat and so are better able to focus in school. Enough time may not have elapsed since the beginning of transfers to evaluate the program's effects on some anthropometrics, which can occur over the longer term. These effects may be difficult for individual service providers in program communities to detect over a relatively short time period. Also, there could be considerable variation in anthropometric impacts, which is difficult to discern at the community level, or may not have been present in the specific communities visited as part of the endline focus groups and in-depth interviews.

Takeaways:

- It is important to evaluate these types of programs over a longer period, to see if these children experience better outcomes in adulthood.
- The pattern of positive estimates suggests that the program had no negative impacts on children's anthropometrics, and that the program may have been mildly beneficial. This is consistent with the fact that we do not observe major changes in consumption, as observed later.

### Education Outcomes

In this section, we discuss how participation in the CB-CCT (that is, treatment) had positive effects on several education outcomes at endline. In table 7.12, we first show that treatment does not have a statistically significant impact on the likelihood that children age 0–18 are literate at endline, a self-reported measure (column 1). Treatment did lead to a higher likelihood that 0–18-year-olds had attended school at some point (column 2). While 69 percent of children age 0–18 had attended school at some point at baseline, treatment made them 4 percentage points more likely to have done so by endline (table 7.12). This echoes our findings at the midline where we discussed that treatment led to a 7 percentage point increase in whether children had ever attended school (significant at the 1 percent level).

Treatment does not seem to have—on average—a statistically significant impact on the likelihood that children age 0–18 enroll in school, miss school, or

**Table 7.12  Effects of CCT on Household Education Outcomes at the Endline**

| | Age 0–18 years | | | | | Age 7–14 years | Age 15–18 years |
|---|---|---|---|---|---|---|---|
| | (1) | (2) | (3) | (4) | (5) | (6) | (7) |
| | Literate | Ever attended school | Currently in school | Missed school last week, if enrolled (own fault) | Took national exam-Standard IV+ | Completed Standard IV or higher | Completed Standard VII or higher |
| Baseline mean | 0.52 | 0.69 | 0.59 | 0.12 | 0.14 | 0.36 | 0.51 |
| *Panel A: Effect of treatment on the treated* | | | | | | | |
| Treatment (ETT) × After | 0.02 | 0.04 | 0.04 | 0.02 | −0.02 | 0.03 | 0.15 |
| | (0.02) | (0.02)** | (0.03) | (0.03) | (0.02) | (0.03) | (0.07)** |
| After | 0.14 | 0.11 | 0.00 | −0.04 | 0.03 | 0.28 | 0.18 |
| | (0.01)*** | (0.01)*** | (0.02) | (0.02)** | (0.01)** | (0.02)*** | (0.04)*** |
| Observations | 6,239 | 6,239 | 6,205 | 3,412 | 1,934 | 3,073 | 852 |
| R-squared | 0.07 | 0.07 | 0.00 | 0.01 | 0.01 | 0.18 | 0.12 |
| *Panel B: Intent to treat* | | | | | | | |
| Treatment (ITT) × After | 0.02 | 0.04 | 0.04 | 0.01 | −0.02 | 0.03 | 0.13 |
| | (0.02) | (0.02) | (0.04) | (0.04) | (0.03) | (0.04) | (0.08) |
| After | 0.14 | 0.11 | 0.00 | −0.04 | 0.03 | 0.28 | 0.18 |
| | (0.02)*** | (0.02)*** | (0.03) | (0.03)* | (0.02) | (0.03)*** | (0.05)*** |

*Source:* World Bank data.
*Note:* Clustered standard errors in parentheses. CCT = conditional cash transfer; ETT = effect of treatment on the treated; ITT = intention to treat.
*** $p < .01$, ** $p < .05$, * $p < 0.1$.

take the national Standard IV exam, nor does it have a statistically significant impact on whether children 7–14 years complete Standard IV or higher at end-line (columns 3–6). At midline (table 4.7), we found that treatment led to a 6 percentage point increase in whether children were currently in school, significant at the 10 percent level. Such differences between midline and endline may be due to changes in perceptions of how rigorously conditions would be imposed, or schools may have become increasingly crowded in treatment communities, disincentivizing attendance.

Nonetheless, treatment seems to have a large impact on grade progression at endline. Figure 7.5 illustrates the relative magnitudes of treatment's impact on several school outcomes. At midline (table 4.7, column 7), we found that children age 15–19 were 13 percentage points more likely to complete Standard VII or higher, significant at the 10 percent level. At endline, treatment continued to have a positive effect. In fact, treatment had an even larger effect at endline as it was associated with, on average, a 15 percentage point increase in children age 15–18 years completing Standard VII or higher education at endline (column 7). This is significant at the 5 percent level.

These results underscore our findings from the midline (table 4.7). At endline we continue to see that the CCT has a statistically significant and positive affect on whether a child has ever attended school, but not whether a child recently attended school. This may indicate that while the program is enrolling new

**Figure 7.5  Effect of Conditional Cash Transfer on School Outcomes**

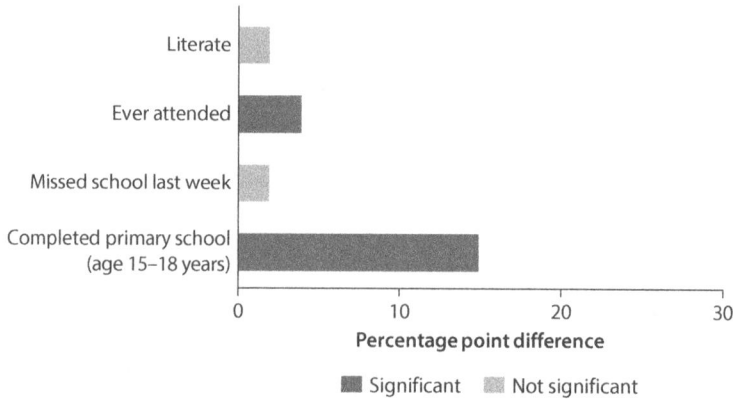

Source: World Bank data.

students, it does not encourage students to spend more time in school then they did previously. One possibility is that the conditions are nonbinding and that students were already attending at the 80 percent attendance rate or higher. At baseline, only 12 percent of enrolled children reported having missed school the previous week. Another possibility is that parents overreported their children's attendance at the baseline, midline, and endline surves.

In table 7.13, we analyze the differences in education outcomes between treated boys and girls. We find that the gains in education seem to be principally concentrated among girls, with the impacts on ever attending school and on completion of Standard 7 high among girls and less strong among boys. That said, we cannot confidently rule out that the impacts are similar across genders. Column (7) and figure 7.6 show that treated girls are 24 percentage points more likely to complete Standard 7 (significant at the 1 percent level). This is a drastic improvement, especially since the baseline survey found that beginning at the age of 15, a large gap existed between boys and girls attending school.

There are also differences in the education outcomes between treated children in the poorest and less poor households at endline (table 7.14). Column (3) shows that the poorest children age 0–18 years had a 7 percentage point increase in their likelihood of being currently enrolled in school at endline (significant at the 10 percent level). In column (7) we find that children age 15–18 from less poor households are now statistically significantly more likely to complete Standard 7. These children saw a major 19 percentage point increase (significant at the 5 percent level). Meanwhile, their poorer peers saw a statistically insignificant and much smaller increase. This suggests that although treatment has a greater effect on keeping the poorest children enrolled in school, the primary completion impacts are concentrated among the less poor children.

Finally, we explored the differences in education outcomes among the various treatment districts. In general, we see that treatment had a positive effect on education outcomes in all three districts—increasing literacy, school attendance, and the likelihood that older children complete primary education.

**Table 7.13 Heterogeneous Gender Treatment Effects of CCT on Household Education Outcomes at Endline**

| | Age 0–18 years | | | | | Age 7–14 years | Age 15–18 years |
|---|---|---|---|---|---|---|---|
| | (1) | (2) | (3) | (4) | (5) | (6) | (7) |
| | Literate | Ever attended school | Currently in school | Missed school last week, if enrolled (own fault) | Took national exam-Standard IV+ | Completed Standard IV or higher | Completed Standard VII or higher |
| Baseline mean: female | 0.52 | 0.69 | 0.60 | 0.12 | 0.96 | 0.38 | 0.52 |
| Baseline mean: male | 0.53 | 0.70 | 0.59 | 0.13 | 0.97 | 0.33 | 0.49 |
| Effect female | 0.02 | 0.05 | 0.04 | 0.01 | −0.04 | 0.03 | 0.24 |
| | −0.02 | (0.03)* | (0.04) | (0.03) | (0.03) | (0.04) | (0.09)*** |
| Effect male | 0.00 | 0.00 | 0.05 | 0.02 | −0.01 | 0.03 | 0.08 |
| | (0.02) | (0.02) | (0.03) | (0.04) | (0.02) | (0.04) | (0.08) |
| Difference effect male and effect female | −0.03 | −0.02 | 0.01 | 0.02 | 0.03 | 0.00 | −0.15 |
| | (0.03) | (0.03) | (0.04) | (0.04) | (0.03) | (0.05) | (0.11) |
| Observations | 6,239 | 6,239 | 6,205 | 3,412 | 1,934 | 3,073 | 852 |

*Source:* World Bank data.
*Note:* Results reported in this table are based on effect of treatment on the treated (ETT) regressions. Clustered standard errors in parentheses. CCT = conditional cash transfer.
Significance level: * = 10 percent, ** = 5 percent, *** = 1 percent.

**Figure 7.6 Effect of Community Cash Transfer on School Outcomes of Females**

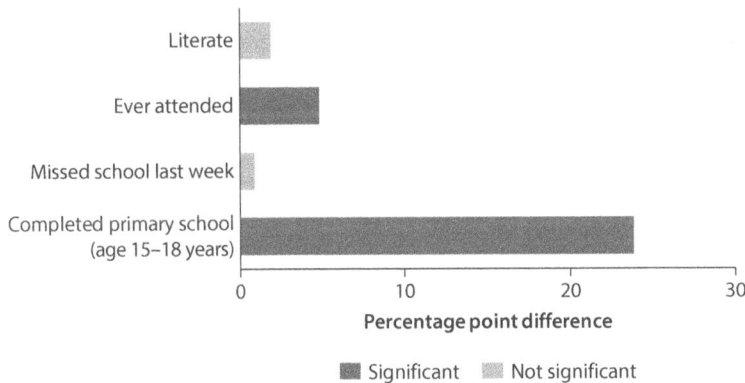

*Source:* World Bank data.

In column (1) of table 7.15, we see that at endline, children age 0–18 years living in Kibaha realized a 4 percentage point increase in their likelihood of being literate (significant at the 10 percent level). Children in Bagamoyo realized a 3 percentage point increase (significant at the 5 percent level). Treatment in Chamwino is correlated with an increased likelihood of being literate, but this result was not statistically significant.

All three districts also realized an increase in attendance, although these results are not statistically significant. For children age 7–14 years in Chamwino we see a statistically significant increase in their likelihood of completing Standard 4 or higher at endline. Column (6) illustrates that these children are

**Table 7.14 Heterogeneous Poverty Treatment Effects of CCT on Household Education Outcomes at Endline**

| | Age 0–18 years | | | | | Age 7–14 years | Age 15–18 years |
|---|---|---|---|---|---|---|---|
| | (1) | (2) | (3) | (4) | (5) | (6) | (7) |
| | Literate | Ever attended school | Currently in school | Missed school last week, if enrolled (own fault) | Took national exam-Standard IV+ | Completed Standard IV or higher | Completed Standard VII or higher |
| Baseline mean: poorest | 0.45 | 0.64 | 0.56 | 0.14 | 0.98 | 0.32 | 0.47 |
| Baseline mean: less poor | 0.59 | 0.74 | 0.63 | 0.10 | 0.98 | 0.32 | 0.54 |
| Effect poorest | 0.03 | 0.04 | 0.07 | 0.07 | −0.01 | 0.04 | 0.04 |
| | (0.03) | (0.03) | (0.04)* | (0.04) | (0.03) | (0.05) | (0.10) |
| Effect less poor | 0.01 | 0.04 | 0.03 | −0.02 | −0.03 | 0.03 | 0.19 |
| | (0.02) | (0.02) | (0.03) | (0.03) | (0.02) | (0.04) | (0.08)** |
| Difference effect less poor and effect poorest | −0.02 | −0.01 | −0.05 | −0.09 | −0.03 | −0.01 | 0.15 |
| | (0.04) | (0.04) | (0.04) | (0.04)** | (0.04) | (0.06) | (0.12) |
| Observations | 6,239 | 6,239 | 6,205 | 3,412 | 1,934 | 3,073 | 852 |

*Source:* World Bank data.

*Note:* Results reported in this table are based on effect of treatment on the treated (ETT) regressions. Clustered standard errors in parentheses. CCT = conditional cash transfer.

Significance level: * = 10 percent, ** = 5 percent, *** = 1 percent.

now 16 percentage points more likely to complete Standard 4 or higher, a 31 percent increase over the baseline mean that is significant at the 5 percent level.

Most striking is that older children, age 15–18, in Bagamoyo and Kibaha enjoyed much larger and significant increases in continuing upper-level primary education (column 7). In Kibaha, these children were 30 percentage points more likely to complete Standard 7 or higher (significant at the 10 percent). Similarly, in Bagamoyo these children realized a 24 percentage point increase in the likelihood of completing Standard 7 or higher (significant at the 5 percent). Though their Chamwino counterparts seemed to have also realized an increase, the result was not significant.

We next divided the population of children age 0–18 into two groups: those in school at baseline and those out of school at baseline. We then estimated the ETT for each group and found that the conditions of the program had a positive effect on three major education outcomes for particularly vulnerable children—those who were not in school at baseline (table 7.16). In column (1), we see that children who were out of school at baseline are now 4 percentage points more likely to be literate at endline, a result that is significant at the 1 percent level. Column (2) reports that children who were out of school are now 3 percentage points more likely to ever have attended school (significant at the 5 percent level) and column (3) shows that they are 4 percentage points more likely to currently be in school (significant at the 10 percent level). Figure 7.7 illustrates the effect of treatment for those out of school at baseline.

**Table 7.15  Heterogeneous Geography Treatment Effects of CCT on Household Education Outcomes at Endline**

| | Age 0–18 years | | | | | Age 7–14 years | Age 15–18 years |
|---|---|---|---|---|---|---|---|
| | (1) | (2) | (3) | (4) | (5) | (6) | (7) |
| | Literate | Ever attended school | Currently in school | Missed school last week, if enrolled (own fault) | Took national exam-Standard IV+ | Completed Standard IV or higher | Completed Standard VII or higher |
| Baseline mean: Kibaha | 0.61 | 0.75 | 0.63 | 0.08 | 0.97 | 0.45 | 0.68 |
| Baseline mean: Bagamoyo | 0.55 | 0.72 | 0.62 | 0.16 | 0.99 | 0.35 | 0.35 |
| Baseline mean: Chamwino | 0.34 | 0.57 | 0.50 | 0.10 | 0.98 | 0.23 | 0.23 |
| Effect Kibaha | 0.04 | 0.04 | 0.02 | 0.06 | −0.01 | 0.05 | 0.30 |
| | (0.02)* | (0.05) | (0.06) | (0.04) | (0.06) | (0.06) | (0.16)* |
| Effect Bagamoyo | 0.035 | 0.028 | 0.13 | −0.018 | −0.018 | 0.082 | 0.240 |
| | (0.02)** | (0.04) | (0.06)** | (0.05) | (0.02) | (.08) | (0.12)** |
| Effect Chamwino | 0.05 | 0.03 | 0.05 | 0.14 | −0 | 0.16 | 0.12 |
| | (0.05) | (0.051) | (0.07) | (0.11) | (0.00) | (0.07)** | (0.17) |
| Difference effect Bagamoyo and effect Kibaha | −0.05 | 0.08 | 0.10 | −0.07 | −0.01 | 0.03 | −0.06 |
| | (0.06) | (0.07) | (0.09) | (0.07) | (0.06) | (0.10) | (0.19) |
| Difference effect Chamwino and effect Kibaha | −0.03 | −0.01 | 0.03 | 0.09 | 0.01 | 0.11 | −0.18 |
| | (0.07) | (0.07) | (0.09) | (0.12) | (0.06) | (0.09) | (0.23) |
| Observations | 3,482 | 3,482 | 3,438 | 1,546 | 444 | 1,730 | 432 |

*Source:* World Bank data.
*Note:* Results reported in this table are based on effect of treatment on the treated (ETT) regressions. Clustered standard errors in parentheses. CCT = conditional cash transfer.
Significance level: * = 10 percent, ** = 5 percent, *** = 1 percent.

**Table 7.16  Heterogeneous Treatment Effects of CCT on Household Education Outcomes at the Endline Based on Baseline Enrollment**

| | (1) | (2) | (3) | (4) | (5) | (6) | (7) |
|---|---|---|---|---|---|---|---|
| | Age 0–18 years | | | | | Age 7–14 years | Age 15–18 years |
| | Literate | Ever attended school | Currently in school | Missed school last week, if enrolled (own fault) | Took national exam-Standard IV+ | Completed Standard IV or higher | Completed Standard VII or higher |
| Effect out of school at baseline | 0.04 | 0.03 | 0.04 | 0.07 | −0.01 | 0.05 | 0.05 |
| | (0.01)*** | (0.02)** | (0.02)* | (0.04) | (0.03) | (0.04) | (0.04) |
| Effect in school at baseline | 0.01 | 0.01 | 0.05 | −0.05 | 0 | 0.09 | 0.09 |
| | 0.03 | 0.03 | 0.04 | 0.08 | 0.00 | 0.06 | 0.06 |
| Difference | −0.03 | −0.03 | 0.00 | −0.12 | 0.01 | 0.03 | 0.03 |
| | (0.04) | (0.04) | (0.04) | (0.08) | (0.03) | (0.07) | (0.07) |
| Observations | 8,887 | 8,877 | 6,344 | 1,546 | 444 | 2,298 | 2,298 |
| *R*-squared | 0.07 | 0.03 | 0.01 | 0.02 | 0.02 | 0.36 | 0.36 |

*Source:* World Bank data.
*Note:* Results reported in this table are based on effect of treatment on the treated (ETT) regressions. Clustered standard errors in parentheses. CCT = conditional cash transfer.
Significance level: * = 10 percent, ** = 5 percent, *** = 1 percent.

**Figure 7.7 Effect of Conditional Cash Transfer on School Outcomes of Children Out of School at Baseline**

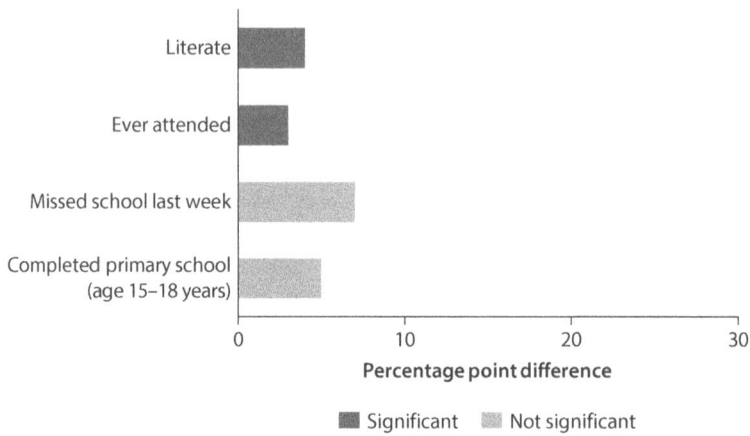

Source: World Bank data.

### Qualitative Findings

One of the most strongly reported results of the program from the qualitative work with both treatment community leaders (including teachers) and beneficiaries was that the program increased the continuation of vulnerable children to secondary school, despite the fact that secondary students were not direct beneficiaries. This is consistent with the impacts on grade progression that are evident in the quantitative data, and especially the large increase in girls completing Standard 7 (the grade immediately prior to the beginning of secondary school). However, the fact that transfers are discontinued when children reach secondary school may explain why there is a large increase in Standard 7 completion for the relatively better-off beneficiaries, but not as large of an increase for the poorest. If these households will no longer receive transfers for their children, they may be unable to afford to send their children to secondary school and so may decide that finishing primary, even if they could afford it, is not as necessary if the child will not continue her schooling. Indeed, a head teacher in Kibaha explained that children may not attend secondary school because parents have a very low income, while secondary school is very expensive.

Another explanation for a larger increase in Standard 7 completion in less poor households comes from a focus group in Bagamoyo district, where it was explained that the number of students completing Standard 7 was greater than the places available for secondary students. This may deter the poorest from continuing their education even to the end of Standard 7, since they may not be able to compete as well with their less poor peers for the limited space available in secondary school. Focus groups that included head teachers with community leaders in Bagamoyo also explained that the program increased attendance because children could afford uniforms, food, supplies, and shoes.

The quantitative analysis suggests increased enrollment for beneficiaries as a result of the program, and in particular presents significant evidence for increased enrollment for the poorest households relative to the less poor. In other words,

School built by TASAF I in a control community in Bagamoyo district.

those most likely to have not attended school at baseline because of a lack of school materials and clothing are now more likely to attend school because of the transfers from the CB-CCT program. One village conceded, consistent with the quantitative findings, that the program may not have reduced the number of days of school that enrolled students are absent, but that it did increase their attentiveness and confidence when they did attend. The qualitative work further clarified that previously, some children had been unable to pay attention due to lack of food, and that they were ashamed of not having the appropriate uniform, but that morale improved after the program began. This may explain some of the impact of the program on grade progression.

The qualitative exercise also found a range of responses from communities on how they encouraged children to attend school. In one village in Kibaha, the village executive officer (VEO) told us that he would receive information from the CMC and school, and if some children were not complying with the conditions of the CB-CCT program, he would contact the family directly. This VEO told us that while the CMC lacked power to induce households to change their behavior, his involvement was enough to ensure that children attended school. However, in other communities village leaders expressed less engagement with monitoring the conditions of the program.

Takeaways:

- It is essential to consider within-household spillover effects when evaluating these types of programs: Impacts on children in the household not covered by the conditions seem to be significant.

- Continuing payments through secondary school would likely improve equity by allowing the poorest children to continue to secondary school; however, it would require looking further into capacity constraints.

## Expenditures

We also examined whether participation in the community-based CCT (that is, treatment) changed the amount and composition of annual expenditures on various items at endline.

In table 7.17, we see that treatment does not lead to many statistically significant changes in non-food expenditures.

One concern with cash transfer programs is that households may misspend transfers on unhealthy items such as tobacco products. The fact that we are not seeing this in the endline analysis is a positive finding: Indeed, if there is any change in spending on these items, it is likely to be a reduction in spending.

Further, we do see that treatment leads to statistically significant higher expenditures on insurance, significant at the 1 percent level (column 1). Households now spend an average of T Sh 1,625 more a year on car, medical, and life insurance. This underscores the midline findings (table 4.8, column 10) and indicates that treatment has a sustained positive effect on whether households purchase insurance. This is also consistent with our findings in table 7.7, which reported that households were more likely to finance medical care with insurance at endline.

Some of the other results, however, do differ slightly from those found at the midline. In table 4.8, columns (4) and (5), we saw that treated households spent more on clothing and footwear for women and girls older than 15 years of age and other personal effects (both significant at the 10 percent level) at the midline. Although these results remain positive at the endline (table 7.17, columns 4 and 5), they appear to be smaller and are no longer significant, although we cannot rule out that the effect sizes are the same. Households may have used the first transfers to purchase basic needs, such as clothing and footwear for women and girls and other personal effects. However, because these are semi-durable goods, subsequent transfers and spending went to other uses by endline. This would explain why our findings were significant at midline, but not at endline.

Next, we discuss how female and male led households responded to treatment at endline. Three significant results come out. First, female-headed households receiving transfers do seem to spend significantly more than male-headed households receiving transfers on tobacco products. Second, female-headed households spend significantly more—almost twice as much—on boarding school expenses for children. Finally, both kinds of households have significantly increased their insurance spending (table 7.18).

In table 7.19, we see that treatment affected households in the top and bottom half of asset ownership differently. Column (6) reports that both sets of households are now spending statistically significantly more money on weddings, parties, funerals, and dowries. The poorest households spent, on average, T Sh 1,363

Table 7.17 **Effects of CCT on Household Non-Food Expenditures at Endline**

| | (1) | (2) | (3) | (4) | (5) | (6) | (7) | (8) | (9) | (10) |
|---|---|---|---|---|---|---|---|---|---|---|
| | | | | | Average annual expenditure on the following goods (T Sh) | | | | | |
| | Cigarettes tobacco, snuff | Children's clothing (all HHs in sample) | Clothing and footwear for men and boys >15 years of age | Clothing and footwear for women and girls >15 years of age | Other personal effects | Weddings parties, funerals, dowries | Modern medical care: services | Modern medical care: medicine | Education for children in boarding school | Insurance (car, medical, life) |
| Baseline mean | 6,347 | 6,389 | 6,407 | 9,252 | 983 | 4,045 | 10,066 | 5,081 | 5,817 | 181 |
| *Panel A: Effect of treatment on the treated* | | | | | | | | | | |
| Treatment (ETT) × After | −1,593 | 212 | −951 | 1,646 | 501 | 969 | −2,708 | −200 | 591 | 1,625 |
| | (2,037) | (1,990) | (1,386) | (1,945) | (544) | (1,019) | (5,080) | (1,249) | (4,734) | (302)*** |
| After | −248.2 | 5,100 | 2,160 | 1,667 | −600 | 953.4 | 7,332 | 1,428.9 | 802.3 | 433.5 |
| | (1,073) | (1,597)*** | (1,046)** | (1,511) | (489) | (782) | (4,034)* | (911) | (3,968) | (102)*** |
| Observations | 3,130 | 3,132 | 3,126 | 3,130 | 3,132 | 3,132 | 3,128 | 3,132 | 3,130 | 3,132 |
| R-squared | 0.00 | 0.03 | 0.00 | 0.01 | 0.00 | 0.01 | 0.00 | 0.00 | 0.00 | 0.18 |
| *Panel B: Intention to treat* | | | | | | | | | | |
| Treatment (ITT) × After | −1,491 | 198.8 | −890 | 1,540 | 469 | 907.05 | −2,534 | −187.35 | 553 | 1,521 |
| | (2,777) | (2,718) | (1,892) | (2,657) | (743) | (1,394) | (6,937) | (1,704) | (6,466) | (412)*** |
| After | −252 | 5,101 | 2,157.9 | 1,672 | −599 | 956 | 7,325 | 1,428 | 804 | 438 |
| | (1,562) | (2,323)** | (1,524) | (2,200) | (711) | (1,138) | (5,871) | (1,326) | (5,773) | (149)*** |

*Source:* World Bank data.

*Note:* Clustered standard errors in parentheses. CCT = conditional cash transfer; ETT = effect of treatment on the treated; ITT = intention to treat; T Sh = Tanzanian shilling.

**Table 7.18 Heterogeneous Gender Treatment Effects of CCT on Household Non-Food Expenditures at Endline**

| | (1) | (2) | (3) | (4) | (5) | (6) | (7) | (8) | (9) | (10) |
|---|---|---|---|---|---|---|---|---|---|---|
| | | | | | *Average annual expenditure on the following goods* | | | | | |
| | Cigarettes, tobacco, snuff | Children's clothing (all HHs in sample) | Clothing and footwear for men and boys >15 | Clothing and footwear for women and girls >15 | Other personal effects | Weddings, parties, funerals, dowries | Modern medical care: services | Modern medical care: medicine | Education for children in boarding school | Insurance (car, medical, life) |
| Baseline mean: female head of household | 4,149 | 5,387 | 3,775 | 8,423 | 863 | 3,114 | 7,617 | 4,359 | 2,154 | 88.19 |
| Baseline mean: male head of household | 7,758 | 7,036 | 8,095 | 9,790 | 1,061 | 4,645 | 11,641 | 5,547 | 8,164 | 240.4 |
| Effect female head of household | 2,984.0 | −422.1 | −2,476 | 1,357 | 329.3 | 2,337 | −3,739 | 530.2 | 8,743 | 1,485 |
| | (2,351) | (3,109) | (1,755) | (2,352) | (726) | (1,548) | (4,167) | (1,385) | (4,219)** | (330)*** |
| Effect male head of household | −4,430 | 757.2 | 42.84 | 1,882 | 636.0 | 133.2 | −2,597 | −655.9 | −4,331 | 1,695 |
| | (2,703) | (1,984) | (2,015) | (2,411) | (675) | (1,261) | (7,219) | (1,690) | (6,642) | (363)*** |
| Difference effect male head of household and effect female head of household | −7,414 | 1,179.3 | 2,518.7 | 524.7 | 306.7 | −2,204 | 1,141.8 | −1,186 | −13,074 | 210.2 |
| | (3,362)** | (3,149) | (2,729) | (2,870) | (881) | (1,907) | (7,122) | (1,979) | (6,831)* | (375) |
| Observations | 3,130 | 3,132 | 3,126 | 3,130 | 3,132 | 3,132 | 3,128 | 3,132 | 3,130 | 3,132 |

*Source:* World Bank data.

*Note:* Results reported in this table are based on effect of treatment on the treated (ETT) regressions. Clustered standard errors in parentheses. CCT = conditional cash transfer.

Significance level: * = 10 percent, ** = 5 percent, *** = 1 percent.

**Table 7.19 Heterogeneous Poverty Treatment Effects of CCT on Household Non-Food Expenditures at Endline**

| | (1) | (2) | (3) | (4) | (5) | (6) | (7) | (8) | (9) | (10) |
|---|---|---|---|---|---|---|---|---|---|---|
| | | | | Average annual expenditure on the following goods: | | | | | | |
| | Cigarettes-tobacco, snuff | Children's clothing (all HHs in sample) | Clothing and footwear for men and boys >15 years of age | Clothing and footwear for women and girls >15 years of age | Other personal effects | Weddings, parties, funerals, dowries | Modern medical care: services | Modern medical care: medicine | Education for children in boarding school | Insurance (car, medical, life) |
| Baseline mean: Poorest | 4,390 | 3,794 | 3,285 | 5,744 | 466 | 2,394 | 6,690 | 3,684 | 3,468 | 105 |
| Baseline mean: less poor | 8,982 | 9,883 | 10,611 | 13,976 | 1,680 | 6,269 | 14,613 | 6,962 | 8,980 | 284 |
| Effect poorest | −1,264 | 1,665 | 135 | 1,709 | −95 | 1,363 | 5,319.73 | 666.57 | 3,456.6 | 1,751 |
| | (2,540) | (1,315) | (1,102) | (1,431) | (208.7) | (756)* | (3,577) | (908) | (2,820) | (306)*** |
| Effect less poor | −1,832 | −605.6 | −1,778 | 1,924 | 1,091 | 830.4 | −10,130 | −868.4 | −1,980 | 1,515 |
| | (2,650) | (3,662) | (2,330) | (3,195) | (945.1) | (1,730) | (8,629) | (2,084) | (8,306) | (364)*** |
| Difference effect less poor and effect poorest | −568 | −2,270 | −1,913 | 214.93 | 1,185.8 | −532.4 | −15,450 | −1,535 | −5,437 | −235 |
| | (3,266) | (3,963) | (2,405) | (3,054) | (877) | (1,746) | (8,943)* | (2,076) | (8,294) | (294) |
| Observations | 3,130 | 3,132 | 3,126 | 3,130 | 3,132 | 3,132 | 3,128 | 3,132 | 3,130 | 3,132 |

Source: World Bank data.

Note: Results reported in this table are based on effect of treatment on the treated (ETT) regressions. Clustered standard errors in parentheses. CCT = conditional cash transfer.

Significance level: * = 10 percent, ** = 5 percent, *** = 1 percent.

more in these categories (significant at the 10 percent level), whereas less poor households spent an average of T Sh 830 more (not significant). However, this is a much larger proportionate increase for the poorest households than for the less poor ones.

In column (10) we see that by endline both the poorest and less poor households are spending statistically significantly more on insurance. At baseline, less poor households spent almost twice as much on insurance than their poorer counterparts. The endline results report that less poor households spent, on average, T Sh 1,751 more on insurance while their less poor counterparts spent T Sh 1,515 more. Both results were significant at the 1 percent.

In table 7.20, we explore how households in the three CCT pilot districts responded to treatment at endline. Across the board, households in Chamwino were much more likely to increase their non-food expenditures, with significant increases in clothing for men and women, both children and adults. Households in Chamwino also spent more on social events (weddings, parties, funerals, and dowries).

We see that spending on insurance significantly increased in all three districts at endline (column 10). Households in Kibaha now spend, on average, T Sh 2,659 more on insurance (significant at the 1 percent level). In Bagamoyo, households now spend an average of T Sh 986 more on insurance a year (significant at the 5 percent level). Households in Chamwino now spend an average of T Sh 1,446 more on insurance a year, an increase that is significant at the 1 percent level. Note that even in the district with the highest baseline insurance expenditures (Kibaha), the program led to substantial and significant impacts on insurance spending.

In table 7.21 we examine the effects of the CCT on household expenditures in households that had suffered from a severe drought since the midline data collection and in those that had not. Approximately 50 percent of households included in the survey had experienced such a shock.

In column (6) we see that nondrought-affected households spent statistically significantly more on weddings, parties, funerals, and dowries. These households spent T Sh 2,680 more at endline in this category, significant at the 1 percent level. Finally, in column (10) we find that both drought and nondrought-affected households spent statistically significantly more on insurance at endline. This seems to suggest that regardless of whether treated households had suffered from a catastrophic event or not, they had a high demand for health insurance.

### Qualitative Findings

Almost every beneficiary focus group and in-depth interview participant across districts stated that the money they received from the CB-CCT program was spent on children's school supplies and on chickens and other livestock, with the remainder used to purchase food (these findings will be discussed in later sections). However, except for indirect inclusion of school uniforms in the categories for men and boys clothing and women and girls clothing, these most common expenditures are largely absent from the standard non-food expenditure catego-

**Table 7.20 Heterogeneous Geography Treatment Effects of CCT on Household Non-Food Expenditures at Endline**

| | (1) | (2) | (3) | (4) | (5) | (6) | (7) | (8) | (9) | (10) |
|---|---|---|---|---|---|---|---|---|---|---|
| | | | | Average annual expenditure on the following goods | | | | | | |
| | Cigarettes, tobacco, snuff (all HHs in sample) | Children's clothing | Clothing and footwear for men and boys >15 | Clothing and footwear for women and girls >15 | Other personal effects | Weddings, parties, funerals, dowries | Modern medical care: services | Modern medical care: medicine | Education for children in boarding school | Insurance (car, medical, life) |
| Baseline mean: Kibaha | 9,426 | 7,859 | 8,077 | 10,848 | 954 | 4,086 | 11,158 | 6,206 | 7,679 | 448 |
| Baseline mean: Bagamoyo | 7,311 | 7,663 | 7,554 | 11,244 | 1,475 | 5,549 | 11,499 | 6,000 | 7,521 | 80.41 |
| Baseline mean: Chamwino | 1,595 | 2,826 | 2,836 | 4,412 | 231 | 1,608 | 6,644 | 2,443 | 1,158 | 62 |
| Effect Kibaha | −7,255 | 1,765 | −961 | 3,322 | 113 | −1,395 | −6,069 | −1,443 | 4,489 | 2,659 |
| | (4,943) | (2,592) | (2,815) | (3,114) | (802) | (1,937) | (8,870) | (2,330) | (5,606) | (313)*** |
| Effect Bagamoyo | 874.9 | −3,407 | −3,635 | 14.34 | 1,007 | 2,225 | −7,254 | 1,525 | −4,984 | 986.2 |
| | (2,740) | (3,911) | (2,024)* | (3,628) | (1,113) | (1,868) | (9,286) | (1,699) | (10,169) | (498)** |
| Effect Chamwino | 792.3 | 4,434 | 3,565 | 2,908 | 153 | 1,432 | 7,900 | −1,513 | 5,207 | 1,446 |
| | (1,536) | (1,533)*** | (1,366)** | (1,168)** | (299) | (773)* | (5,794) | (2,634) | (2,057)** | (497)*** |
| Difference effect Bagamoyo and effect Kibaha | 8,130 | −5,172 | −2,674 | −3,308 | 893 | 3,620 | −1,185 | 2,968 | −9,474 | −1,672 |
| | (5,652) | (4,692) | (3,467) | (4,781) | (1,372) | (2,691) | (12,841) | (2,884) | (11,612) | (588)*** |
| Difference effect Chamwino and effect Kibaha | 8,047 | 2,669 | 4,526 | −415 | 40.2 | 2,827 | 13,969 | −70.3 | 718 | −1,213 |
| | (5,177) | (3,011) | (3,129) | (3,326) | (856) | (2,085) | (10,595) | (3,517) | (5,971) | (587)** |
| Observation | 3,130 | 3,132 | 3,126 | 3,130 | 3,132 | 3,132 | 3,128 | 3,132 | 3,130 | 3,132 |

Source: World Bank data.

Note: Results reported in this table are based on effect of treatment on the treated (ETT) regressions. Clustered standard errors in parentheses. CCT = conditional cash transfer.

Significance level: * = 10 percent, ** = 5 percent, *** = 1 percent.

**Table 7.21 Heterogeneous Shock Treatment Effects of CCT on Non-Food Expenditures at Endline**

| | (1) | (2) | (3) | (4) | (5) | (6) | (7) | (8) | (9) | (10) |
|---|---|---|---|---|---|---|---|---|---|---|
| | | | | Average annual expenditure on the following goods | | | | | | |
| | Cigarettes-tobacco, snuff | Children's clothing (all HHs in sample) | Clothing and footwear for men and boys >15 years of age | Clothing and footwear for women and girls >15 years of age | Other personal effects | Weddings,-parties, funerals, dowries | Modern medical care: services | Modern medical care: medicine | Education for children in boarding school | Insurance (car, medical, life) |
| Effect no drought | 184.1 | −634 | −115 | 2,650 | 669.6 | 2,680 | −4,597 | 1,711 | 2,506 | 1,682 |
| | (2,025) | (2,893) | (1,789) | (2,466) | (764) | (1,180)** | (7,764) | (1,400) | (6,853) | (321)*** |
| Effect drought | −4,486 | 1,556 | −2,190 | 611.6 | 261.6 | −1,197 | −308.9 | −2,541 | −1,773 | 1,522 |
| | (3,765) | (2,434) | (2,016) | (2,492) | (592) | (1,729) | (4,609) | (2,185) | (4,632) | (382)*** |
| Difference effect drought and effect no drought | −4,670 | 2,190 | −2,075 | −2,038 | −408 | −3,877 | 4,288 | −4,252 | −4,279 | −160.5 |
| | (3,935) | (3,696) | (2,546) | (3,002) | (869) | (2,018)* | (8,694) | (2,571)* | (7,469) | (349) |
| Observations | 3,130 | 3,132 | 3,126 | 3,130 | 3,132 | 3,132 | 3,128 | 3,132 | 3,130 | 3,132 |
| R-squared | 0.00 | 0.03 | 0.01 | 0.01 | 0.00 | 0.01 | 0.01 | 0.01 | 0.00 | 0.18 |

Source: World Bank data.

Note: Results reported in this table are based on effect of treatment on the treated (ETT) regressions. Clustered standard errors in parentheses. CCT = conditional cash transfer.

Significance level: * = 10 percent, ** = 5 percent, *** = 1 percent.

ries considered in this section. Since there are few significant quantitative impacts of the program on non-food expenditures at endline, the explanation may relate to the fact that since the transfers are relatively small, there was not enough money to use for additional purchases outside of the most common expenditures on livestock and school supplies. An alternative explanation is that since we do find a significant increase for expenditures on clothing and footwear for women and girls at midline, it may be that uniforms were purchased immediately with the transfers, and so no longer needed to be bought at endline.

Where the quantitative analysis does find significant impacts of the program on non-food expenditures is increased expenditures on modern medical care, education of children in boarding schools, and clothing for men and boys in the poorest households. The findings are supported by the qualitative evidence. For example, one head of a health facility in Kibaha said that many more people are coming to the health facility that could not previously afford to visit. One man in Kibaha also said that the transfers had helped him to pay for medication when the dispensary was out of drugs. Thus, it may be true that the program enabled households that faced binding constraints on purchases of modern medical care or boys' uniforms, for example, to purchase more of these goods.

The quantitative finding that beneficiary households spend significantly more on insurance corresponds with the health care results (described above) that beneficiary households are much more likely to participate in the CHF, and that the CMC and health facility staff encourage them to pay for health insurance when they receive transfers. The qualitative exercise additionally did not find evidence for problems with the money being spent unproductively, such as on purchases like tobacco and alcohol, which is supported by no evidence that these expenditures increased in the quantitative analysis.

Takeaways:

- The program did not increase expenditures on less socially desirable goods such as tobacco and cigarettes.
- If the goal is to increase non-food consumption, more specific targeting is likely to be necessary: We find more measurable effects on expenditures for poorer households and those in Chamwino, where consumption is most likely to have been suboptimal originally.
- The one consistent increase in expenditure is for insurance, most likely driven by participation in the community health fund.

## Food Consumption

In this next section, we evaluate how participation in the CCT program affected weekly food consumption and find no systematic impacts on food consumption. Table 7.22 shows the effects of treatment on both the purchased value and the home-produced value of six of the most common food consumption items: Super Sembe maize flour, husked rice, sugar, Dona maize flour, dried beans, and other flour. In the case of two of these goods—sugar and dried beans—we consider only

Table 7.22 Effects of CCT on Household Food Consumption at Endline

| | (1) | (2) | (3) | (4) | (5) | (6) | (7) | (8) | (9) | (10) |
|---|---|---|---|---|---|---|---|---|---|---|
| | | | | | Value of Food Consumption in the Past Week | | | | | |
| | Maize (flour) super/sembe- purchased | Maize (flour) super/sembe- produced | Maize (flour) Dona- purchased | Maize (flour) Dona- produced | Other flour (millet, cassava, sorghum, barley)- purchased | Other flour (millet, cassava, sorghum, barley)-produced | Rice (husked)- purchased | Rice (husked)- produced | Dried beans- purchased | Sugar- purchased |
| Baseline mean | 3,600 | 216 | 700 | 371 | 166 | 424 | 263 | 61 | 551 | 580 |
| **Panel A: Effect of treatment on the treated** | | | | | | | | | | |
| Treatment (ETT) × After | 84.3 | 600.93 | −55.7 | −108.55 | −70.06 | −415 | −100 | −341 | −50.2 | 131 |
| | (620.9) | (593) | (226.1) | (175) | (82) | (227)* | (294) | (386) | (144) | (124) |
| After | −2,380 | 1,584 | −481.09 | 243.04 | −30.69 | 299.29 | 914 | 1,138 | 404.8 | 617 |
| | (398)*** | (419)*** | (136)*** | (89)*** | (48) | (205) | (232)*** | (264)*** | (102)*** | (78)*** |
| Observations | 3,286 | 3,286 | 3,286 | 3,286 | 3,286 | 3,286 | 3,286 | 3,286 | 3,286 | 3,286 |
| R-squared | 0.17 | 0.15 | 0.04 | 0.01 | 0.01 | 0.01 | 0.06 | 0.08 | 0.03 | 0.10 |
| **Panel B: Intention to treat** | | | | | | | | | | |
| Treatment (ITT) × After | 78.60 | 560.30 | −51.97 | −101.21 | −65.32 | −387 | −93.32 | −318 | −46.8 | 122.4 |
| | (835) | (798) | (304.00) | (235.38) | (110) | (306) | (395) | (520) | (193) | (167) |
| After | −2,380 | 1,586.7 | −481 | 243 | −31.0 | 297.6 | 913.6 | 1,137 | 405 | 617.2 |
| | (571)*** | (602)** | (195)** | (128)* | (68.9) | (294) | (333)*** | (379)*** | (146)*** | (112)*** |

Source: World Bank data.

Note: Results reported in this table are based on effect of treatment on the treated (ETT) regressions. Clustered standard errors in parentheses. CCT = conditional cash transfer; ETT = effect of treatment on the treated; ITT = intention to treat.

Significance level: * = 10 percent; ** = 5 percent; *** = 1 percent.

the value purchased and not the value produced at home, since home production of these two goods is negligible. These 10 items jointly account for over half of total food consumption value in our study villages. The values in table 7.22 have been adjusted to take into account inflation that occurred between the baseline and endline surveys, so that all amounts are in 2010 Tanzanian shillings.

Analyzing table 7.22, we see that in general treatment is not associated with statistically significant changes in food consumption. In column (6), we see the only statistically significant result: that treated households are now producing roughly T Sh 415 less "other" flour (that is, nonmaize, coming from millet, cassava, sorghum, and barley)—a finding significant at the 10 percent level. Point estimates are large relative to baseline values, with large standard errors, so challenges in measurement may make it more difficult to estimate changes in food consumption precisely.

While we find no statistically significant changes in household food consumption overall, when we analyzed various subgroups of households, we did find significant results. Table 7.23 shows that less poor (that is, those in the top half of the distribution on the poverty index) treated households, in particular, had statistically significant changes in food consumption.

Less poor households spent T Sh 446 more per week on maize dona at endline, as shown in column (3) (significant at the 10 percent level). Furthermore, less poor households spent T Sh 1,949 fewer on husked rice at endline, as shown in column (7) (significant at the 5 percent level). For husked risk in particular, the difference between the effect of treatment on the less poor and the poorest is statistically significant at the 5 percent level.

We also see minor differences across the three pilot districts (table 7.24). In particular, treated households in Chamwino spent T Sh 492 per week less at endline on other flour (that is, nonmaize flour), and T Sh 224 per week more on husked rice—findings significant at the 10 percent and the 5 percent levels, respectively. The net effects of these two differences in consumption, however, largely cancel one another out (and may actually suggest a very modest reduction in overall food spending across the basket of goods measured here in Chamwino). Households in other districts did not see statistically significant impacts of treatment on food consumption.

In table 7.25 we analyze differences in the effects of treatment on food consumption at endline for households that suffered droughts since the midline (1 year earlier) and households that did not. The only statistically significant finding is in column (10). It shows that households unaffected by recent drought spent T Sh 323 more per week on sugar at endline (statistically significant at the 10 percent level). The difference between drought and nondrought households is also significant in column (10); treatment led drought-affected households to spend T Sh 430 per week less on sugar than it did their nonaffected counterparts at endline (significant at the 10 percent level).

Overall, the quantitative findings suggest that treatment had little impact on the food consumption of households overall. There is always the possibility that households increase food consumption of commodities not considered in the

**Table 7.23 Heterogeneous Poverty Treatment Effects of CCT on Household Food Consumption at Endline**

| | (1) | (2) | (3) | (4) | (5) | (6) | (7) | (8) | (9) | (10) |
|---|---|---|---|---|---|---|---|---|---|---|
| | | | | | Value of Food Consumption in the Past Week | | | | | |
| | Maize (flour) super/sembe-purchased | Maize (flour) super/sembe-produced | Maize (flour) Dona-purchased | Maize (flour) Dona-produced | Other flour (millet, cassava, sorghum, barley)-purchased | Other flour (millet, cassava, sorghum, barley)-produced | Rice (husked)-purchased | Rice (husked)-produced | Dried beans-purchased | Sugar-purchased |
| Baseline mean: poorest | 2,191 | 112.05 | 660 | 369 | 210 | 478 | 93 | 18.51 | 284 | 334 |
| Baseline mean: less poor | 5,496 | 356 | 754 | 374 | 108 | 353 | 492 | 119 | 911 | 910 |
| Effect poorest | 61.40 | 724.45 | 17.07 | 443 | −105.59 | −80.51 | 348 | −142 | 157.39 | 109 |
| | (433) | (818) | (307) | (277) | (111) | (212) | (308.1) | (170) | (119) | (190) |
| Effect less poor | 354.3 | 562.0 | 446.4 | 165.0 | −36.96 | 183.4 | −1,949 | −99 | −48.82 | 232.3 |
| | (925.2) | (1,190) | (248)* | (316) | (110.6) | (175) | (973)** | (692) | (173) | (202) |
| Difference effect less poor and effect poorest | 292.95 | −162 | 429.38 | −278 | 68.64 | 263.94 | −2,297 | 43.2 | 206.2 | 123.3 |
| | (934) | (949) | (339) | (273) | (143) | (285) | (1,054)** | (618) | (194) | (233) |
| Observations | 2,230 | 1,644 | 2,604 | 2,828 | 2,530 | 2,920 | 2,759 | 2,188 | 3,031 | 2,994 |

*Source:* World Bank data.

*Note:* Results reported in this table are based on effect of treatment on the treated (ETT) regressions. Clustered standard errors in parentheses. CCT = conditional cash transfer.
Significance level: * = 10 percent; ** = 5 percent; *** = 1 percent.

**Table 7.24 Heterogeneous Geography Treatment Effects of CCT on Household Food Consumption at Endline**

|  | (1) | (2) | (3) | (4) | (5) | (6) | (7) | (8) | (9) | (10) |
|---|---|---|---|---|---|---|---|---|---|---|
|  | Value of food consumption in the past week | | | | | | | | | |
|  | Maize (flour) super/sembe-purchased | Maize (flour) super/sembe-produced | Maize (flour) Dona-purchased | Maize (flour) Dona-produced | Other flour (millet, cassava, sorghum, barley)-purchased | Other flour (millet, cassava, sorghum, barley)-produced | Rice (husked)-purchased | Rice (husked)-produced | Dried beans-purchased | Sugar-purchased |
| Baseline mean- Kibaha | 3,841 | 154 | 718 | 44 | 123 | 421 | 331 | 62 | 733 | 818 |
| Baseline mean: Bagamoyo | 5,510 | 350 | 781 | 239 | 48 | 48 | 367 | 100 | 717 | 765 |
| Baseline mean: Chamwino | 305 | 66 | 552 | 922 | 399 | 399 | 26 | 0 | 96 | 36 |
| Effect Kibaha | 897.68 | 1,851 | 356.33 | 302.17 | 8.64 | 185.87 | −1,003 | −862.87 | −261.6 | −181.7 |
|  | (1,197) | (1,880) | (311) | (248.5) | (110.5) | (221.02) | (828.3) | (1,197) | (234) | (371) |
| Effect Bagamoyo | −261.4 | 76.86 | 190.0 | −82.46 | 103.9 | −42.40 | −1,645 | −58.78 | 108.9 | 284.8 |
|  | (907.9) | (992.5) | (342) | (393.2) | (86.78) | (158.8) | (992.6) | (336.2) | (198) | (223) |
| Effect Chamwino | −110.1 | −127.8 | 311.3 | 977.7 | −492 | 69.06 | 224.5 | 23.85 | 168 | 245.1 |
|  | (321.5) | (444.8) | (483) | (649.7)* | (274.1)* | (329.3) | (105)** | (23.57) | (140) | (181) |
| Difference effect Bagamoyo and effect Kibaha | −1,159 | −1,774 | −166 | −385 | 95.25 | −228.27 | −642.6 | 804.09 | 370.53 | 370.53 |
|  | (1,502) | (2,126) | (462) | (465) | (140.48) | (272.13) | (1,293) | (1,243) | (306) | (306) |
| Difference effect Chamwino and effect Kibaha | −1,008 | −1,979 | −45.1 | 675.52 | −500.60 | −116.81 | 1,227 | 886.72 | 429.70 | 429.70 |
|  | (1,239) | (1,932) | (575) | (696) | (295.6)* | (396.62) | (834.98) | (1,197) | (273) | (273) |
| Observations | 2,230 | 1,644 | 2,604 | 2,828 | 2,530 | 2,920 | 2,759 | 2,188 | 3,031 | 2,994 |

Source: World Bank data.

Note: Results reported in this table are based on effect of treatment on the treated (ETT) regressions. Clustered standard errors in parentheses. CCT = conditional cash transfer.

Significance level: * = 10 percent, ** = 5 percent, *** = 1 percent.

**Table 7.25  Heterogeneous Shock Treatment Effects of CCT on Food Consumption at Endline**

| | (1) | (2) | (3) | (4) | (5) | (6) | (7) | (8) | (9) | (10) |
|---|---|---|---|---|---|---|---|---|---|---|
| | | | | | Value of food consumption in the past week | | | | | |
| | Maize (flour) super/sembe-purchased | Maize (flour) super/sembe-produced | Maize (flour) Dona-purchased | Maize (flour) Dona-produced | Other flour (millet, cassava, sorghum, barley)-purchased | Other flour (millet, cassava, sorghum, barley)-produced | Rice (husked)-purchased | Rice (husked)-produced | Dried beans-purchased | Sugar-purchased |
| Effect no drought | −285.71 | 781.00 | 231.1 | 326.20 | −102.3 | 121.62 | −1,015 | −67.56 | 27.99 | 323.1 |
| | (523) | (1,167) | (247) | (274) | (119) | (195.15) | (771) | (354) | (176) | (192)* |
| Effect drought | 824.1 | 462.3 | 249.5 | 235.6 | −8.686 | −27.56 | −699.2 | −169.0 | 14.67 | −107.0 |
| | (895.1) | (1,267) | (310) | (351.0) | (85.88) | (148.4) | (446.8) | (523.4) | (179) | (229.0) |
| Difference effect drought and effect no drought | 1,110 | −318.75 | 18.39 | −90.59 | 93.61 | −149.18 | 315.4 | −101.4 | −13.3 | −430.1 |
| | (904) | (1,238) | (342) | (319.5) | (132.8) | (248.8) | (762) | (477) | (200) | (249)* |
| Observations | 2,230 | 1,644 | 2,604 | 2,828 | 2,530 | 2,920 | 2,759 | 2,188 | 3,031 | 2,994 |
| R-squared | 0.02 | 0.25 | 0.01 | 0.04 | 0.01 | 0.01 | 0.05 | 0.06 | 0.31 | 0.20 |

*Source:* World Bank data.

*Note:* Results reported in this table are based on effect of treatment on the treated (ETT) regressions. Clustered standard errors in parentheses. CCT = conditional cash transfer.

Significance level: * = 10 percent, ** = 5 percent, *** = 1 percent.

analysis of this section. While these food commodities comprise over 50 percent of the food consumption value of surveyed households, there are many unmeasured commodities. Furthermore, consumption is more challenging to measure than many other outcomes, increasing the probability of impacts being masked by noise in the data. On the whole, however, the quantitative evidence suggests that households spent transfers predominately on non-food items. We examine these types of expenditures shortly.

### Qualitative Findings

While the quantitative analysis found little evidence of an increase in food consumption across diverse categories due to the CB-CCT program, beneficiaries across focus groups and in-depth interviews in all three districts claimed that they had increased their food consumption as a part of the program. However, when asked for a breakdown of their expenditures with the last transfer, the food portion was generally small. As such, any increase in food consumption in beneficiary households relative to control households may be too small to outweigh any time, seasonality, and recall noise in the consumption data. Another possible explanation for the fact that so many people reported increases in food consumption is that consumption actually did increase. However, this occurred in both villages that received the program and those that did not, as shown by the fact that the "after" coefficient is large and significant for most of the food items in table 7.22. While beneficiaries may attribute their increased food consumption to the program, increased food consumption occurred in control villages as well.

Takeaways:

- If the principal goal of the program is to increase food consumption, then it may be necessary to provide more explicit conditions or provide in-kind transfers rather than cash. However, this may not be desirable since the most reasonable assumption, if households are not increasing food consumption, is that households are already consuming a sufficient amount of food.
- Food consumption is a clear example of the importance of having a set of control villages. Although treatment households attributed increases to the program, food consumption increases in fact were widespread across treatment and comparison households and not clearly attributable to the program.

### Children's Activities and Assets

Next, we explore whether participation in the CB-CCT changes the types of activities children perform, and whether it affects ownership of two assets associated with health improvements: children's shoes and children's slippers (also known as flip-flops or sandals). We define children as anyone age 0–18.

In table 7.26, we show that treatment had no statistically significant impact on a variety of children's activities at endline. This is consistent with the midline result of minimal changes in measured children's activities (table 4.10).

**Table 7.26  Effects of CCT on Children's Activities and Assets at Endline**

|  | (1) | (2) | (3) | (4) | (5) | (6) | (7) | (8) |
|---|---|---|---|---|---|---|---|---|
|  | Did the children do the following activities last week? | | | | | | Does the child have ... | |
|  | Fetch water | Cut wood | Clean toilet | Cook | Provide child care | Provide elderly care | Shoes | Slippers |
| Baseline mean | 0.57 | 0.28 | 0.13 | 0.26 | 0.16 | 0.28 | 0.42 | 0.63 |
| *Panel A: Effect of treatment* | | | | | | | | |
| Treatment (ETT) × After | −0.00 | 0.04 | 0.01 | 0.01 | −0.01 | −0.01 | 0.07 | 0.04 |
|  | (0.04) | (0.04) | (0.03) | (0.03) | (0.02) | (0.04) | (0.04)* | (0.03) |
| After | −0.02 | −0.02 | 0.03 | 0.02 | −0.04 | −0.08 | 0.07 | 0.11 |
|  | (0.03) | (0.03) | (0.02)* | (0.02) | (0.02)** | (0.03)*** | (0.03)*** | (0.02)*** |
| Observations | 6,109 | 6,109 | 6,109 | 6,109 | 6,109 | 6,109 | 7,568 | 7,568 |
| *R*-squared | 0.00 | 0.00 | 0.00 | 0.00 | 0.01 | 0.01 | 0.02 | 0.03 |
| *Panel B: Intent to treat* | | | | | | | | |
| Treatment (ITT) × After | −0.00 | 0.04 | 0.00 | 0.01 | −0.01 | −0.01 | 0.06 | 0.03 |
|  | (0.06) | (0.05) | (0.04) | (0.04) | (0.03) | (0.05) | (0.05) | (0.03) |
| After | −0.02 | −0.02 | 0.03 | 0.02 | −0.04* | −0.08** | 0.07** | 0.11*** |
|  | (0.04) | (0.04) | (0.03) | (0.03) | (0.02) | (0.04) | (0.04) | (0.03) |

*Source:* World Bank data.

*Note:* Results reported in this table are based on effect of treatment on the treated (ETT) regressions. Clustered standard errors in parentheses. CCT = conditional cash transfer; ETT = effect of treatment on the treated; ITT = intention to treat. Significance level: * = 10 percent, ** = 5 percent, *** = 1 percent.

Treatment did have a statistically significant impact on shoe ownership at endline (table 7.26, column 7). We see that treated children were 7 percentage points more likely to own shoes at endline (significant at the 10 percent level). This is an important effect, given the recognized health benefits of wearing shoes. This finding underscores our results at midline (table 4.10). We do not see a statistically significant increase in slipper ownership at endline.

Table 7.27 shows that most of the effects of treatment on shoe ownership come from increases in shoe ownership among children in the poorest half of beneficiary households. Treatment did not lead children in less poor households to be significantly more likely to own shoes at endline. In column (7), we see that the poorest children are 10 percentage points more likely to own shoes at end-line. This result is statistically significant at the 5 percent level, and likely reflects the fact that the poorest children were less likely to already own shoes at baseline, making the purchase of shoes a particularly good investment. Less poor children may have not needed new shoes. Figure 7.8 shows the share of poor children in treatment and in comparison communities that owned shoes at baseline (in red) and at endline (in green or grey). Green indicates statistically significant differences from the baseline. The difference between treatment and comparison households is noticeably larger among the poorest half of households than it is overall (that is, for all households).

Looking across districts (table 7.28), we observe no systematic differences in the effects of treatment on children's activities. Indeed, at endline, the only

**Table 7.27 Heterogeneous Poverty Treatment Effects of CCT on Children's Activities and Assets at Endline**

| | (1) | (2) | (3) | (4) | (5) | (6) | (7) | (8) |
|---|---|---|---|---|---|---|---|---|
| | Did the children do the following activities last week? | | | | | | Does the child have … | |
| | Fetch water | Cut wood | Clean toilet | Cook | Child care | Elderly care | Shoes | Slippers |
| Baseline mean: poorest | 0.55 | 0.31 | 0.10 | 0.25 | 0.15 | 0.29 | 0.30 | 0.57 |
| Baseline mean: less poor | 0.59 | 0.25 | 0.15 | 0.27 | 0.17 | 0.28 | 0.53 | 0.68 |
| Effect poorest | 0 | 0.04 | 0.00 | −0.02 | 0.00 | −0.04 | 0.10 | 0.05 |
| | (0.06) | (0.05) | (0.04) | (0.04) | −0.03 | (0.05) | (0.05)** | (0.04) |
| Effect less poor | −0.00 | 0.04 | 0.01 | 0.02 | −0.01 | 0.02 | 0.05 | 0.03 |
| | (0.07) | (0.05) | (0.04) | (0.04) | (0.03) | (0.04) | (0.04) | (0.03) |
| Difference effect less poor and effect poorest | 0.00 | 0.00 | 0.00 | 0.04 | −0.01 | 0.06 | −0.05 | −0.02 |
| | (0.07) | (0.06) | (0.05) | (0.05) | (0.04) | (0.06) | (0.06) | (0.05) |
| Observations | 6,109 | 6,109 | 6,109 | 6,109 | 6,109 | 6,109 | 7,568 | 7,568 |

*Source:* World Bank data.
*Note:* Results reported in this table are based on effect of treatment on the treated (ETT) regressions. Clustered standard errors in parentheses. CCT = conditional cash transfer.
Significance level: * = 10 percent, ** = 5 percent, *** = 1 percent.

**Figure 7.8 Effect of CCT on Whether Child Has Shoes**

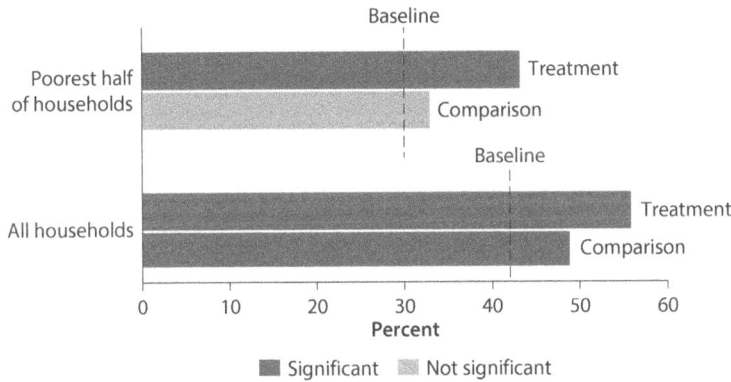

*Source:* World Bank data.
*Note:* CCT = conditional cash transfer.

notable effect of treatment is an increase in the likelihood of a child from Kibaha participating in wood cutting in the past week (a 17 percentage point increase due to treatment).

Treatment significantly increases child shoe ownership in all three districts (and slipper ownership in none of the three). The impact of treatment on shoe ownership in Chamwino is especially striking: only 24 percent of children in Chamwino owned shoes at baseline, but treatment led to a 26 percentage point increase in shoe ownership at endline, which is a doubling of the baseline rate, purely due to the program. Kibaha and Bagamoyo also saw large increases in shoe ownership, of 15 and 20 percentage points, respectively.

Community-Based Conditional Cash Transfers in Tanzania • http://dx.doi.org/10.1596/978-1-4648-0141-9

**Table 7.28 Heterogeneous Geography Treatment Effects of CCT on Children's Activities and Assets at the Endline**

|  | (1) | (2) | (3) | (4) | (5) | (6) | (7) | (8) |
|---|---|---|---|---|---|---|---|---|
|  | *Did the children do the following activities last week?* | | | | *Does the child have* | | | |
|  | *Fetch water* | *Cut wood* | *Clean toilet* | *Cook* | *Child care* | *Elderly care* | *Shoes* | *Slippers* |
| Baseline mean: Kibaha | 0.54 | 0.23 | 0.14 | 0.22 | 0.12 | 0.20 | 0.48 | 0.66 |
| Baseline mean: Bagamoyo | 0.59 | 0.30 | 0.15 | 0.27 | 0.21 | 0.33 | 0.47 | 0.63 |
| Baseline mean: Chamwino | 0.57 | 0.31 | 0.07 | 0.28 | 0.12 | 0.30 | 0.24 | 0.61 |
| Effect Kibaha | 0.07 | 0.17 | −0.04 | 0.03 | −0.01 | −0.05 | 0.15 | 0.10 |
|  | (0.09) | (0.07)** | (0.05) | (0.05) | (0.05) | (0.07) | (0.09)* | (0.06) |
| Effect Bagamoyo | −0.01 | −0.06 | −0.04 | 0.03 | −0.03 | −0.03 | 0.20 | 0.09 |
|  | (0.09) | (0.05) | (0.07) | (0.04) | (0.07) | (0.08) | (0.07)*** | (0.08) |
| Effect Chamwino | −0.04 | −0.01 | 0.06 | −0.09 | 0.02 | 0.08 | 0.26 | 0.08 |
|  | (0.05) | (0.05) | (0.06) | (0.05) | (0.06) | (0.09) | (0.10)** | (0.06) |
| Difference effect Bagamoyo and effect Kibaha | −0.09 | −0.22 | 0.01 | −0.00 | −0.01 | 0.02 | 0.05 | −0.00 |
|  | (0.13) | (0.09)*** | (0.09) | (0.07) | (0.08) | (0.11) | (0.12) | (0.10) |
| Difference effect Chamwino and effect Kibaha | −0.11 | −0.18 | 0.10 | −0.12 | 0.03 | 0.12 | 0.10 | −0.02 |
|  | (0.10) | (0.09)** | (0.08) | (0.07) | (0.07) | (0.12) | (0.14) | (0.09) |
| Observations | 2,696 | 2,696 | 2,696 | 2,696 | 2,696 | 2,696 | 3,570 | 3,570 |

*Source:* World Bank data.

*Note:* Results reported in this table are based on effect of treatment on the treated (ETT) regressions. Clustered standard errors in parentheses. CCT = conditional cash transfer.

Significance level: * = 10 percent, ** = 5 percent, *** = 1 percent.

## Qualitative Findings

Both the quantitative and qualitative analyses found clear evidence of a significant impact of the CB-CCT program on children's ownership of shoes. Every head teacher in the focus groups and in-depth interviews across districts stated that more of the beneficiary children were able to own school materials as a result of the program, including notebooks, uniforms, and shoes. Many teachers also emphasized that students need shoes to go to school: One teacher explained that while teachers may be lenient in the first few schools day of the year, students will very soon be turned away from school if they do not wear shoes.

One school girl who was interviewed said that her mother had bought her the uniform she was wearing, books, and shoes with the transfer money. A head teacher in a focus group in Bagamoyo explained that before the program, some of the beneficiaries were very poor, and so were not going to school because they felt ashamed not to have shoes and books next to the other children. However, after receiving transfers through the program, these children were able to dress correctly and so feel more comfortable and attend school. This change in behavior and attitude among beneficiary children was verified by a beneficiary in the same village, who described in a focus group how before the program, two of her children were bad and did not attend school, but after the program began, once she was able to buy them shoes and books, they were not so jealous of the other children and now regularly attend school.

Community-Based Conditional Cash Transfers in Tanzania • http://dx.doi.org/10.1596/978-1-4648-0141-9

The teachers' observation that more children owned shoes corresponds with the quantitative finding that the poorest children are relatively more likely to increase their ownership of shoes as a result of the program. These would have been the children that were most likely to have been unable to purchase shoes prior to the start of the CB-CCT. The qualitative exercise did not find any evidence of significant changes in student behavior and activities outside of school.

Takeaways:

- The program did not clearly shift children's activities or time use, but it unambiguously increased the proportion of children with shoes—in some cases dramatically.
- Households invested in shoes across all study districts, especially among the poorest households. Despite this not being a condition of the program, this is an indicator that households are making positive, child-friendly investments with recognized health benefits.
- The transfers may be encouraging children to remain school, but they do not appear to affect the nonschool activities in which children engage.

## Savings and Credit

Next, we examine how treatment affected household savings and credit decisions. As we can see from table 7.29, treatment did not significantly impact savings and credit decisions at endline. Specifically, treatment does not impact the likelihood that someone in the household has a bank account, that they have nonbank savings, or that they have taken out a loan in the last year.

These results are slightly different from those found at midline. At midline (table 4.11), treated households saw an increase in whether someone had nonbank savings. The endline estimate is the same but no longer significant.

However, the poorest half of treated households are significantly more likely to have a household member with nonbank savings at endline, as shown in table 7.30. Column (2) demonstrates that these very poor households realized a 5 percentage point increase in the rate of nonbank savings at endline, significant at the 1 percent level. The effect for the less poor is smaller and not precisely estimated. While treatment did not significantly affect the overall likelihood that a household would have nonbank savings, the effect on the poorest is indeed significant (figure 7.9).

The results in table 7.31 suggest that in the three pilot districts, treatment had varying effects on household savings and credit decisions. Column (2) shows that households in Chamwino realized a 9 percentage point increase in their likelihood of having nonbank savings, significant at the 5 percent level. This is a major increase, as less than 1 percent of households in Chamwino had nonbank savings at baseline. In other districts, however, there were no effects of treatment on nonbank savings, bank savings, or loans taken out in the past year. Further, there were no impacts of treatment on bank savings or loans taken out in the past year in Chamwino district.

**Table 7.29  Effects of CCT on Household Savings and Credit at the Endline**

|  | (1) | (2) | (3) |
|---|---|---|---|
|  | Does someone in the household have a bank account? | Does someone in the household have nonbank savings? | Has someone in the household taken out a loan in the last year? |
| Baseline mean | 0.02 | 0.01 | 0.20 |
| *Panel A: Effect of treatment on the treated* |  |  |  |
| Treatment (ETT) × After | 0.00 | 0.03 | −0.00 |
|  | (0.01) | (0.02) | (0.04) |
| After | 0.00 | 0.06 | 0.05 |
|  | (0.01) | (0.01)*** | (0.03)** |
| Observations | 3,132 | 3,128 | 3,132 |
| *R*-squared | 0.00 | 0.06 | 0.01 |
| *Panel B: Intent to treat* |  |  |  |
| Treatment (ITT) × After | −0.00 | 0.03 | −0.00 |
|  | (0.01) | (0.03) | (0.05) |
| After | 0.00 | 0.06*** | 0.05 |
|  | (0.01) | (0.02) | (0.04) |

*Source:* World Bank data.
*Note:* Clustered standard errors in parentheses. CCT = conditional cash transfer; ETT = effect of treatment on the treated; ITT = intention to treat.
Significance level: * = 10 percent, ** = 5 percent, *** = 1 percent.

**Table 7.30  Heterogeneous Poverty Treatment Effects of CCT on Household Savings and Credit at the Endline**

|  | (1) | (2) | (3) |
|---|---|---|---|
|  | Does someone in the household have a bank account? | Does someone in the household have nonbank savings? | Has someone in the household taken out a loan in the last year? |
| Baseline mean: poorest | 0.01 | 0.01 | 0.21 |
| Baseline mean: less poor | 0.04 | 0.02 | 0.17 |
| Effect poorest | 0.00 | 0.05 | 0.01 |
|  | (0.01) | (0.02)*** | (0.04) |
| Effect less poor | −0.01 | 0.01 | −0.02 |
|  | (0.02) | (0.03) | (0.06) |
| Difference effect less poor and effect poorest | −0.01 | −0.03 | −0.03 |
|  | (0.02) | (0.03) | (0.06) |
| Observations | 3,132 | 3,128 | 3,132 |

*Source:* World Bank data.
*Note:* Results reported in this table are based on effect of treatment on the treated (ETT) regressions. Clustered standard errors in parentheses. CCT = conditional cash transfer.
Significance level: * = 10 percent, ** = 5 percent, *** = 1 percent.

In table 7.32, we present the effects of treatment on households who had suffered from a drought since midline and those who had not. In column (2), we see that households not affected by drought are now 3 percentage points more

**Figure 7.9 Effect of Treatment on Likelihood that Someone in Household Has Nonbank Savings at Endline**

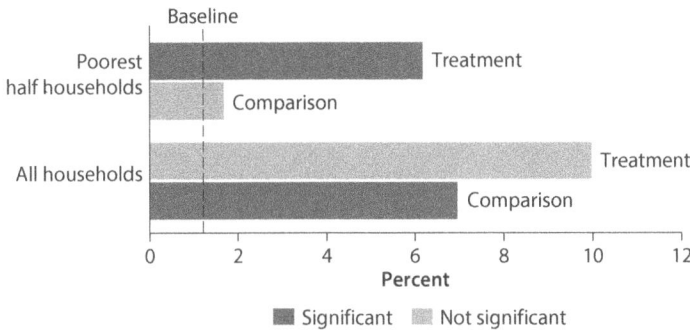

Source: World Bank data.
Note: Baseline average in red. HHs = households.

**Table 7.31 Heterogeneous Geography Treatment Effects of CCT on Household Savings and Credit at Endline**

| | (1) | (2) | (3) |
|---|---|---|---|
| | Does someone in the household have a bank account? | Does someone in the household have nonbank savings? | Has someone in the household taken out a loan in the last year? |
| Baseline mean- Kibaha | 0.03 | 0.02 | 0.22 |
| Baseline mean- Bagamoyo | 0.02 | 0.01 | 0.19 |
| Baseline mean- Chamwino | 0.00 | 0.01 | 0.16 |
| Effect Kibaha | −0.03 | −0.05 | −0.01 |
| | (0.02) | (0.04) | (0.08) |
| Effect Bagamoyo | 0.02 | 0.04 | −0.00 |
| | (0.02) | (0.03) | (0.07) |
| Effect Chamwino | −0.01 | 0.09 | −0.01 |
| | (0.01) | (0.03)** | (0.05) |
| Difference effect Bagamoyo and effect Kibaha | 0.05 | 0.09 | 0.01 |
| | (0.03)* | (0.05)* | (0.10) |
| Difference effect Chamwino and effect Kibaha | 0.03 | 0.14 | 0.01 |
| | (0.02) | (0.06)** | (0.10) |
| Observations | 3,132 | 3,128 | 3,132 |

Source: World Bank data.
Note: Results reported in this table are based on effect of treatment on the treated (ETT) regressions. Clustered standard errors in parentheses. CCT = conditional cash transfer; HH = household.
Significance level: * = 10 percent, ** = 5 percent, *** = 1 percent.

likely to have nonbank savings, significant at the 10 percent level. Drought-affected households, however, were no more likely to have nonbank savings as a result of treatment. This is intuitive; it suggests that drought-affected treatment households were more likely to have exhausted their nonbank savings in the wake of the drought.

**Table 7.32 Heterogeneous Shock Treatment Effects of CCT on Household Savings and Credit at the Endline**

|  | (1) | (2) | (3) |
|---|---|---|---|
|  | Does someone in the HH have a bank account? | Does someone in the HH have nonbank savings? | Has someone in the HH taken out a loan in the last year? |
| Effect no drought | −0.01 | 0.03 | −0.04 |
|  | (0.01) | (0.02)* | (0.05) |
| Effect drought | 0.01 | 0.02 | 0.05 |
|  | 0.02 | 0.03 | 0.06 |
| Difference effect drought and effect no drought | 0.02 | −0.02 | 0.10 |
|  | (0.02) | (0.03) | (0.07) |
| Observations | 3,132 | 3,128 | 3,132 |
| R-squared | 0.00 | 0.06 | 0.01 |

*Source:* World Bank data.

*Note:* Results reported in this table are based on effect of treatment on the treated (ETT) regressions. Clustered standard errors in parentheses. CCT = conditional cash transfer.

Significance level: * = 10 percent, ** = 5 percent, *** = 1 percent

### Qualitative Findings

The qualitative fieldwork supports the quantitative findings of few significant effects of treatment on savings by endline. Most beneficiaries in both focus groups and in-depth interviews said that money from CB-CCT transfers was enough to pay their necessary expenses but not more, or even that they would often run out of money before the next transfer. Thus, while some households may have been able to increase their nonbank savings, this was not common across treatment households, and is consistent with the quantitative findings of a positive but insignificant effect on nonbank savings overall.

The significant increase in savings in the poorest households gives a good indication of the increased security that beneficiaries feel as a result of the program. For example, one woman in Bagamoyo who was a beggar before the program had been able to buy chickens and support herself and her grandchildren, and even gave TASAF one of her chickens as a token of her gratitude for the program. For certain households, this increased security may manifest in having some savings.

The results of the qualitative interviews and focus groups were more nuanced in terms of the effects on credit, as were the quantitative findings of a significant increase in borrowing for treatment households at midline, but no impact on borrowing at endline. Various focus groups and interviewees reported a range of contrasting impacts of the program on their likelihood of borrowing money. One focus group of community leaders in Bagamoyo district described how the community as a whole had reduced borrowing, since there was now more money in circulation. One beneficiary in Bagamoyo district and another in Kibaha said that they still needed to borrow money to cover expenses before receiving a transfer, although they were able to pay off these debts as soon as they received the money.

Other beneficiaries mentioned that they no longer needed to borrow money since they received sufficient money from the program. Thus, the finding of no change in the likelihood of taking out a loan due to the program at endline is likely due to the heterogeneous, opposite effects of the program on borrowing behavior.

Takeaways:

- The program has a clear impact on nonbank savings for the very poorest of households, suggesting that the program is especially good at helping poor people shield themselves from risk in ways they were not able to before the program.
- Households affected by drought are—unsurprisingly—unable to maintain savings. However, the fact that nondrought-affected households do maintain savings is a sign that program households use transfer payments to insure themselves against risk.
- To encourage saving, it would make sense to coordinate with a savings program, encouraging households to save at the time they receive the transfers.
- Banking networks are very poorly developed in these areas: To encourage their use it could be useful to create an account for beneficiaries where the money is directly deposited, since so few households already have bank accounts.

## Community Trust

Next, we examine the impacts of treatment at endline on household members' reported trust of people overall, people in their community, and leaders in their community.

Treatment led to significantly higher trust in community leaders at endline (from 80 percent at baseline to 81 percent in treatment communities at endline versus only 75 percent in comparison communities at endline), as shown in table 7.33. This 6 percentage point difference in trust of community leaders at endline, attributable to treatment, is statistically significant at the 5 percent level. It is the exact same impact of treatment on trust of leaders measured at midline. At endline, however—unlike at midline, where we saw negative impacts of treatment on trust in most people—we see no significant impacts of treatment on trust in most people or trust in people from the community.

Trust in community leaders increased in some treatment subpopulations more than others. In particular, trust in community leaders was especially raised by treatment in villages unaffected by drought, in Kibaha, and in the poorest half of households. These findings are detailed below.

Turning to table 7.34, we see that the increase in trust of community leaders is concentrated among the poorest half of households: In column (3), we observe that these households reported a 9 percentage point increase in trust of their community leaders, which is significant at the 5 percent level. In contrast, less poor households saw no impact of treatment on their trust in community leaders. However, both the poorest and less poor households saw a neutral

**Table 7.33  Effects of CCT on Household Members' Trust of their Community at the Endline**

|  | (1) | (2) | (3) |
|---|---|---|---|
|  | Can most people be trusted? | Can people in the community be trusted? | Can community leaders be trusted? |
| Baseline mean | 0.24 | 0.56 | 0.80 |
| *Panel A: Effect of treatment on the treated* | | | |
| Treatment (ETT) × After | 0.02 | 0.03 | 0.06 |
|  | (0.04) | (0.05) | (0.03)** |
| After | −0.11 | 0.11 | −0.05 |
|  | (0.03)*** | (0.03)*** | (0.02)*** |
| Observations | 3,069 | 3,061 | 3,082 |
| *R*-squared | 0.03 | 0.04 | 0.01 |
| *Panel B: Intent to treat* | | | |
| Treatment (ITT) × After | 0.02 | 0.03 | 0.05 |
|  | (0.06) | (0.06) | (0.04) |
| After | −0.11 | 0.11 | −0.05 |
|  | (0.04)*** | (0.04)** | (0.02)** |

*Source:* World Bank data.
*Note:* Results reported in this table are based on effect of treatment on the treated (ETT) regressions. Clustered standard errors in parentheses. CCT = conditional cash transfer; ETT = effect of treatment on the treated; ITT = intention to treat.
Significance level: * = 10 percent, ** = 5 percent, *** = 1 percent

**Table 7.34  Heterogeneous Poverty Treatment Effects of CCT on Household Members' Trust of their Community at the Endline**

|  | (1) | (2) | (3) |
|---|---|---|---|
|  | Can most people be trusted? | Can people in the community be trusted? | Can community leaders be trusted? |
| Baseline mean- poorest | 0.29 | 0.59 | 0.83 |
| Baseline mean- less poor | 0.17 | 0.51 | 0.77 |
| Effect poorest | 0.08 | −0.02 | 0.09 |
|  | (0.06) | (0.05) | (0.04)** |
| Effect less poor | −0.03 | 0.09 | 0.03 |
|  | (0.04) | (0.06) | (0.04) |
| Difference effect less poor and effect poorest | −0.11 | 0.10 | −0.06 |
|  | (0.06)* | (0.07) | (0.06) |
| Observations | 3,069 | 3,061 | 3,082 |

*Source:* World Bank data.
*Note:* Results reported in this table are based on effect of treatment on the treated (ETT) regressions. Clustered standard errors in parentheses. CCT = conditional cash transfer.
Significance level: * = 10 percent, ** = 5 percent, *** = 1 percent

**Table 7.35  Heterogeneous Geography Treatment Effects of CCT on Household Members' Trust of their Community at the Endline**

|  | (1) | (2) | (3) |
|---|---|---|---|
|  | Can most people be trusted? | Can people in the community be trusted? | Can community leaders be trusted? |
| Baseline mean- Kibaha | 0.16 | 0.52 | 0.77 |
| Baseline mean- Bagamoyo | 0.21 | 0.51 | 0.79 |
| Baseline mean- Chamwino | 0.38 | 0.67 | 0.86 |
| Effect Kibaha | 0.10 | 0.11 | 0.18 |
|  | (0.08) | (0.09) | (0.05)*** |
| Effect Bagamoyo | −0.11 | 0.05 | 0.02 |
|  | (0.06)* | (0.08) | (0.04) |
| Effect Chamwino | 0.12 | −0.06 | −0.02 |
|  | (0.06)* | (0.07) | (0.04) |
| Difference effect Bagamoyo and effect Kibaha | −0.21 | −0.06 | −0.17 |
|  | (0.10)** | (0.12) | (0.06)** |
| Difference effect Chamwino and effect Kibaha | 0.03 | −0.17 | −0.21 |
|  | (0.10) | (0.11) | (0.06)*** |
| Observations | 3,069 | 3,061 | 3,082 |

*Source:* World Bank data.
*Note:* Results reported in this table are based on effect of treatment on the treated (ETT) regressions. Clustered standard errors in parentheses. CCT = conditional cash transfer.
Significance level: * = 10 percent, ** = 5 percent, *** = 1 percent

impact of treatment on their trust of people in general or of people in their community.

In table 7.35 we see that at endline, treated households in Bagamoyo reported decreases in trusting most people while treated households in Chamwino reported increases, and treated households in Kibaha did not see statistically significant changes in trust of most people. Specifically, column (1) demonstrates that treated households in Bagamoyo reported an 11 percentage point *decrease* in trust of most, while households in Chamwino reported a 12 percentage point *increase*. Both these results were significant at the 10 percent level.

In column (3), we see that at endline the impact of treatment on trust in community leaders was concentrated in Kibaha. There, treated households experienced an 18 percentage point increase in their trust of community leaders. This finding is significant at the 1 percent level. The changes in other districts are small in magnitude and statistically insignificant.

We find that treated households that were not affected by drought since midline reported a statistically significant increase in trusting their community leaders at endline, as shown in table 7.36. Column (3) shows that these nondrought-afflicted households reported a statistically significant 7 percentage point increase in trust of community leaders. These heterogeneous effects are summarized in figure 7.10 below.

**Table 7.36  Heterogeneous Shock Treatment Effects of CCT on Household Members' Trust of their Community at the Endline**

|  | (1) | (2) | (3) |
|---|---|---|---|
|  | Can most people be trusted? | Can people in the community be trusted? | Can community leaders be trusted? |
| Effect no drought | 0.05 | 0.05 | 0.07 |
|  | (0.06) | (0.05) | (0.03)** |
| Effect drought | −0.02 | 0.01 | 0.03 |
|  | 0.05 | 0.07 | 0.04 |
| Difference effect drought and effect no drought | −0.07 | −0.03 | −0.05 |
|  | (0.07) | (0.08) | (0.05) |
| Observations | 3,069 | 3,061 | 3,082 |
| R-squared | 0.03 | 0.04 | 0.01 |

*Source:* World Bank data.

*Note:* Results reported in this table are based on effect of treatment on the treated (ETT) regressions. Clustered standard errors in parentheses. CCT = conditional cash transfer.
Significance level: * = 10 percent, ** = 5 percent, *** = 1 percent

**Figure 7.10  Heterogeneous Effects of Conditional Cash Transfer on Trust in Community Leaders**

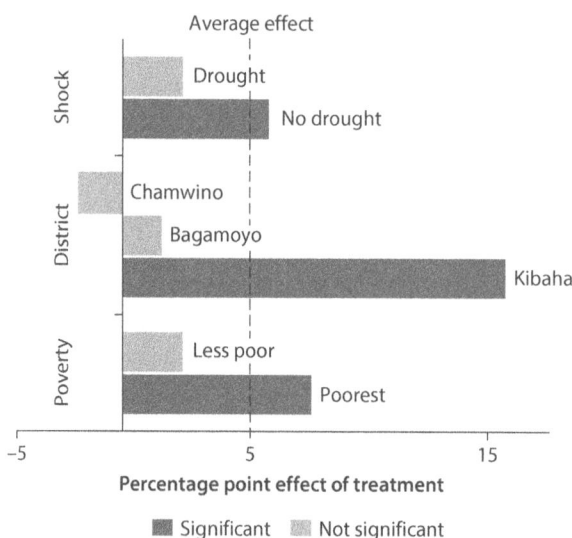

*Source:* World Bank data.

## Qualitative Findings

The qualitative exercise found complex effects of the program on community dynamics and trust across villages. In some of the focus groups in Bagamoyo, beneficiaries stated that the program had made people feel that their leaders and community cared about them, and so improved community dynamics. This finding of increased trust in leaders corresponds to the quantitative findings of increased trust in treatment villages, and especially the finding that the poorest households were more likely to increase their trust in community leaders. These households expressed that they were largely ignored until the start of the program, and the program made huge changes in their lives.

However, we also heard from some leaders and nonbeneficiaries that the poorest households were not always selected. One man in Kibaha district told us that while some of the community leaders benefited from the program, he had not been chosen even though he did not have much money, and this may have been due to the fact that he was from a different tribe. We also heard from one CMC member in Kibaha and a focus group of nonbeneficiaries in Bagamoyo that the process had not been completely fair in those communities, and that some of the poorest households had been left out of the selection process. Even if based purely on perception rather than reality, such sentiments would tend to erode some of the trust within the community. This may account for the short-term reduction in trust of others in the community, captured in the midline survey. However, those effects disappeared on average by the time of the endline survey.

Takeaways:

- At the design of the project, there was significant concern that the community administration of this conditional cash transfer program would decrease social capital in the community. There is no evidence that this is the case, with levels of trust in others in the community unmoved by endline, and in fact an increase in the level of trust in community leaders.
- Kibaha may be a useful case for further study, to understand factors that drive increase in trust of leaders. Most of the significant impacts on trust of leaders are driven by findings from this district.

## Community Participation and Perception of Public Service Quality

In this next section, we examine whether participation in the CB-CCT (that is, treatment) changes community participation or perceptions of public service quality. Our measure of community participation is whether household members contributed to community development projects. To measure perceptions of public service quality, we asked about the perceived quality of health and education facilities and whether their community has a parents' association or a health committee.

As table 7.37 shows, treatment is not associated with statistically significant increases in either participation in community development projects (column 1) or positive ratings of the community's school and health facilities (columns 2–4). These results stand in contrast to the midline results, where we observed statistically significant increases in the likelihood that treated households rated their school and health facilities positively (table 4.13). This change may be due to expectation adjustments. While at midline, households were pleased to find their community school and health facilities in good condition, by endline they had become accustomed to the facilities. In columns (5) and (6), we see that treatment communities are not more likely to have a community health committee or a parents' association at endline.

While treatment was not associated with significant increases in household participation in community development projects overall, treated households headed by women did see an increase in their likelihood to contribute. In

**Table 7.37  CCT Effects on Community Participation and Perceptions of Public Service Quality at Endline**

|  | (1) | (2) | (3) | (4) | (5) | (6) |
|---|---|---|---|---|---|---|
|  | HH contributed labor to CD project | Rates schooling good or excellent | Rates health facilities good or excellent | Rates schooling and health facilities good or excellent | Community has a parents' association | Community has a health committee |
| Baseline mean | 0.36 | 0.85 | 0.71 | 0.65 | 0.11 | 0.57 |
| *Panel A: Effect of treatment on the treated* | | | | | | |
| Treatment | 0.00 | 0.05 | 0.04 | 0.06 | 0.02 | 0.04 |
| (ETT) × After | (0.04) | (0.04) | (0.05) | (0.05) | (0.04) | (0.04) |
| After | −0.22 | −0.23 | −0.13 | −0.17 | 0.11 | 0.11 |
|  | (0.03)*** | (0.03)*** | (0.03)*** | (0.03)*** | (0.02)*** | (0.03)*** |
| Observations | 3,132 | 3,130 | 3,132 | 3,130 | 3,130 | 3,132 |
| R-squared | 0.12 | 0.12 | 0.03 | 0.05 | 0.05 | 0.05 |
| *Panel B: Intent to treat* | | | | | | |
| Treatment | 0.00 | 0.05 | 0.03 | 0.06 | 0.02 | 0.04 |
| (ITT) × After | (0.06) | (0.05) | (0.06) | (0.06) | (0.05) | (0.06) |
| After | −0.22*** | −0.23*** | −0.13*** | −0.17*** | 0.11*** | 0.11** |
|  | (0.04) | (0.03) | (0.04) | (0.04) | (0.03) | (0.04) |

*Source:* World Bank data.
*Note:* Clustered standard errors in parentheses. CCT = conditional cash transfer; ETT = effect of treatment on the treated; ITT = intention to treat.
Significance level: * = 10 percent, ** = 5 percent, *** = 1 percent

table 7.38, column (1), we see that female-headed households realized a 12 percentage point gain in their likelihood of contributing labor to community development projects. This result is a 40 percent increase over their baseline mean and is significant at the 5 percent level. We observe no significant differences for male-headed households at endline.

Column (2) reports that treated households headed by women were by endline 9 percentage points more likely to rate schooling as excellent or good (significant at the 10 percent level). Male-headed households realized a smaller and statistically insignificant increase.

We next examine differences in how the poorest and less poor treated households responded to treatment at endline (table 7.39). In column (2), we see that the poorest households are now 9 percentage points more likely to rate schooling as good or excellent, which is significant at the 5 percent level. Similarly, column (4) shows that the poorest households are now 11 percentage points more likely to rate school and health facilities (together) as good or excellent, significant at the 10 percent. As there are no separate impacts of treatment on the poorest households' perceptions of health facilities being good or excellent at endline (column 3), this suggests that the results in column 4 are driven by positive impacts of treatment on perceptions of schooling quality.

Positive impacts of treatment are not found for less poor households. Furthermore, neither the poorest nor less poor households saw impacts of treatment on contributions to community development projects, or reports that their community has an active parents' association or health committee.

**Table 7.38 Heterogeneous Gender Treatment Effect of CCT on Community Participation and Perceptions of Public Service Quality at Endline**

| | (1) | (2) | (3) | (4) | (5) | (6) |
|---|---|---|---|---|---|---|
| | HH contributed labor to CD project | Rates schooling good or excellent | Rates health facilities good or excellent | Rates schooling and health facilities good or excellent | Community has a parents' association | HH contributed labor to CD project |
| Baseline mean- female head of household | 0.30 | 0.87 | 0.74 | 0.61 | 0.08 | 0.51 |
| Baseline mean- male head of household | 0.40 | 0.84 | 0.69 | 0.63 | 0.13 | 0.61 |
| Effect female head of household | 0.12 | 0.09 | 0.03 | 0.06 | 0.03 | 0.08 |
| | (0.05)** | (0.05)* | (0.06) | (0.07) | (0.05) | (0.06) |
| Effect male head of household | −0.06 | 0.03 | 0.04 | 0.06 | 0.01 | 0.01 |
| | (0.05) | (0.05) | (0.05) | (0.05) | (0.04) | (0.05) |
| Difference effect male head of household and effect female head of household | −0.18 | −0.06 | 0.01 | −0.00 | −0.02 | −0.07 |
| | (0.07)*** | (0.06) | (0.08) | (0.08) | (0.06) | (0.07) |
| Observations | 3,132 | 3,130 | 3,132 | 3,130 | 3,130 | 3,132 |

*Source:* World Bank data.
*Note:* Results reported in this table are based on effect of treatment on the treated (ETT) regressions. Clustered standard errors in parentheses. CCT = conditional cash transfer; HH = household.
Significance level: * = 10 percent, ** = 5 percent, *** = 1 percent

**Table 7.39 Heterogeneous Poverty Treatment Effect of CCT on Community Participation and Perceptions of Public Service Quality at Endline**

| | (1) | (2) | (3) | (4) | (5) | (6) |
|---|---|---|---|---|---|---|
| | HH contributed labor to CD project | Rates schooling good or excellent | Rates health facilities good or excellent | Rates schooling and health facilities good or excellent | Community has a parents' association | Community has a health committee |
| Baseline mean- poorest | 0.27 | 0.88 | 0.75 | 0.70 | 0.11 | 0.55 |
| Baseline mean- less poor | 0.48 | 0.82 | 0.65 | 0.60 | 0.11 | 0.60 |
| Effect poorest | −0.02 | 0.09 | 0.04 | 0.11 | −0.01 | 0.05 |
| | (0.06) | (0.05)** | (0.06) | (0.06)* | (0.04) | (0.05) |
| Effect less poor | 0.03 | 0.01 | 0.03 | 0.02 | 0.05 | 0.03 |
| | (0.05) | (0.05) | (0.06) | (0.06) | (0.04) | (0.05) |
| Difference effect less poor and effect poorest | 0.05 | −0.08 | −0.01 | −0.09 | 0.07 | −0.02 |
| | (0.06) | (0.05) | (0.07) | (0.07) | (0.05) | (0.06) |
| Observations | 3,132 | 3,130 | 3,132 | 3,130 | 3,130 | 3,132 |

*Source:* World Bank data.
*Note:* Results reported in this table are based on effect of treatment on the treated (ETT) regressions. Clustered standard errors in parentheses. CCT = conditional cash transfer; HH = household.
*** $p<.01$, ** $p<.05$, * $p<.1$

Finally, in table 7.40, we analyze the differences in treatment effects between the three pilot districts at endline. In column (2) we see that in Kibaha, treated households were 15 percentage points more likely to rate schooling as good or excellent (significant at the 10 percent level). In Kibaha, treated households were also 11 percentage points more likely to report the existence of a health committee in their community. No other regions saw statistically significant impacts of treatment.

Figure 7.11 summarizes these overall impacts of treatment on perceptions of schools as well as impacts for particular subgroups of households explored in the heterogeneous treatment effects regressions. Overall, we see that female-headed households, households in the poorest half, and households in Kibaha were those perceiving program-induced improvements in the quality of schools. There were no effects of treatment on such perceptions overall (that is, across all households).

### Qualitative Findings

The quantitative analysis did not find evidence for consistent impacts of the program on households' participation in community projects and organizations, or on their likelihood to hold positive views of the quality of schools and health

**Table 7.40 Heterogeneous Geography Treatment Effect of CCT on Community Participation and Perceptions of Public Service Quality at Endline**

|  | (1) | (2) | (3) | (4) | (5) | (6) |
|---|---|---|---|---|---|---|
|  | HH contributed labor to CD project | Rates schooling good or excellent | Rates health facilities good or excellent | Rates schooling and health facilities good or excellent | Community has a parents' association | Community has a health committee |
| Baseline mean- Kibaha | 0.52 | 0.82 | 0.71 | 0.64 | 0.10 | 0.65 |
| Baseline mean- Bagamoyo | 0.37 | 0.87 | 0.66 | 0.62 | 0.13 | 0.52 |
| Baseline mean- Chamwino | 0.18 | 0.87 | 0.78 | 0.72 | 0.10 | 0.58 |
| Effect Kibaha | 0.07 | 0.15 | 0.07 | 0.10 | 0.05 | 0.11 |
|  | (0.06) | (0.09)* | (0.08) | (0.08) | (0.05) | (0.05)** |
| Effect Bagamoyo | −0.06 | 0.06 | 0.09 | 0.12 | 0.05 | −0.01 |
|  | (0.06) | (0.05) | (0.07) | (0.07) | (0.05) | (0.07) |
| Effect Chamwino | 0.04 | −0.05 | −0.07 | −0.05 | −0.08 | 0.03 |
|  | (0.05) | (0.06) | (0.07) | (0.07) | (0.07) | (0.08) |
| Difference effect Bagamoyo and effect Kibaha | −0.13 | −0.09 | 0.02 | 0.02 | 0.00 | −0.12 |
|  | (0.09) | (0.10) | (0.10) | (0.11) | (0.07) | (0.09) |
| Difference effect Chamwino and effect Kibaha | −0.03 | −0.20 | −0.14 | −0.14 | −0.12 | −0.08 |
|  | (0.08) | (0.10)* | (0.10) | (0.11) | (0.09) | (0.10) |
| Observations | 3,132 | 3,130 | 3,132 | 3,130 | 3,130 | 3,132 |

Source: World Bank data.
Note: Results reported in this table are based on effect of treatment on the treated (ETT) regressions. Clustered standard errors in parentheses. CCT = conditional cash transfer.
Significance level: * = 10 percent, ** = 5 percent, *** = 1 percent

**Figure 7.11 Various Heterogeneous Treatment Effects on Likelihood of Rating School Good or Excellent**

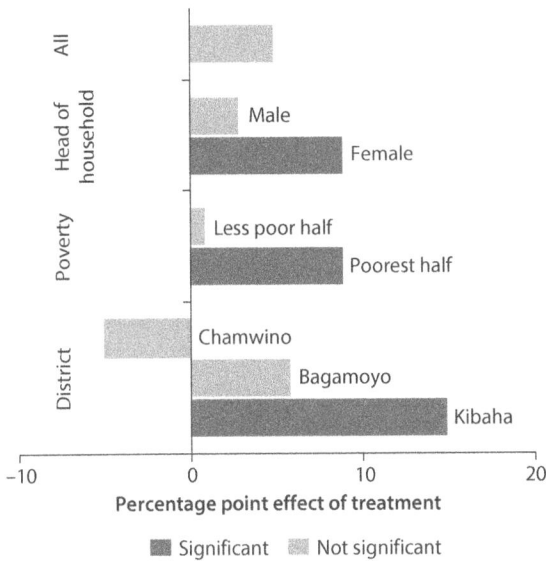

*Source:* World Bank data.

facilities in their communities. The qualitative exercise found little evidence for an impact of the program on community participation by beneficiaries, although there was some evidence for increased participation in village-level affairs for specific subgroups within communities. For example, a pastoralist in one village in Kibaha became involved in the community management committee (CMC), which served as a way to increase participation in the program by this group. It is possible that working with diverse members of the community in the CMC can be a way to increase communication and cooperation between different social groups at a higher level than individual participation in community projects.

Effects on perceptions of public service quality were varied. One focus group of leaders in Bagamoyo said that there is now a shortage of teachers, since enrollment has increased. Similarly, this group mentioned a shortage of health workers. Beneficiaries in a focus group in Bagamoyo mentioned that the program made them feel more secure in their decisions to attend the clinic since the CB-CCT was supporting them and the health staff were encouraging their participation in the community health fund (the government-subsidized health insurance program). Yet participants also mentioned that some problems of overcrowding and medication shortages may have increased due to higher demand from the program. However, one health facility leader in an in-depth interview explained that while patient numbers had increased, the actual work was easier because now the beneficiaries were insured, so the paperwork and administrative aspects of treating patients were much easier.

One significant finding of the quantitative analysis that is corroborated by the qualitative fieldwork is that both female-headed and the poorest households are more likely to rate school facilities as good or excellent as a result of the program. These types of households may have had more limited exposure to schools at baseline. For example, two beneficiaries in female-headed households in a focus group in Bagamoyo reported that their children are now attending school when they did not before. They could now observe and enjoy the schooling facilities— which seemed to raise their estimation of their quality. Another explanation is that these households feel more respected by the school as a result of the program, since they are now able to afford the necessary or expected school supplies for their children. This might in turn generate positive feelings towards the schools.

Takeaways:

- There is no evidence that the program has reduced social capital as measured in the existence of community groups. On the contrary, for certain kinds of households, the program has increased participation in community work projects.
- That the program increases perceptions of school quality most among some of the most marginalized groups (female-headed households and the poorest of the poor) is positive; it suggests that these individuals may be accessing and appreciating these facilities for the first time.

## Additional Results on Trust and Political Participation, with Endline Data Only

To better understand the effects of the CB-CCT on trust and political participation, we added some questions to the endline survey which were not included at the baseline. To estimate the effect of the program on these outcomes, we conducted ward fixed effect regressions (that is, comparing treatment and comparison villages within administrative divisions in Tanzania). We divided the various pilot communities into 34 separate wards, based on existing state administrative divisions.

As we see in table 7.41 and figure 7.12, treatment is associated with statistically significant increases in households' trust towards other individuals in their community at endline. In the first three columns we see that treated households are now statistically significantly more likely to trust their local government leaders. Column (1) shows that treated households are now 8 percentage points more likely to trust their Village Chairman (significant at the 10 percent level). Similarly, columns (2) and (3) show that treated households are now 11 percentage points more likely to trust their Village Council (significant at the 5 percent level) and 8 percentage points more likely to trust their VEO (significant at the 10 percent level). Column (5) shows that treated households are now 27 percentage points more likely to trust their community management committee, that is, the group the implements the program (significant at the 1 percent level).

Columns (4), (6), (7), and (8) show that these increases in trust are not limited to local leaders. In column (4) we find that treated households are now

**Table 7.41 Ward Fixed Effects of CCT on Household Trust of Community at Endline**

| | (1) | (2) | (3) | (4) | (5) | (6) | (7) | (8) |
|---|---|---|---|---|---|---|---|---|
| | Chair | VC | VEO | Strangers | CMC | Shopkeeper | Teachers | Health Workers |
| **Panel A: Effect of treatment on treated** | | | | | | | | |
| Treatment (ETT) × After | 0.08 | 0.11 | 0.08 | 0.08 | 0.27 | 0.12 | 0.10 | 0.09 |
| | (0.04)* | (0.05)** | (0.04)* | (0.04)* | (0.04)*** | (0.04)*** | (0.04)** | (0.04)** |
| Observations | 1,596 | 1,596 | 1,596 | 1,596 | 1,595 | 1,596 | 1,596 | 1,596 |
| R-squared | 0.02 | 0.02 | 0.03 | 0.01 | 0.07 | 0.03 | 0.03 | 0.02 |
| **Panel B: Intention to treat** | | | | | | | | |
| Treatment (ITT) × After | 0.07 | 0.10 | 0.08 | 0.08 | 0.26 | 0.12 | 0.09 | 0.08 |
| | (0.04)* | (0.05)* | (0.04)* | (0.04)* | (0.04)*** | (0.03)*** | (0.04)** | (0.04)** |
| Observations | 1,596 | 1,596 | 1,596 | 1,596 | 1,595 | 1,596 | 1,596 | 1,596 |
| R-squared | 0.08 | 0.09 | 0.09 | 0.07 | 0.16 | 0.07 | 0.07 | 0.06 |

*Source:* World Bank data.
*Note:* Clustered standard errors in parentheses. CCT = conditional cash transfer; CMC = community management committee; ETT = effect of treatment on the treated; ITT = intention to treat; VC = village council; VEO = village executive officer.
Significance level: * = 10 percent, ** = 5 percent, *** = 1 percent

**Figure 7.12 Effect of Conditional Cash Transfer on Community Trust**

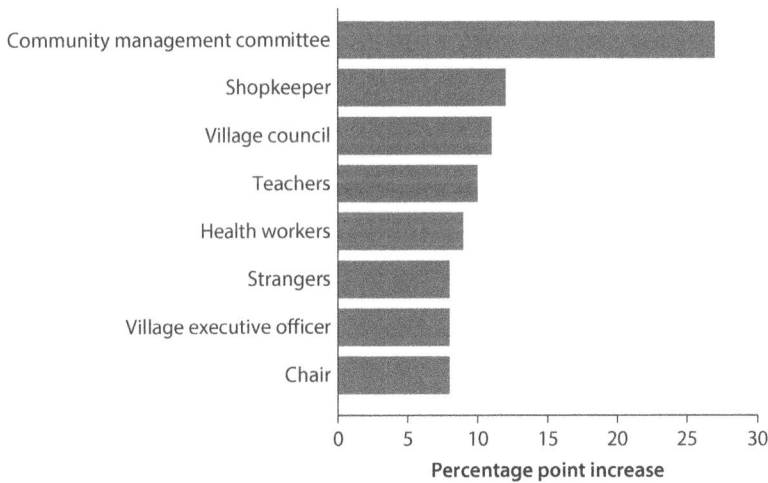

*Source:* World Bank data.

8 percentage points more likely to trust strangers (significant at the 10 percent level). Treated households are also 12 percentage points more likely to trust shopkeepers (significant at the 1 percent level) and 10 percentage points more likely to trust teachers (significant at the 5 percent level). Column (8) shows that they are 9 percentage points more likely to trust health care workers at endline (significant at the 5 percent level). This may be due to the conditions associated with the program. As treated households interact with education and medical professionals more, trust in them may increase.

Community-Based Conditional Cash Transfers in Tanzania • http://dx.doi.org/10.1596/978-1-4648-0141-9

These results should be interpreted with caution. Although we do not have baseline data on these specific questions, treatment households were six percentage points more likely to say that they could trust people in their community at baseline than control households. However, note that the point estimates for every estimate of trust in table 7.41 are greater than six percentage points, suggesting—at least—that trust was not eroded in the context of this program.

In table 7.42, we show the extent to which treated household members trust of others changed by endline. We find that treated households are now statistically significantly more likely to trust others in their community enough to leave their children in their care for a day or two: Column (2) shows that treated household are 13 percentage points more likely to know someone willing to care for their children, a result that is significant at the 1 percent level.

In table 7.43, we analyze the effects of treatment on household members' likelihood of participating in collective action opportunities. Columns (1) and (3) demonstrate that treated households were statistically significantly more likely to participate in village groups and organizations and are more willing to donate funding to village projects that do not directly benefit the households. As we see, treated households are 3 percentage points more willing to participate in village groups (significant at the 1 percent) and they are 5 percentage points more likely to willingly commit funding to village projects (significant at the 5 percent level).

Conversely, column (5) shows that treatment is associated with a statistically significant decrease in the likelihood that households have petitioned the government in the year preceding the endline survey. We find that members of these households are now 6 percentage points less likely to petition to government for something that benefits the community, significant at the 10 percent level.

**Table 7.42  Ward Fixed Effects of CCT on Household Extent of Trust at Endline**

|  | (1) | (2) | (3) |
|---|---|---|---|
|  | HH can turn to three or more people for T Sh 15,000 | HH has someone who would be willing to take care of their children for a day or two | HH has turned to others for assistance in the last year |
| *Panel A: Effect of treatment on treated* | | | |
| Treatment (ETT) × After | −0.01 | 0.13 | 0.01 |
|  | (0.04) | (0.03)*** | (0.02) |
| Observations | 1,780 | 1,780 | 1,780 |
| *R*-squared | 0.03 | 0.03 | 0.03 |
| *Panel B: Intention to treat* | | | |
| Treatment (ITT) × After | −0.01 | 0.11 | 0.01 |
|  | (0.04) | (0.03)*** | (0.02) |
| Observations | 1,780 | 1,780 | 1,780 |
| *R*-squared | 0.05 | 0.07 | 0.06 |

*Source:* World Bank data.
*Note:* Clustered standard errors in parentheses. CCT = conditional cash transfer; ETT = effect of treatment on the treated; HH = household; ITT = intention to treat.
Significance level: * = 10 percent, ** = 5 percent, *** = 1 percent

**Table 7.43 Ward Fixed Effects of CCT on Household Collective Action at Endline**

| | (1) | (2) | (3) | (4) | (5) |
|---|---|---|---|---|---|
| | Compared to three years ago, HH willing to participate in a village group or organization | HH willing to commit time to a village project that does not benefit them directly | HH willing to commit money to village projects that does not benefit them directly | HH has participated with others to benefit the community | HH has gotten together 1 or more times in the past 12 months with others to petition government officials for something to benefit the community |
| **Panel A: Effect of treatment on treated** | | | | | |
| Treatment (ETT) × After | 0.03 | 0.05 | 0.05 | 0.02 | −0.06 |
| | (0.01)*** | (0.03) | (0.02)** | (0.01) | (0.03)* |
| Observations | 1,780 | 1,780 | 1,780 | 1,780 | 1,780 |
| R-squared | 0.04 | 0.06 | 0.05 | 0.06 | 0.03 |
| **Panel B: Intention to treat** | | | | | |
| Treatment (ITT) × After | 0.03 | 0.04 | 0.05 | 0.02 | −0.05 |
| | (0.01)*** | (0.03) | (0.02)** | (0.01) | (0.03)* |
| Observations | 1,780 | 1,780 | 1,780 | 1,780 | 1,780 |
| R-squared | 0.06 | 0.08 | 0.08 | 0.11 | 0.09 |

*Source:* World Bank data.
*Note:* Clustered standard errors in parentheses. CCT = conditional cash transfer; ETT = effect of treatment on the treated; HH = household; ITT = intention to treat.
Significance level: * = 10 percent, ** = 5 percent, *** = 1 percent

In table 7.44, we analyze the effect of the CB-CCT on household political participation at endline and find that treatment led to statistically significant increases in whether household members had attended village council meetings in the past 12 months and whether they had voted in the most recent community management committee election.

In column (1) we see that treated household members were 7 percentage points more likely to have attended a village council meeting in the past 12 months, significant at the 5 percent level. Column (5) shows an even larger effect of treatment. It shows that treated households were 22 percentage points more likely to vote in the most recent CMC election at endline, significant at the 1 percent level, unsurprising given that the CMC is the body that directly administers the CCT.

Finally, in table 7.45 we analyze the effects of the CCT on household perceptions of their local leaders and find some statistically significant increases. In column (1) we see that households are 8 percentage points more likely to believe that local leaders take into account concerns voiced by community members when making decisions. This result is significant at the 1 percent level and indicates that treatment led to increased accountability, or at the very least, increased perceptions of accountability.

In column (2) we see that at endline, treated households were 8 percentage points more likely to believe that local government leaders' honesty had improved compared to three years ago, a result that is significant at the 1 percent level.

**Table 7.44 Ward Fixed Effects of CCT on Political Participation at Endline**

| | (1) | (2) | (3) | (4) | (5) |
|---|---|---|---|---|---|
| | HH member attended VC meeting past 12 months | HH member attended VC meeting 3 months | HH member talked with a VC member about community affairs in past 12 months | HH member voted in most recent VA election | HH voted in most recent CMC election |
| **Panel A: Effect of treatment on treated** | | | | | |
| Treatment (ETT) × After | 0.07 | −0.04 | −0.02 | 0.05 | 0.22 |
| | (0.03)** | (0.03) | (0.03) | (0.04) | (0.05)*** |
| Observations | 1,780 | 1,780 | 1,780 | 1,780 | 1,780 |
| R-squared | 0.08 | 0.02 | 0.05 | 0.05 | 0.07 |
| **Panel B: Intention to treat** | | | | | |
| Treatment (ITT) × After | 0.06 | −0.03 | −0.02 | 0.05 | 0.21 |
| | (0.03)** | (0.03) | (0.03) | (0.03) | (0.05)*** |
| Observations | 1,780 | 1,780 | 1,780 | 1,780 | 1,780 |
| R-squared | 0.12 | 0.04 | 0.10 | 0.09 | 0.12 |

Source: World Bank data.
Note: Clustered standard errors in parentheses. CCT = conditional cash transfer; ETT = effect of treatment on the treated; HH = household; ITT = intention to treat; VC = village council.
Significance level: * = 10 percent, ** = 5 percent, *** = 1 percent

**Table 7.45 Ward Fixed Effects of CCT on Household Perceptions of Quality of Leaders at Endline**

| Variables | (1) | (2) | (3) | (4) |
|---|---|---|---|---|
| | Local government leaders take into account concerns voiced by community | Honesty of local government leaders has improved since 3 years ago | HH has paid money to local government official to get something done | HH very satisfied with work of VC |
| **Panel A: Effect of treatment on treated** | | | | |
| Treatment (ETT) × After | 0.08 | 0.08 | −0.01 | 0.02 |
| | (0.03)*** | (0.02)*** | (0.02) | (0.02) |
| Observations | 1,780 | 1,780 | 1,780 | 1,169 |
| R-squared | 0.02 | 0.03 | 0.03 | 0.02 |
| **Panel B: Intention to treat** | | | | |
| Treatment (ITT) × After | 0.08 | 0.07 | −0.01 | 0.02 |
| | (0.03)** | (0.02)*** | (0.02) | (0.01) |
| Observations | 1,780 | 1,780 | 1,780 | 1,169 |
| R-squared | 0.07 | 0.06 | 0.05 | 0.05 |

Source: World Bank data.
Note: Clustered standard errors in parentheses. CCT = conditional cash transfer; ETT = effect of treatment on the treated; HH = household; ITT = intention to treat; VC = village council.
Significance level: * = 10 percent, ** = 5 percent, *** = 1 percent

Takeaway:

- As was demonstrated in the previous sections, far from undermining social cohesion, this program has—if anything—increased trust in the community for beneficiaries. It has also increased political participation, positive perceptions of leaders, and reported willingness to engage in community projects.

## Transfers Paid Out and Received

When the project was designed, the possibility arose that participation in the CB-CCT (that is, treatment) might affect what benefits treatment households receive from other sources. The findings in table 7.46 explore this concern. In columns (1) and (4) we see that treatment has a large and statistically significant impact on whether households receive transfers from the government, as well as on the size of the transfer received: This is most likely simply capturing the fact that households are participating in the program. Treatment households are now 95 percentage points more likely to receive a transfer of at least T Sh 5,000 from the government or TASAF (column 1). In fact, column (4) shows that treated households are, on average, receiving about T Sh 94,000 more from the government and TASAF. Both of these results are significant at the 1 percent level.

**Table 7.46  Effects of CCT on Transfers Received (by Source) and Paid Out at Endline**

| | (1) | (2) | (3) | (4) | (5) | (6) | (7) |
|---|---|---|---|---|---|---|---|
| | Household received at least T Sh 5,000 from group, last 12 months | | | Value of all transfers received (cash, food, and other in-kind) from group, last 12 months | | | Value of all transfers given out, last 12 months |
| | Gov't / TASAF | NGO/ FBO | Individuals | Gov't / TASAF | NGO/ FBO | Individuals | |
| Baseline mean | 0.04 | 0.05 | 0.40 | 648 | 1,038 | 20,229 | 1,523 |
| *Panel A: Effect of treatment on the treated* | | | | | | | |
| Treatment (ETT) × After | 0.95 | 0.00 | −0.02 | 94,368 | −983 | −5,049 | 341 |
| | (0.02)*** | (0.03) | (0.05) | (3,610)*** | (1,171) | (8,181) | (785) |
| After | −0.02 | −0.01 | 0.09 | −597 | 1,283 | 28,636 | 1,354 |
| | (0.01)*** | (0.02) | (0.03)*** | (209)*** | (890) | (6,395)*** | (571)** |
| Observations | 3,128 | 3,132 | 3,132 | 3,128 | 3,132 | 3,132 | 3,132 |
| R-squared | 0.79 | 0.00 | 0.02 | 0.71 | 0.00 | 0.05 | 0.01 |
| *Panel B: Intent to Treat* | | | | | | | |
| Treatment (ITT) × After | 0.89*** | 0.00 | −0.02 | 88,298 | −920.2 | −4,724.7 | 318.9 |
| | (0.03) | (0.03) | (0.06) | (5,300)*** | (1,599) | (11,172) | (1,071) |
| After | −0.02 | −0.01 | 0.09 | −349 | 1,281 | 28,623 | 1,355 |
| | (0.01)** | (0.03) | (0.05)* | (199)* | (1,296) | (9,303)*** | (830.35) |

*Source:* World Bank data.
*Note:* Clustered standard errors in parentheses. CCT = conditional cash transfer; ETT = effect of treatment on the treated; FBO = faith-based organization; ITT = intention to treat; NGO = nongovernmental organization; TASAF = Tanzania Social Action Fund. Significance level: * = 10 percent, ** = 5 percent, *** = 1 percent

At endline, there is no evidence of significant crowding out of other transfers as a result of the program. This varies from the midline finding that treatment had some negative impact on transfers from other individuals in the community. In other words, the crowding out of other transfers seems to have been a short-term phenomenon. At endline, there is no evidence of individual crowding out in any of the project districts.

In table 7.47, we analyze the different effects treatment had on households headed by women and men at endline. Of particular note, in column (4) we observe that male-headed households received larger transfers from the government/TASAF than female-led households. Treatment households led by women received about T Sh 82,015 at endline, but those led by men received about T Sh 101,200 from the government and TASAF. Both of these findings are significant at the 1 percent level. If we look at the difference between effect of male head of household and effect of female head of household we see that male-headed households received T Sh 19,243 more from the government in the form of transfers, significant at the 1 percent level. This could be driven by differences in household composition.

From table 7.48, we see that treatment has slightly different effects on the poorest and less poor households. In columns (6) and (7) we observe no significant

**Table 7.47 Heterogeneous Gender Treatment Effects of CCT on Transfers Received (by Source) and Paid Out at Endline**

| | (1) | (2) | (3) | (4) | (5) | (6) | (7) |
|---|---|---|---|---|---|---|---|
| | Household received at least T Sh 5,000 from group, last 12 months | | | Value of all transfers received (cash, food, and other in-kind) from group, last 12 months | | | Value of all transfers given out, last 12 months |
| | Gov't / TASAF | NGO/ FBO | Individuals | Gov't / TASAF | NGO/ FBO | Individuals | |
| Baseline mean- female head of household | 0.04 | 0.05 | 0.48 | 624 | 1,206 | 22,646 | 1,324 |
| Baseline mean- male head of household | 0.03 | 0.05 | 0.36 | 663 | 931 | 18,684 | 1,651 |
| Effect female head of household | 0.94 | −0.00 | −0.05 | 82,015 | 737.85 | −4,030 | 464.72 |
| | (0.03)*** | (0.03) | (0.06) | (3,851)*** | (2,294) | (8,074) | (1,465.10) |
| Effect male head of household | 0.96 | 0.00 | 0.00 | 101,259 | −2,037 | −6,327 | 175.8 |
| | (0.02)*** | (0.03) | (0.05) | (4,039)*** | (1,266) | (11,334) | (1,007) |
| Difference effect male head of household and female head of household | 0.02 | 0.00 | 0.05 | 19,243.73 | −2,775 | −2,296.8 | −288.95 |
| | (0.03) | (0.03) | (0.07) | (3,544)*** | (2,577) | (12,503) | (1,920.40) |
| Observations | 3,128 | 3,132 | 3,132 | 3,128 | 3,132 | 3,132 | 3,132 |

*Source:* World Bank data.

*Note:* Results reported in this table are based on effect of treatment on the treated (ETT) regressions. Clustered standard errors in parentheses. CCT = conditional cash transfer; ETT = effect of treatment on the treated; FBO = faith-based organization; ITT = intention to treat; NGO = nongovernmental organization; TASAF = Tanzania Social Action Fund; T Sh = Tanzanian shilling.
Significance level: * = 10 percent, ** = 5 percent, *** = 1 percent

**Table 7.48 Heterogeneous Poverty Treatment Effects of CCT on Transfers Received (by Source) and Paid Out at Endline**

| | (1) | (2) | (3) | (4) | (5) | (6) | (7) |
|---|---|---|---|---|---|---|---|
| | Household received at least T Sh 5,000 from group, last 12 months | | | Value of all transfers received (cash, food, and other in-kind) from group, last 12 months | | | Value of all transfers given out, last 12 months |
| | Gov't / TASAF | NGO/ FBO | Individuals | Gov't / TASAF | NGO/ FBO | Individuals | |
| Baseline mean- poorest | 0.04 | 0.04 | 0.39 | 628 | 605 | 15,239 | 1,155 |
| Baseline mean- less poor | 0.04 | 0.07 | 0.43 | 675 | 1,621 | 26,942 | 2,018 |
| Effect poorest | 0.98 | 0.00 | −0.02 | 92,294 | −310 | 901 | −200.8 |
| | (0.02)*** | (0.02) | (0.06) | (4,143)*** | (1,528) | (8,822) | (1,019) |
| Effect less poor | 0.92 | 0.00 | −0.02 | 96,564 | −1,695 | −11,008 | 1,162 |
| | (0.03)*** | (0.03) | (0.06) | (3,965)*** | (1,275) | (12,009) | (1,716) |
| Difference effect less poor and effect poorest | −0.06 | 0.00 | −0.00 | 4,269.68 | −1,385 | −11,910 | 1,363 |
| | (0.03)** | (0.03) | (0.07) | (3,707.6) | (1,585) | (13,510) | (2,361) |
| Observations | 3,128 | 3,132 | 3,132 | 3,128 | 3,132 | 3,132 | 3,132 |

*Source:* World Bank data.

*Note:* Clustered standard errors in parentheses. CCT = conditional cash transfer; FBO = faith-based organization; NGO = nongovernmental organization; TASAF = Tanzania Social Action Fund; T Sh = Tanzanian shilling.

*** $p<.01$, ** $p<.05$, * $p<.1$

differences, but the estimates suggest that if any crowding out of individual transfers is taking place, it is most likely only taking place among the less poor beneficiary households.

We also see that there is a statistically significant difference between the effect on less poor and the effect on the poorest with regards to their likelihood to receive transfers from the Government/TASAF. In column (1) we see that less poor households are 6 percentage points less likely than their poorest counterparts to receive these transfers, significant at the 5 percent level. This suggests that communities are successful in identifying the most vulnerable members of their community for treatment.

In table 7.49 the only striking effect in the context of a recent drought is that households were much more likely to receive their government payments (significant at the 5 percent level).

When we decompose the transfers into cash, food, and in-kind, we see no significant impacts of the program outside of the government (TASAF) transfers. We likewise see no pattern of significant effects when we examine these decomposed transfers across gender of household head, poverty level of the household, and whether the household was affected by drought.

### Qualitative Findings

The endline quantitative analysis shows generally muted effects on transfers to and from treatment households, except for an expected, significant increase in

**Table 7.49 Heterogeneous Shock Treatment Effects of CCT on Transfers Received (by Source) and Paid Out at Endline**

| | (1) | (2) | (3) | (4) | (5) | (6) | (7) |
|---|---|---|---|---|---|---|---|
| | Household received at least T Sh 5,000 from group, last 12 months | | | Value of all transfers received (cash, food, and other in-kind) from group, last 12 months | | | Value of all transfers given out, last 12 months |
| | Gov't / TASAF | NGO/ FBO | Individuals | Gov't / TASAF | NGO/ FBO | Individuals | |
| Effect no drought | 0.92 | 0.01 | −0.07 | 89,093 | −81.23 | 101.93 | −178.42 |
| | (0.03)*** | (0.03) | (0.06) | (4,073)*** | (1,309) | (7,490) | (765) |
| Effect drought | 0.99 | −0.01 | 0.07 | 102,978 | −2,418 | −11,782 | 1,163 |
| | (0.03)*** | (0.03) | (0.06) | (4,520)*** | (1,987) | (14,150) | (1,652) |
| Difference effect drought and effect no drought | 0.08 | −0.02 | 0.14 | 13,884 | −2,336 | −11,884 | 1,342 |
| | (0.04)** | (0.04) | (0.08)* | (4,904)*** | (2,361.42) | (14,676) | (1,885.37) |
| Observations | 3,128 | 3,132 | 3,132 | 3,128 | 3,132 | 3,132 | 3,132 |
| R-squared | 0.79 | 0.01 | 0.02 | 0.71 | 0.00 | 0.06 | 0.01 |

*Source:* World Bank data.

*Note:* Results reported in this table are based on effect of treatment on the treated (ETT) regressions. Clustered standard errors in parentheses. CCT = conditional cash transfer; FBO = faith-based organization; NGO = nongovernmental organization; TASAF = Tanzania Social Action Fund; T Sh = Tanzanian shilling.

Significance level: * = 10 percent, ** = 5 percent, *** = 1 percent

transfers from the government. In contrast to the midline analysis, the endline quantitative analysis shows no significant indication of crowding out on average, although this does not rule out reductions in some cases. The qualitative fieldwork supports the finding that in beneficiary households there may be occasional reductions in transfers from individuals. One nonbeneficiary in a focus group in Bagamoyo district said that she was very grateful for the transfers, since now she did not need to worry so much about supporting her parents.

In-depth interviews with village leaders in a treatment village in Kibaha revealed that a few of the elderly females had no other source of income aside from the program. Similarly, participants in a focus group for community leaders in Bagamoyo said that there are very few people in their village that receive money from outside. This reflects the quantitative findings of the small amount of all types of transfers before the program (T Sh 20,229 received from individuals on average prior to the program), relative to the much larger transfers (an increase of T Sh 94,368 for treatment households) received from the government as a result of the CB-CCT program.

Takeaway:

- Over time, there is little evidence that these transfers are crowding out other kinds of transfers. This suggests positive targeting, as the total needs of these households likely exceed the size of the transfers.

## Livestock, Land, and Other Durable Assets

In this section we discuss the effects of the CB-CCT on ownership of land and other major durable assets.[1] Analyzing table 7.50, we see that treatment does not have a statistically significant effect on ownership of land or durable assets at endline on average.

The coefficients in table 7.51 suggest few significant effects. However, in column (2) we see a 2 percentage point increase in the likelihood that a female-headed household owned a sewing machine (significant at the 10 percent level), while male-headed households saw no significant change.

In table 7.52 we observe few differences across the poorest and less poor households. The one exception is that in column (6) we see that treatment had an opposite effect on the two sets of households with regards to bicycle ownership. The poorest households are now 5 percentage points less likelihood to own a bicycle, significant at the 5 percent level. Meanwhile, less poor households are now 10 percentage points more likely to own a bicycle, significant at the 5 percent level. The difference between effect less poor and effect poorest is also statistically significant. One explanation is that less poor households may already be meeting some of their basic needs and thus they were able to use the TASAF transfer to purchase a larger asset, such as a bicycle.

In table 7.53 we explore the different treatment effects realized by the three pilot districts. Column (1) shows that households in Kibaha had 1.1 fewer acres of land at endline, significant at the 5 percent level. Meanwhile, households in

**Table 7.50  Effects of CCT on Land and Durable Asset Ownership at Endline**

| | (1) | (2) | (3) | (4) | (5) | (6) |
|---|---|---|---|---|---|---|
| | Acres of land | Sewing machine | Stove | Radio | Mobile phone | Bicycle |
| Baseline mean | 4.15 | 0.01 | 0.10 | 0.33 | 0.11 | 0.19 |
| *Panel A: Effect of treatment on the treated* | | | | | | |
| Treatment (ETT) × After | −0.25 | 0.00 | 0.02 | 0.04 | −0.02 | 0.02 |
| | (0.47) | (0.01) | (0.03) | (0.04) | (0.03) | (0.03) |
| After | −0.23 | 0.01 | 0.05 | −0.05 | 0.19 | 0.01 |
| | (0.21) | (0.00) | (0.02)*** | (0.02)** | (0.02)*** | (0.02) |
| Observations | 3,128 | 3,132 | 3,132 | 3,132 | 3,132 | 3,132 |
| R-squared | 0.00 | 0.00 | 0.02 | 0.01 | 0.12 | 0.00 |
| *Panel B: Intent to treat* | | | | | | |
| Treatment (ITT) × After | −0.23 | 0.00 | 0.02 | 0.04 | −0.02 | 0.01 |
| | (0.64) | (0.01) | (0.04) | (0.05) | (0.04) | (0.04) |
| After | −0.23 | 0.01 | 0.05** | −0.05 | 0.19*** | 0.01 |
| | (0.30) | (0.01) | (0.03) | (0.03) | (0.03) | (0.03) |

*Source:* World Bank data.
*Note:* Clustered standard errors in parentheses. CCT = conditional cash transfer; ETT = effect of treatment on the treated; ITT = intention to treat.
Significance level: * = 10 percent, ** = 5 percent, *** = 1 percent

**Table 7.51 Heterogeneous Gender Treatment Effects of CCT on Land and Durable Asset Ownership at Endline**

|  | (1) | (2) | (3) | (4) | (5) | (6) |
|---|---|---|---|---|---|---|
|  | Acres of land | Sewing machine | Stove | Radio | Mobile phone | Bicycle |
| Baseline mean: female head of household | 2.77 | 0.007 | 0.08 | 0.19 | 0.06 | 0.07 |
| Baseline mean: male head of household | 5.03 | 0.005 | 0.12 | 0.42 | 0.13 | 0.27 |
| Effect female head of household | 0.24 | 0.02 | 0.02 | 0.06 | 0.01 | 0.05 |
|  | (0.38) | (0.01)* | (0.04) | (0.04) | (0.05) | (0.03) |
| Effect male head of household | −0.49 | −0.00 | 0.02 | 0.03 | −0.04 | 0.00 |
|  | (0.64) | (0.01) | (0.03) | (0.05) | (0.03) | (0.04) |
| Difference effect male head of household and effect female head of household | −0.73 | −0.02 | −0.00 | −0.03 | −0.04 | −0.04 |
|  | (0.65) | (0.01) | (0.05) | (0.06) | (0.05) | (0.05) |
| Observations | 3,128 | 3,132 | 3,132 | 3,132 | 3,132 | 3,132 |

*Source:* World Bank data.
*Note:* Clustered standard errors in parentheses. CCT = conditional cash transfer.
*** p < .01, ** p < .05, * p < .1.

**Table 7.52 Heterogeneous Poverty Treatment Effects of CCT on Land and Durable Asset Ownership at Endline**

|  | (1) | (2) | (3) | (4) | (5) | (6) |
|---|---|---|---|---|---|---|
|  | Acres of land | Sewing machine | Stove | Radio | Mobile phone | Bicycle |
| Baseline mean: poorest | 3.37 | 0 | 0 | 0.04 | 0 | 0 |
| Baseline mean: less poor | 5.20 | 0.01 | 0.23 | 0.71 | 0.25 | 0.45 |
| Effect poorest | 0.27 | −0.00 | 0.02 | 0.02 | −0.02 | −0.05 |
|  | (0.49) | (0.00) | (0.02) | (0.04) | (0.01) | (0.03)** |
| Effect less poor | −0.77 | 0.01 | 0.04 | 0.07 | 0.02 | 0.10 |
|  | (0.72) | (0.01) | (0.04) | (0.05) | (0.05) | (0.05)** |
| Difference effect less poor and effect poorest | −1.04 | 0.01 | 0.03 | 0.05 | 0.03 | 0.16 |
|  | (0.80) | (0.01) | (0.05) | (0.06) | (0.05) | (0.05)*** |
| Observations | 3,128 | 3,132 | 3,132 | 3,132 | 3,132 | 3,132 |

*Source:* World Bank data.
*Note:* Results reported in this table are based on effect of treatment on the treated (ETT) regressions. Clustered standard errors in parentheses. CCT = conditional cash transfer.
Significance level: * = 10 percent, ** = 5 percent, *** = 1 percent.

Chamwino realized statistically significant increases in land ownership at endline. These households now have 1.27 more acres of land, significant at the 10 percent level. For the most part, other differences across districts are not statistically significant.

Although treatment did not have a statistically significant impact on durable asset ownership, in table 7.54 we see that treatment households did acquire some new assets at endline. Following treatment, households purchased additional

**Table 7.53 Heterogeneous Geographic Treatment Effects of CCT on Land and Durable Asset Ownership at Endline**

| | (1) | (2) | (3) | (4) | (5) | (6) |
|---|---|---|---|---|---|---|
| | Acres of land | Sewing machine | Stove | Radio | Mobile phone | Bicycle |
| Baseline mean—Kibaha | 3.45 | 0.16 | 0.12 | 0.36 | 0.12 | 0.19 |
| Baseline mean—Bagamoyo | 5.08 | 0.00 | 0.12 | 0.45 | 0.15 | 0.27 |
| Baseline mean—Chamwino | 3.39 | 0 | 0.03 | 0.10 | 0.02 | 0.06 |
| Effect Kibaha | −1.10 | 0.01 | 0.04 | 0.05 | −0.07 | 0.03 |
| | (0.49)** | (0.02) | (0.04) | (0.06) | (0.05) | (0.07) |
| Effect Bagamoyo | −0.68 | 0.00 | 0.00 | 0.03 | 0.03 | −0.02 |
| | (0.85) | (0.01) | (0.05) | (0.07) | (0.04) | (0.05) |
| Effect Chamwino | 1.27 | 0.00 | 0.04 | 0.04 | −0.04 | 0.05 |
| | (0.70)* | (0.00) | (0.04) | (0.03) | (0.04) | (0.03)* |
| Difference effect Bagamoyo and effect Kibaha | 0.42 | −0.01 | −0.04 | −0.02 | 0.10 | −0.05 |
| | (0.98) | (0.20) | (0.06) | (0.09) | (0.07) | (0.08) |
| Difference effect Chamwino and effect Kibaha | 2.37 | −0.01 | −0.00 | −0.01 | 0.03 | 0.02 |
| | (0.85)*** | (0.02) | (0.05) | (0.07) | (0.07) | (0.07) |
| Observations | 3,128 | 3,132 | 3,132 | 3,132 | 3,132 | 3,132 |

*Source:* World Bank data.
*Note:* Clustered standard errors in parentheses. CCT = conditional cash transfer.
*** $p < .01$, ** $p < .05$, * $p < .1$.

**Table 7.54 Effects of CCT on Livestock Ownership at Endline**

| | (1) | (2) | (3) | (4) | (5) | (6) | (7) | (8) |
|---|---|---|---|---|---|---|---|---|
| | Indigenous Cows (including calves) | Dairy goats (including kids) | Indigenous goats (including kids) | Local chickens (excluding chicks) | Foreign chickens (excluding chicks) | Sheep | Pigs | Turkey and ducks |
| Baseline mean | 0.80 | 0.005 | 0.25 | 2.37 | 0.10 | 0.21 | 0.19 | 0.14 |
| *Panel A: Effect of treatment on the treated* | | | | | | | | |
| Treatment (ETT) × After | −0.03 | 0.02 | 0.38 | 1.09 | −0.06 | −0.02 | −0.02 | −0.07 |
| | (0.14) | (0.03) | (0.16)** | (0.37)*** | (0.04) | (0.03) | (0.02) | (0.08) |
| After | 0.15 | 0.01 | 0.12 | −0.14 | 0.07 | 0.06 | 0.01 | 0.08 |
| | (0.08)* | (0.02) | (0.07)* | (0.19) | (0.03)** | (0.02)*** | (0.02) | (0.05)* |
| Observations | 3,132 | 3,132 | 3,132 | 3,130 | 3,132 | 3,132 | 3,132 | 3,132 |
| *R*-squared | 0.00 | 0.00 | 0.02 | 0.01 | 0.00 | 0.01 | −0.00 | 0.00 |
| *Panel B: Intent to treat* | | | | | | | | |
| Treatment (ITT) × After | −0.03 | 0.02 | 0.36 | 1.02 | −0.05 | −0.02 | −0.02 | −0.06 |
| | (0.19) | (0.04) | (0.23) | (0.51)** | (0.06) | (0.05) | (0.03) | (0.10) |
| After | 0.15 | 0.01 | 0.12 | −0.14 | 0.07 | 0.06 | 0.01 | 0.08 |
| | (0.12) | (0.02) | (0.09) | (0.28) | (0.05) | (0.03)** | (0.03) | (0.07) |

*Source:* World Bank data.
*Note:* Clustered standard errors in parentheses. CCT = conditional cash transfer; ETT = effect of treatment on the treated; ITT = intention to treat.
Significance level: * = 10 percent, ** = 5 percent, *** = 1 percent.

dairy goats, indigenous goats, and local chickens. Column (3) shows that treatment households own 0.38 more indigenous goats (significant at the 5 percent level), while column (4) shows that these households own 1.1 more chickens (significant at the 1 percent level). As clarified during the qualitative exercises, households preferred to buy chickens because they are affordable and they are easier to sell than other animals. Figure 7.13 illustrates the baseline average ownership, and effect of treatment for the animals significantly affected.

In table 7.55, we found some differences in livestock ownership between treated female and male-led households at endline. Specifically, male-headed households are more likely to increase their ownership of goats, whereas female-headed households are more likely to increase their ownership of chickens. Male-headed households saw an ownership increase of 0.5 goats, significant at the 5 percent level. Female-headed households now own 1.62 more local chickens, significant at the 1 percent level.

Analyzing table 7.56, we observe few differences in livestock investments between the poorest and less poor treated households. In column (3) we see that the poorest households now own 0.59 more indigenous goats, significant at the 10 percent level, whereas investments in dairy goats are more concentrated among the less poor households.

Next, in table 7.57 we examine some of the differences in treatment effects in the three pilot districts at endline. Note that column (2) is blank for Chamwino as no treated household in this district owned a dairy goat either before or after treatment.

In column (3) we see that treated households in Chamwino had a statistically significant increase in indigenous goat ownership. Households in this community now own 0.97 more goats, significant at the 1 percent level. Likewise, in column (4) we see that treated households in Bagamoyo and Chamwino made statistically significant investments in local chicken ownership. In Bagamoyo, treated

**Figure 7.13 Effects of Conditional Cash Transfer on Livestock Assets**

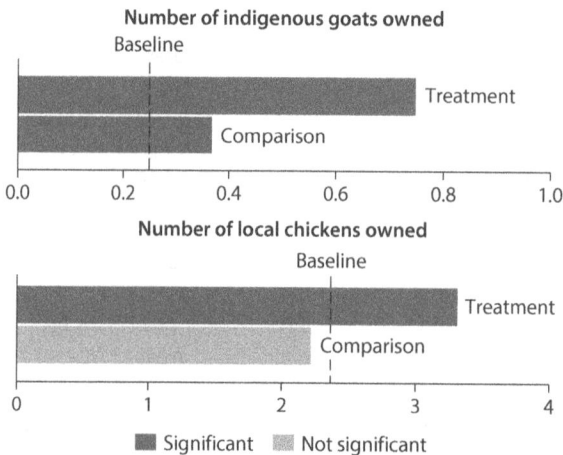

**Table 7.55 Heterogeneous Gender Treatment Effects of CCT on Livestock Ownership at Endline**

| | (1) | (2) | (3) | (4) | (5) | (6) | (7) | (8) |
|---|---|---|---|---|---|---|---|---|
| | Indigenous Cows (including calves) | Dairy goats (including kids) | Indigenous goats (including kids) | Local chickens (excluding chicks) | Foreign chickens (excluding chicks) | Sheep | Pigs | Turkey and ducks |
| Baseline mean- female head of household | 0.04 | 0 | 0.13 | 1.63 | 0.01 | 0.01 | 0.02 | 0.12 |
| Baseline mean- male head of household | 0.10 | 0.01 | 0.33 | 2.84 | 0.16 | 0.03 | 0.02 | 0.14 |
| Effect female head of household | 0.19 | 0.02 | 0.23 | 1.62 | −0.12 | 0.02 | 0.02 | −0.04 |
| | (0.24) | (0.01) | (0.16) | (0.36)*** | (0.08) | (0.08) | (0.04) | (0.12) |
| Effect male head of household | −0.16 | 0.02 | 0.47 | 0.82 | −0.02 | −0.04 | −0.04 | −0.08 |
| | (0.18) | (0.04) | (0.23)** | (0.51) | (0.06) | (0.03) | (0.02)** | (0.10) |
| Difference effect male head of household and effect female head of household | −0.35 | 0.01 | 0.23 | −0.80 | 0.09 | −0.07 | −0.06 | −0.04 |
| | (0.30) | (0.05) | (0.27) | (0.59) | (0.10) | (0.08) | (0.05) | (0.16) |
| Observations | 3,132 | 3,132 | 3,132 | 3,130 | 3,132 | 3,132 | 3,132 | 3,132 |

*Source:* World Bank data.
*Note:* Clustered standard errors in parentheses. CCT = conditional cash transfer.
*** p<.01, ** p<.05, * p<.1

**Table 7.56 Heterogeneous Poverty Treatment Effects of CCT on Livestock Ownership at Endline**

| | (1) | (2) | (3) | (4) | (5) | (6) | (7) | (8) |
|---|---|---|---|---|---|---|---|---|
| | Indigenous Cows (including calves) | Dairy goats (including kids) | Indigenous goats (including kids) | Local chickens (excluding chicks) | Foreign chickens (excluding chicks) | Sheep | Pigs | Turkey and ducks |
| Baseline mean- poorest | 0.08 | 0 | 0.15 | 1.44 | 0.011 | 0.02 | 0.008 | 0.07 |
| Baseline mean- less poor | 0.07 | 0.001 | 0.38 | 3.61 | 0.22 | 0.25 | 0.03 | 0.22 |
| Effect poorest | −0.04 | 0.00 | 0.59 | 0.60 | −0.06 | 0.01 | 0.00 | 0.01 |
| | (0.18) | (0.04) | (0.18)*** | (0.38) | (0.07) | (0.05) | (0.01) | (0.07) |
| Effect less poor | −0.02 | 0.036 | 0.181 | 1.596 | −0.06 | −0.05 | −0.037 | −0.13 |
| | (0.02) | (0.02)* | (0.263) | (0.689) | (0.05) | (0.06) | (0.04) | (0.12) |
| Difference effect less poor and effect poorest | 0.02 | 0.03 | −0.41 | 0.99 | −0.00 | −0.06 | −0.04 | −0.14 |
| | (0.239) | (0.040) | (0.305) | (0.827) | (0.084) | (0.073) | (0.04) | (0.13) |
| Observations | 3,132 | 3,132 | 3,132 | 3,130 | 3,132 | 3,132 | 3,132 | 3,132 |

*Source:* World Bank data.
*Note:* Results reported in this table are based on effect of treatment on the treated (ETT) regressions. Clustered standard errors in parentheses. CCT = conditional cash transfer.
Significance level: * = 10 percent, ** = 5 percent, *** = 1 percent

**Table 7.57 Heterogeneous Geographic Treatment Effects of CCT on Livestock Ownership at Endline**

| | (1) | (2) | (3) | (4) | (5) | (6) | (7) | (8) |
|---|---|---|---|---|---|---|---|---|
| | Indigenous Cows (including calves) | Dairy goats (including kids) | Indigenous goats (including kids) | Local chickens (excluding chicks) | Foreign chickens (excluding chicks) | Sheep | Pigs | Turkey and ducks |
| Baseline mean- Kibaha | 0.13 | 0 | 0.08 | 2.50 | 0.33 | 0.02 | 0 | 0.11 |
| Baseline mean- Bagamoyo | 0.06 | 0.0 | 0.44 | 2.97 | 0.01 | 0.02 | 0.02 | 0.20 |
| Baseline mean- Chamwino | 0.05 | 0 | 0.14 | 1.26 | 0.01 | 0.02 | 0.04 | 0.06 |
| Effect Kibaha | 0.10 | −0.00 | 0.18 | 0.21 | −0.21 | 0.05 | 0.00 | −0.34 |
| | (0.33) | (0.00) | (0.11) | (0.67) | (0.11)* | (0.08) | (.) | (0.17)* |
| Effect Bagamoyo | 0.00 | 0.00 | 0.13 | 1.26 | 0.03 | −0.04 | −0.05 | −0.01 |
| | (0.12) | (0.00) | (0.27) | (0.58)** | (0.07) | (0.03) | (0.03) | (0.11) |
| Effect Chamwino | −0.21 | --- | 0.97 | 1.77 | −0.03 | −0.06 | 0.01 | 0.11 |
| | (0.29) | --- | (0.26)*** | (0.58)*** | (0.03) | (0.05) | (0.06) | (0.09) |
| Difference effect Bagamoyo and effect Kibaha | −0.09 | 0.00 | −0.05 | 1.05 | 0.24 | −0.09 | −0.04 | 0.32 |
| | (0.35) | (0.00) | (0.29) | (0.88) | (0.13)* | (0.09) | (0.03) | (0.21) |
| Difference effect Chamwino and effect Kibaha | −0.31 | 0.07 | 0.79 | 1.56 | 0.18 | −0.11 | 0.01 | 0.44 |
| | (0.44) | (0.09) | (0.28)*** | (0.89)* | (0.11) | (0.10) | (0.06) | (0.20)** |
| Observations | 3,132 | 3,132 | 3,132 | 3,130 | 3,132 | 3,132 | 3,132 | 3,132 |

*Source:* World Bank data.

*Note:* Results reported in this table are based on effect of treatment on the treated (ETT) regressions. Clustered standard errors in parentheses. CCT = conditional cash transfer.

Significance level: * = 10 percent, ** = 5 percent, *** = 1 percent

households own 1.26 more chickens (significant at the 5 percent) at endline and those in Chamwino own 1.77 more chickens (significant at the 1 percent). Meanwhile, column (5) shows that households in Kibaha had a statistically significant decrease in the number of foreign chickens they own. These households own 0.21 fewer foreign chickens (significant at the 10 percent level) at endline.

In column (8) we see that households in Kibaha saw a statistically significant decrease in the number of turkeys and ducks they own, suggesting that they shifted investments away from turkeys and ducks.

Finally, in table 7.58 we see significant investments in livestock were concentrated among nondrought-affected households. In column (3) we see that treatment is associated with nondrought-affected households owning 0.63 more indigenous goats, significant at the 1 percent level. Column (4) reports that treatment is associated with nondrought-affected households owning 1.56 more local chickens, significant at the 1 percent level.

### Qualitative Findings

Consistent with the quantitative findings of significant, large increases in goat and chicken ownership, almost every beneficiary participant in the focus group and

**Table 7.58 Heterogeneous Shock Treatment Effects of CCT on Livestock Ownership at Endline**

| | (1) | (2) | (3) | (4) | (5) | (6) | (7) | (8) |
|---|---|---|---|---|---|---|---|---|
| | Indigenous Cows (including calves) | Dairy goats (including kids) | Indigenous goats (including kids) | Local chickens (excluding chicks) | Foreign chickens (excluding chicks) | Sheep | Pigs | Turkey and ducks |
| Effect no drought | −0.05 | 0.05 | 0.63 | 1.56 | −0.05 | −0.03 | −0.02 | −0.09 |
| | (0.24) | (0.03) | (0.22)*** | (0.44)*** | (0.06) | (0.05) | (0.03) | (0.10) |
| Effect drought | −0.02 | −0.02 | −0.02 | 0.39 | −0.08 | −0.01 | −0.02 | −0.04 |
| | (0.10) | (0.04) | (0.20) | (0.54) | (0.06) | (0.05) | (0.03) | (0.10) |
| Difference effect drought and effect no drought | 0.03 | −0.06 | −0.65 | −1.18 | −0.03 | 0.02 | −0.00 | 0.05 |
| | (0.27) | (0.05) | (0.28)** | (0.66)* | (0.08) | (0.08) | (0.04) | (0.14) |
| Observations | 3,132 | 3,132 | 3,132 | 3,130 | 3,132 | 3,132 | 3,132 | 3,132 |
| R-squared | 0.00 | 0.01 | 0.02 | 0.01 | 0.00 | 0.01 | 0.00 | 0.00 |

*Source:* World Bank data.

*Note:* Results reported in this table are based on effect of treatment on the treated (ETT) regressions. Clustered standard errors in parentheses. CCT = conditional cash transfer.

Significance level: * = 10 percent, ** = 5 percent, *** = 1 percent

in-depth interview discussions mentioned that they had bought chickens, goats, or even ducks with the transfer money. This use of the transfer money seemed to be widespread knowledge in the villages: even one focus group of nonbeneficiaries in Bagamoyo explained that the beneficiaries used the transfer money to invest in chickens. This seemed to be the most prevalent store of value in these villages, and functions as a type of savings for these vulnerable households. For example, one old man in a focus group in Bagamoyo said that he had used the money from the transfers to purchase a chicken, which he then sold to have money to pay for someone to cultivate his land. Another woman in Bagamoyo mentioned that she had created a business of cooking and selling the meat from chickens she was able to buy with the CB-CCT transfers. A man in Kibaha described how the transfer money had allowed him to buy chickens and ducks, which had then reproduced so that he could sell the chicks and ducklings for income.

One possible explanation for the lack of significant effects of the program on non-livestock asset purchases in the quantitative analysis is that the types of assets purchased were too diverse to register in the analysis of individual items. For example, one man in a focus group in Bagamoyo described how he used the transfer income to purchase a hammer, which he uses to make gravel that he sells for additional income. While this reflects a productive investment in a durable asset, the categories in the quantitative data may not capture every diverse investment.

One focus group of beneficiaries in Bagamoyo explained that some of the elderly are now able to pay people to cultivate their land, which allows them to generate additional income. Several elderly beneficiaries in different villages in Kibaha also said that they used the money to clear land or assist with farming. Therefore, while the program may not increase land ownership, it may serve to increase the returns beneficiaries are able to get from land they already own.

Takeaways:

- The program, overall, led to both increases in some types of livestock (chickens and goats) and—depending on the group—some shifts in the composition of livestock owned.
- Qualitative work highlights that most households view these as productive assets: The chickens, ducks, and goats are used for reproducing and selling. While there are not many significant effects on direct food and non-food consumption, effects on livestock are at least equally valuable. This can be a means of ensuring adequate consumption in the future.

## Infrastructure

In this next section we turn our discussion towards household infrastructure developments at endline. As we see from table 7.59, treatment is not associated with any statistically significant improvement in household infrastructure. In fact, the quality of housing materials in treatment households improved significantly more slowly than in control households. In column (2) we see that treated households were 8 percentage points less likely to have improved walls at endline, significant at the 5 percent level. Column (3) shows that treated households are now 4 percentage points less likely to have an improved floor, significant at the 10 percent level. Here we are defining "improved" as households having anything other than the dirt wall or dirt floor they had at baseline. Finally, in column (4)

**Table 7.59  Effects of CCT on Infrastructure at Endline**

|  | (1) | (2) | (3) | (4) | (5) |
|---|---|---|---|---|---|
|  | Improved Roof | Improved Walls | Improved Floors | Piped Water | Improved Toilet |
| Baseline mean | 0.82 | 0.14 | 0.06 | 0.31 | 0.72 |
| *Panel A: Effect of treatment on the treated* | | | | | |
| Treatment (ETT) × After | −0.03 | −0.08 | −0.04 | −0.13 | 0.05 |
|  | (0.02) | (0.03)** | (0.02)* | (0.04)*** | (0.03) |
| After | 0.02 | 0.15 | 0.16 | 0.12 | 0.11 |
|  | (0.01) | (0.02)*** | (0.02)*** | (0.03)*** | (0.02)*** |
| Observations | 3,482 | 3,482 | 3,482 | 3,132 | 3,132 |
| R-squared | 0.00 | 0.06 | 0.11 | 0.04 | 0.08 |
| *Panel B: Intention to treat* | | | | | |
| Treatment (ITT) × After | −0.04 | −0.03 | −0.08* | −0.12** | 0.05 |
|  | (0.03) | (0.03) | (0.05) | (0.06) | (0.04) |
| After | 0.16*** | 0.02 | 0.15*** | 0.12*** | 0.11*** |
|  | (0.02) | (0.02) | (0.03) | (0.04) | (0.03) |

*Source:* World Bank data.
*Note:* Clustered standard errors in parentheses. CCT = conditional cash transfer; ETT = effect of treatment on the treated; ITT = intention to treat.
Significance level: * = 10 percent, ** = 5 percent, *** = 1 percent

we see that treated households are now 13 percentage points less likely to have piped water in their homes, significant at the 1 percent level.

It is crucial to note that while the program appears to have reduced the rate of improvement in household infrastructure quality, housing quality is still improving in treatment villages. This is shown by the size of the "after" coefficient in table 7.59, which more than outweighs the negative coefficient on treatment for both the likelihood of having improved walls and improved floors.

The fact that the transfers are provided frequently in relatively small amounts (as opposed to a larger grant less frequently) may discourage larger infrastructure investments, especially as few households have savings accounts. As a result, households may be more likely to invest in a chicken or goat than a new roof or floor.

### Qualitative Findings

The findings of the qualitative exercise differ from the quantitative results that treatment households experience a significant decrease in their likelihood of having improved housing quality relative to control households. One man in a Bagamoyo focus group said that when he gets money from the program he tries to work on his house. Several other beneficiaries mentioned that they had used some of the transfer income to make improvements to their roofs. One of the men in an in-depth interview in Kibaha said that whenever he had extra money from the transfers he would purchase one iron sheet at a time, while a woman in Bagamoyo mentioned that she had bought new thatch. While new thatch or part of a roof would constitute an improvement in infrastructure, it may not be captured in the quantitative measures of an improved roof. Another beneficiary mentioned that while her life had improved, she still did not have enough money to buy her own house.

Takeaway:

- The program does not seem to have improved household infrastructure on average, although many individuals suggest that it did have these effects.

## Note

1. We excluded cars and motorcycles from the list of durable assets because less than 1 percent of the population has each of these assets.

# CHAPTER 8

# Conclusions

This report describes the design and implementation of the impact evaluation of a community-based conditional cash transfer (CB-CCT) program, which began in January 2010. The evaluation instruments include household surveys carried out at baseline (late 2009), midline (mid 2011), and endline (late 2012); a community score card exercise carried out in 20 treatment communities in late 2010–early 2011; two rounds of focus groups (in six villages following the midline survey and in nine villages following the endline); and a set of 39 in-depth interviews in six communities following the endline.

The baseline survey showed that the households in treatment and control communities were comparable across a broad range of characteristics: household size, access to financial services, household infrastructure, school enrollment, health-seeking behavior, and involvement in community activities. The midline survey, carried out after 18–21 months of transfers had been realized, showed a range of significant impacts. Members of participating households were much more likely to visit health clinics in the previous year; this was especially true for the elderly. Illness rates for the previous month were not significantly lower, but children were more likely to be currently enrolled in school. The program also led households to enroll children in school at younger ages, and improved grade progression.

At endline, significant impacts are observed across a broad array of areas, including health, education, and various risk-reducing behaviors: use of health insurance, insurance expenditures, nonbank savings (for the poorest households), and the purchase of livestock such as goats and chickens. In addition, the program has led to significant increases in spending on certain children's goods (especially children's shoes). Results on trust suggest that the program is associated with an increase in trust in community leaders as well as increased trust in some subgroups of community members.

Despite these positive program impacts, the community score card exercise revealed significant deficiencies in the provision of public health and education services. However, individuals participating in those discussions were unclear on who was responsible for implementing changes. Communities participating in the community score card exercise reported very high impacts of the program on a range of outcomes. The focus groups and in-depth interviews likewise revealed high perceptions of impact, and explored the ways that households have put the benefits to use, such as investing in improved household infrastructure. A common element of feedback from the qualitative data collection (community score cards, focus groups, and in-depth interviews) was that the transparency of the household selection process could be improved in future implementation.

The perception of impact between qualitative exercises and the quantitative survey differs in a few areas. The qualitative exercises identified massive impacts on school attendance, for example, whereas the quantitative analysis did not find the same impacts—most likely because reported school attendance was already relatively high. Likewise, households reported using transfers to increase consumption, but this was not picked up in the quantitative measures of food consumption. This may point to the importance of balancing self-reported impacts with impact evaluation results, as the former may be biased when participating households attribute all changes in outcomes to the program without recognizing that conditions may improve over time for other reasons. Alternatively, the quantitative survey may not capture deeply heterogeneous investments: For example, if households improve consumption across a wide range of goods, some of which are not measured in the household survey, then the quantitative analysis may not capture those impacts.

Concerns about the potential adverse impact of the program on community trust seem unfounded. While some crowding out of individual transfers and a reduction in trust in the community were observed at midline, by endline there was no evidence of either. In fact, trust in community leaders and various communities members appears to have increased substantially. Recipient households reported being more willing to participate in village organizations and to contribute to community projects (although we did not observe an increase in actual contributions), and they were more likely to attend village council meetings.

Overall, the program has shown strong impacts in many areas: health outcomes, education outcomes, risk-reducing behaviors, and investments in livestock to improve livelihoods. This suggests that CB-CCTs are a promising investment to reduce risk and improve human capital investments for the most vulnerable households in Tanzania.

# Attrition

## Attrition at the Midline

We were unable to gather data on 9 percent of original households at the time of the midline survey. We define attrition as meaning that neither the original household nor a split-off household from the original household was successfully tracked and interviewed, as split-off households are identified with the same household number as their original households in our regressions. Table A.1 below shows the correlates of attrition at midline (columns 1–3). The dependent variable is a dummy equal to one if the household had attrited by the time of the midline survey (July–September 2011), and we include a number of control variables. All attrition regressions are estimated using a linear probability (ordinary least squares, or OLS) model. (The results are substantively the same with probit estimation.) In all specifications, standard errors are clustered at the village level, just as they are in all of our panel data analysis.

Most important, column (1) shows that living in a treatment village does not predict attrition. column (2) shows that this is robust to controlling for a number of baseline household characteristics: the head's gender, the head's age and age squared, dummies for the head's education level, and dummies for the household having an improved roof, improved floor, toilet facilities, and piped water. From both models, we see that having a male head, toilet facilities, and not having an improved floor at baseline increase the probability of attrition, though none of the other controls are significant predictors. By interacting each of these control variables with treatment, column (3) examines whether household characteristics differentially affect attrition in treated versus control communities. We see that in treatment communities, only the head having upper primary (standards 5–8) education predicts attrition; no other controls have a significant impact on attrition. In control communities, only the head having secondary education (in the OLS specification) predicts attrition.

**Table A.1  Predictors of Attrition at the Midline**

| | Attrition at midline | | | Attrition at endline | | |
|---|---|---|---|---|---|---|
| | (1) | (2) | (3) | (4) | (5) | (6) |
| HH located in treatment village | 0.002 | 0.001 | −0.219 | 0.023 | 0.022 | 0.151 |
| | (0.016) | (0.015) | (0.185) | (0.020) | (0.019) | (0.276) |
| Male HH head | | 0.031** | 0.032 | | 0.047*** | 0.035 |
| | | (0.014) | (0.020) | | (0.017) | (0.022) |
| HH head age | | 0.005 | 0.002 | | 0.009** | 0.012* |
| | | (0.003) | (0.004) | | (0.004) | (0.006) |
| HH head age (squared) | | −0.000* | −0.000 | | −0.000** | −0.000** |
| | | (0.000) | (0.000) | | (0.000) | (0.000) |
| HH head has primary education (Std 1–4) | | 0.005 | 0.007 | | −0.030 | −0.020 |
| | | (0.015) | (0.019) | | (0.020) | (0.028) |
| HH head has primary education (Std 5–8) | | 0.004 | −0.045 | | −0.020 | −0.051 |
| | | (0.024) | (0.041) | | (0.027) | (0.041) |
| HH head has secondary education | | 0.063*** | 0.074*** | | −0.030 | −0.100 |
| | | (0.018) | (0.027) | | (0.118) | (0.231) |
| Dummy—improved roof | | 0.013 | 0.013 | | 0.013 | 0.028 |
| | | (0.015) | (0.025) | | (0.021) | (0.034) |
| Dummy—improved floor | | −0.053* | −0.024 | | −0.042 | −0.035 |
| | | (0.028) | (0.030) | | (0.036) | (0.039) |
| Dummy—toilet facilities | | 0.039** | 0.019 | | 0.050*** | 0.056* |
| | | (0.017) | (0.025) | | (0.018) | (0.032) |
| Dummy—piped water | | −0.002 | −0.016 | | −0.021 | −0.058* |
| | | (0.015) | (0.023) | | (0.021) | (0.032) |
| Treatment × Male head | | | −0.002 | | | 0.021 |
| | | | (0.027) | | | (0.032) |
| Treatment × Head age | | | 0.005 | | | −0.005 |
| | | | (0.006) | | | (0.009) |
| Treatment × Head age squared | | | −0.000 | | | 0.000 |
| | | | (0.000) | | | (0.000) |
| Treatment × Head has primary education (Std 1–4) | | | −0.005 | | | −0.020 |
| | | | (0.031) | | | (0.040) |
| Treatment × Head has primary education (Std 5–8) | | | 0.086* | | | 0.056 |
| | | | (0.049) | | | (0.053) |
| Treatment × Head has secondary education | | | −0.035 | | | 0.150 |
| | | | (0.034) | | | (0.232) |
| Treatment × Dummy—improved roof | | | 0.001 | | | −0.026 |
| | | | (0.031) | | | (0.042) |
| Treatment × Dummy—improved floor | | | −0.074 | | | −0.008 |
| | | | (0.070) | | | (0.081) |
| Treatment × Dummy—toilet facilities | | | 0.038 | | | −0.010 |
| | | | (0.034) | | | (0.038) |
| Treatment × Dummy—piped water | | | 0.029 | | | 0.076* |
| | | | (0.030) | | | (0.041) |

*table continues next page*

**Table A.1  Predictors of Attrition at the Midline** *(continued)*

|  | Attrition at midline | | | Attrition at endline | | |
|---|---|---|---|---|---|---|
|  | *(1)* | *(2)* | *(3)* | *(4)* | *(5)* | *(6)* |
| Constant | 0.913*** | 0.780*** | 0.907*** | 0.857*** | 0.591*** | 0.517** |
|  | (0.013) | (0.100) | (0.114) | (0.015) | (0.135) | (0.211) |
| Observations | 1,764 | 1,756 | 1,756 | 1,764 | 1,756 | 1,756 |
| *R*-squared | 0.000 | 0.017 | 0.021 | 0.001 | 0.022 | 0.027 |

*Source:* World Bank data.
*Notes:* Clustered standard errors in parentheses. HH = household.
Significance level: * = 10 percent, ** = 5 percent, *** = 1 percent.

## Attrition at Endline

We were unable to gather data on 13 percent of original households at the endline survey. Table A.1 shows the correlates of attrition at endline (columns 4–6). The dependent variable is now a dummy for the household having attrited by the time of the endline survey (August–October 2012), and we include the same set of control variables. As at midline, living in a treatment village does not predict attrition (column 4). Column (5) shows that this is robust to controlling for the same set of baseline household characteristics used in the midline attrition analysis. We observe that having a male head, an older head, and toilet facilities at baseline increase the probability of attrition. By interacting each of these control variables with treatment, column (6) examines whether household characteristics differentially affect attrition in treated versus control communities. We see that in treatment communities, only having piped water at baseline predicts attrition; no other controls have a significant impact on attrition. In control communities, only having toilet facilities, not having piped water, and having an older head predict attrition.

Overall, these balanced rates of attrition across treatment and comparison suggest that the impact evaluation results are unlikely to be affected by attrition.

# References

Akresh, Richard, Damien de Walque, and Harounan Kazianga. 2012. "Alternative Cash Transfer Delivery Mechanisms: Impacts on Routine Preventative Health Clinic Visits in Burkina Faso." NBER Working Paper No. 17785, Cambridge, MA.

———. 2013. "Cash Transfers and Child Schooling: Evidence from a Randomized Evaluation of the Role of Conditionality." World Bank Policy Research Working Paper, Washington, DC.

Angelucci, Manuela, and Giacomo De Giorgi. 2009. "Indirect Effects of an Aid Program: How Do Cash Transfers Affect Ineligibles' Consumption?" *American Economic Review* 99 (1): 486–508.

Baird, Sarah, Craig McIntosh, and Berk Özler. 2011. "Cash or Condition? Evidence from a Cash Transfer Experiment." *Quarterly Journal of Economics* 126 (4): 1709–53.

Baird, Sarah, Francisco Ferreira, Berk Özler, and Michael Woolcock. 2013. "Relative Effectiveness of Conditional and Unconditional Cash Transfers for Schooling Outcomes in Developing Countries: A Systematic Review." *Campbell Systematic Reviews* 9 (8).

Behrman, Jere, and John Hoddinott. 2001. "An Evaluation of the Impact of PROGRESA on Preschool Child Height." Food Consumption and Nutrition Division Discussion Paper, IFPRI, Washington DC.

Behrman, Jere, Piyali Sengupta, and Petra Todd. 2005. "Progressing through PROGRESA: An Impact Assessment of a School Subsidy Experiment in Rural Mexico." *Economic Development and Cultural Change* 54 (1): 237–75.

Fiszbein, Ariel, and Norbert Schady. 2009. *Conditional Cash Transfers: Reducing Present & Future Poverty*. Washington DC: World Bank.

Garcia, Marito, and Charity M. T. Moore. 2012. *The Cash Dividend: The Rise of Cash Transfer Programs in Sub-Saharan Africa*. Washington DC: World Bank.

Gassmann, Franziska, and Christina Behrendt. 2006. "Cash Benefits in Low-Income Countries: Simulating the Effects on Poverty Reduction for Senegal and Tanzania." International Labour Office Discussion Paper No. 15, International Labour Office, Geneva.

Grosh, Margaret E., and Judy L. Baker. 1995. *Proxy Means Tests for Targeting Social Programs: Simulations and Speculation*. LSMS Working Paper Series. Washington DC: World Bank.

Public Affairs Foundation. 2011. *An Evaluation of the Conditional Cash Transfer Program in Tanzania*. Bangalore: Public Affairs Foundation.

Rawlings, Laura, and Gloria Rubio. 2005. "Evaluating the Impact of Conditional Cash Transfer Programs." *World Bank Research Observer* 20 (1): 29–55.

Svensson, Jakob, and Martina Bjorkman. 2009. "Power to the People: Evidence from a Randomized Field Experiment of a Community-Based Monitoring Project in Uganda." *Quarterly Journal of Economics* 124 (2): 735–69.

"Tanzanian German Programme to Support Health." n.d. http://www.tgpsh.or.tz/home/download-section/ (accessed October 22, 2013).

World Bank. 2009. "Social Funds." *The World Bank*, August 12. www.worldbank.org/socialfunds (accessed December 9, 2012).

## Environmental Benefits Statement

The World Bank is committed to reducing its environmental footprint. In support of this commitment, the Publishing and Knowledge Division leverages electronic publishing options and print-on-demand technology, which is located in regional hubs worldwide. Together, these initiatives enable print runs to be lowered and shipping distances decreased, resulting in reduced paper consumption, chemical use, greenhouse gas emissions, and waste.

The Publishing and Knowledge Division follows the recommended standards for paper use set by the Green Press Initiative. Whenever possible, books are printed on 50 percent to 100 percent postconsumer recycled paper, and at least 50 percent of the fiber in our book paper is either unbleached or bleached using Totally Chlorine Free (TCF), Processed Chlorine Free (PCF), or Enhanced Elemental Chlorine Free (EECF) processes.

More information about the Bank's environmental philosophy can be found at http://crinfo.worldbank.org/wbcrinfo/node/4.

green press
INITIATIVE